THE FRUIT OF THE SPIRIT

Transformation in the Image of Jesus

Raymond L. Fox

m•agine!

Copyright © 2017 Raymond L. Fox.

All rights reserved. No part of this book may be reproduced, stored, or transmitted by any means—whether auditory, graphic, mechanical, or electronic—without written permission of the author, except in the case of brief excerpts used in critical articles and reviews. Unauthorized reproduction of any part of this work is illegal and is punishable by law.

m·agine!
407 Myrtle Drive · Farmerville, LA 71241

ISBN: 978-0-5781-8462-3 (sc)
ISBN: 978-0-5781-8757-0 (e)

Cover artwork used by permission from Shutterstock.

Scripture taken from the Holy Bible,
NEW INTERNATIONAL VERSION®.
Copyright © 1973, 1978, 1984, 2011 by Biblica, Inc.
All rights reserved worldwide. Used by permission.
NEW INTERNATIONAL VERSION® and NIV® are registered trademarks of Biblica, Inc. Use of either trademark for the offering of goods or services requires the prior written consent of Biblica US, Inc.

Rev. date: 3/13/2017

CONTENTS

PREFACE v

MAKING DISCIPLES 1

LIVING IN LOVE 15

CELEBRATING JOY 45

PURSUING PEACE 81

PRACTICING PATIENCE 119

KINDNESS SHINING IN THE DARKNESS 155

GOODNESS: LIVING THE BENEFICIAL LIFE 181

INCREASE OUR FAITH! 217

GROWING IN GENTLENESS 253

SELF-CONTROL: POWER FOR A NEW LIFE 275

CONCLUDING THOUGHTS 337

PREFACE

Among Christians who regularly read the New Testament and listen to sermons about Christian living, there can be surprisingly little understanding of the precise meaning and practice of those qualities that disciples ought to "put on" in the image of their Lord. Perhaps we assume we commonly understand terms such as gentleness or self-control and therefore pay little attention to deepening our knowledge, especially in the context of Jesus' teaching. Maybe we believe that the fruit of the Spirit simply develop in our character by attending worship and surrounding ourselves with other believers without the need for the discipline of practice. In reality, growth in the image of Jesus flows from conscious practice, empowered by the Lord's Spirit. Conscious practice must be rooted in understanding.

Since transformation in the image of Jesus is the central goal of each disciple, the literature available about the practice of the fruit of the Spirit should be rich and classical. These qualities define disciples of Jesus and provide the reason and motivation for everything we do as we follow him. Nevertheless, the literature dedicated to these character traits is relatively sparse. I hope to add something that will be beneficial for practice.

These chapters on the fruit of the Spirit began as a series of studies I worked through with each person I met who wanted to grow as a disciple. My purpose was to teach Christians to feel secure in examining themselves, imagine and be creative in their practice, and enjoy the excitement of growing as followers of Jesus. I presented these studies in a variety of cultural settings in my own country, in Europe, and in the Spanish-speaking ministry I conduct in Latin America. In my own community, I became involved in juvenile detention facilities and adult jails working as a teacher, counselor, and chaplain. My work focuses especially on young men and their adult counterparts who want to leave street gangs and learn to live a healthy life. Teaching these qualities in such an environment can meet with much skepticism and negativity. But the truth is that when the teachings of Jesus concerning, for instance, peace, patience, self-control, and love are taught in a positive, practical manner, they are powerful to change the most stubborn spirit.

But the teacher is also a student. My experiences in the classroom and in discussions with Christians from different cultures created a dialectic that challenged me to think more deeply, more carefully, and more expansively. I read, thought, listened, went out to practice, and revised my thinking, in a continuous cycle of learning, all the while loving the experience of transformation. Learning and living as a disciple is a very exciting, joyous endeavor. I hope this writing communicates this joy. What you will find in these pages is not definitive because our experience of practice ought always to reveal more creative practice. This too, is my hope—that your creativity as a disciple to practice the Lord's teaching will blossom and flourish.

INTRODUCTION

MAKING DISCIPLES
"TEACHING THEM TO OBEY
EVERYTHING I HAVE COMMANDED YOU"
(MATTHEW 28:18-20)

After his resurrection Jesus met with his disciples on a mountaintop somewhere in Galilee to explain the work that would forever transform them and the multitudes who would come to follow him. He told them, "All authority in heaven and on earth has been given to me. Therefore go and make disciples of all nations, baptizing them in the name of the Father, and of the Son and the Holy Spirit, teaching them to obey everything I have commanded you" (Matthew 28:18-20). According to the words of Jesus, becoming his disciple includes two steps—one that happens in a moment and another that lasts a lifetime.

The first step, baptism, begins our new life as disciples of Jesus. It is a transforming experience. Just as Jesus, after dying on the cross, was buried in the tomb, we surrender in baptism to put to death the sinful self. We are immersed beneath the water to represent the burial of the person we were before coming to the Lord. Then, as Paul explains in Romans 6:3-4, the baptized believer rises from the water to begin a new life, as a disciple of Jesus. By the grace of God, a believer becomes a new, spiritual creation, with a new, spiritual relationship as a child of God, to live a new, spiritually directed life as a disciple of Jesus Christ. But the new birth is only the beginning.

The second step requires a lifetime of learning and practice, living in close fellowship with Jesus. Jesus told his followers to make disciples by "teaching them to obey everything I have commanded." When Jesus gave that instruction to the ones who had accompanied him for three-and-a-half years, those who had listened carefully to his teachings, discussed them, meditated on them, and haltingly began to follow them, what would they have thought about? When Jesus said "everything I have commanded," what images would have come to their minds? What were the teachings that they would have remembered at that stage in their lives as his disciples? The Gospels give us the answer.

The four gospels, Matthew, Mark, Luke, and John, record four perspectives of the life of Christ from the eyes of the earliest witnesses of Jesus. Jesus had promised the apostles that the Holy Spirit would come to help them remember everything he had taught them. Their words show us what these disciples recalled most about the teachings of Jesus. What images came to their minds? They remembered Jesus' gentle generosity toward the poor, the sick, the paralyzed, and the spiritually depressed. They recalled his Sermon on the Mount in which he described the sincerity of heart and purity of life his disciples ought to cultivate in his kingdom. They remembered the parables of Jesus that taught the value of a lost soul, the self-deceit of trusting in riches, the power of faith, the meaning of loving one's neighbor, and the beauty of living in humility. They thought about Jesus, wrapping himself with a towel, taking a basin of water, and washing the disciples' feet, the Master serving the servants in a visible parable of humility. They recalled teachings about forgiveness, faithfulness, gratitude, sacrificial service, self-discipline, and moral purity. They had witnessed how often and in how many ways Jesus taught people to practice a level of love that asked for nothing in return. Interestingly, we might be surprised by the lack of attention that Jesus himself paid to questions of theology, ritual, and ceremony when he was first training his disciples. During his earthly ministry, he focused on the character of life in his kingdom.

LEARNING TO PRACTICE

This second step in making disciples is a continuous project. One does not learn to love in a moment but through many trials and errors, only after much perseverance and self-discipline. Then after years of loving, there are still new lessons to learn about love. Toward the close of the first century, the apostle John, after having written his gospel account of the life of Christ, returned to the theme of love. He wrote his first letter, 1 John, to Christians to remind them about God's love for them and their love for one another. These Christians were still learning. As life's circumstances change, we learn new lessons. Economic or social conditions around us change, either for the better or for the worse, and we learn new truths about compassion and generosity. Life progresses and, as we grow older and more mature, we learn a deeper, more abiding sense of humility. One of the beauties of being a disciple of Jesus is that life is never boring since there are always new challenges that call us to an even higher and holier life.

The second step is also a very practical step. When Jesus told his followers to make disciples, "teaching them to obey," the teaching they were to do must have also included the *how*. Teaching to obey implies teaching people how to obey. Making disciples does not just consist of telling people, "You must do this," "You need to do that," or "You should do this." This language is, unfortunately, often the language of the pulpit. Standing behind a speaker's stand and telling people what they ought to do may sound powerful in the moment but is not practical in the long run. After listening to such a sermon, people leave the assembly certainly believing they ought to do those things, but, in the back of their minds, the question of *how* still remains. How do I practice these character qualities? Where do I begin? What exactly do I do? Making disciples involves providing the answers to these questions so that confusion or simple ignorance does not extinguish enthusiasm for the new life in Christ. At the same time, discipleship does not consist of following an endless list of specific, detailed rules concerning how to practice Jesus' teaching. Instead, the goal is to develop a practical mentality that looks for and creates opportunities to practice. Training to look at the world through the lens of practice takes more than a moment.

The second step of making disciples also happens most dramatically and profoundly during times of testing when challenges call into question how disciples view the practice of Jesus' teaching. Disciples might have the tendency to place limits on their abilities to practice based on their cultural, social, or even economic perceptions of his teachings. The problem of perceptions caused even the very first disciples to stumble. The earliest Christians, coming from a Jewish background, could easily love and respect their fellow Christians who shared the same antecedents. Later, when these Jewish Christians found themselves in the same congregation, sharing the same spiritual meal with Christians from other cultures, they faced a challenge. Of course, they knew they should love everyone, but the challenge of worshiping together forced them to extend the practical limits of love they had placed on themselves. Now they had to practice love for people whom they had never loved before.

In a similar way, generosity may come easier under certain economic circumstances. From a position of wealth, generosity appears to be natural for some Christians. In reality these Christians may be unconsciously placing limits on their generosity. They convince themselves that they are giving a lot, measured in terms of monetary value, but the amount of actual sacrifice is minimal. They protect themselves with a series of reasons why they cannot be too generous to avoid sacrificing the style of life they are accustomed to living. Jesus, however, measured generosity not by the actual monetary amount given but by the amount of sacrifice involved in the act of giving. The disciples recalled Jesus' commentary on the poor widow who gave very little—two small copper coins—to the temple treasury in comparison to what the rich gave. But as Jesus watched the people cast their money into the treasury, he commended the widow for her generosity because the small amount she gave represented a tremendous sacrifice.

When disciples place artificial and even unconscious limits on their generosity, they also limit the possibility of deepening their understanding of generosity. Then, at some point in their lives, they may face some new and challenging experience by which they come to understand the profound need of another human being. Helping the person in need would require great sacrifice, but this particular case of suffering, for some reason, breaks through the protective shell that the disciple hides behind to avoid being overly generous. Filled with a new compassion, the disciple acts by faith and gives more than he or she has ever given before. Taking the leap of faith and giving, without regard for the consequences that might result from such generosity, surprises disciples with a sense of freedom, a liberation from selfishness and greed. In such moments disciples of Jesus can advance by great strides in the practice of generosity. In fact, any experience that challenges cultural or social perceptions of the Christian life gives disciples the chance to learn to follow Jesus on a much more profound level. We have to open ourselves up and allow Jesus to question what we believe about the humility, gentleness, compassion, and patience that should define us as disciples.

If discipleship consists of learning to practice the teachings of Jesus about character, learning to practice the character of Jesus consists of discipleship. Discipleship is a relationship between student and teacher. For a Christian, building character is not just about learning to practice certain principles in daily living, as if we can consider those qualities without considering who the teacher is and our relationship to him. These teachings are not principles that can stand alone without Jesus. Jesus gives life to these principles and to his disciples as they struggle to practice them. The moments that challenge false perceptions especially require a living relationship with him.

The practice of forgiveness is a good example. In many situations forgiveness may be a simple matter of easily forgetting what someone has done to offend us. But then there are moments when the offense is especially painful and destructive or other moments when repeated offenses cause us to question the need to forgive. Why should I forgive? Who says I should forgive such things? For the disciple the answer is Jesus. Disciples of Jesus take the leap of faith and extend the limits of character traits such as forgiveness because, instead of relying on their own wisdom, they trust in Jesus as teacher and Lord. They will practice beyond what they could have imagined practicing because Jesus is Lord.

Everyone, believer and non-believer alike, follows some norm or some authority as he or she decides to what extent to practice a particular character quality. Cultural expectations in general or the expectations of social relationships, such as friends or family, give people the confidence to follow accepted norms for such qualities as generosity or forgiveness. When Peter asked Jesus how many times he should forgive someone who sins against him, he was asking how Jesus would view the practice of forgiveness in contrast to the generally accepted views about forgiveness in Jewish culture at that time. Jesus answered that one ought to forgive "seventy-seven times." If this new and essentially unlimited perspective of forgiveness sounded difficult to follow, Peter would have to trust Jesus' wisdom, committing himself to follow Jesus as Lord. Through faith in Jesus, Peter would have to surrender himself to the process of transformation, no matter where it took him. Discipleship is a relationship of faith in the wisdom, power, and authority of the teacher.

Making disciples through teaching what Jesus commanded also must begin with the heart. A brilliant thread that courses through all of Jesus' teaching is the need to start with the heart. Jesus was especially critical of the Jewish religious leaders of the Pharisee sect for their lack of sincere devotion. On the outside they appeared to be devoted, but, on the inside, in their hearts, they were corrupt. Jesus compared them to whitened tombs, clean on the outside but full of dead men's bones on the inside. Obedience to the teachings of Jesus cannot be routine or robotic, as in simply practicing some external rules for conduct without really changing the attitude of the heart. Imagine practicing humility without a humble heart by just following some rules for humble speech and humble actions. Some salesmen and politicians know how to tilt their heads in just the right way, how to lower the tone of their voices and use gentle language to appear humble, yet in their hearts they are thinking about how to take advantage of their audience. Humility is first an attitude of the heart, and then, starting from the heart, humility changes one's words and actions.

This principle is also true of other character traits for Christians. The word *heart* represents our deepest emotions and attitudes. The heart is a good symbol of emotions because one of the first physical feelings that humans experience in response to fear, anxiety, love, anger, or other emotions is a change in the heart's beating and rhythm. To say that character has to start with the heart means that any attempt to change behavior has to begin with our desires and emotions. What do we really want to be or really want to do? What do we care most about? What will gives us inner peace and contentment? If, for instance, we have a deep desire to be faithful and being faithful gives us a very important feeling of peace, then we will fiercely struggle at being faithful in every relationship and in every work. Change that comes from the heart, motivated by strong emotions, will be consistent from day to day and will persevere. Jesus further taught that change comes from the inside by emphasizing repentance. The word *repentance* means *to change one's mind*. A change of mind must precede a change of life. Practicing the character of Jesus can only come after we change our ways of thinking, desiring with our whole hearts to imitate the Lord. A change of practice, consistently practicing the character qualities of Jesus with full devotion, will then naturally follow our transformed hearts.

THE FRUIT OF THE SPIRIT

The Gospels reveal what the earliest disciples most remembered about the teachings of Jesus. These four books take a biographical approach to Jesus' teaching. For this reason the books are not systematic in their approach to the character qualities that ought to distinguish Christians. For example, there are no chapters or sections dedicated solely to specific character traits like honesty, faithfulness, or generosity. The Gospels treat character traits as they arise in different moments during the teaching that Jesus did while he was physically with his disciples. This approach gives life to his teachings by creating real-life images of humility, compassion, and forgiveness through the conversations Jesus had with a variety of people.

Later, in the letters of the New Testament, writers such as Paul and Peter brought those qualities together by listing them and, in some places, giving a brief explanation of the qualities. The "fruit of the Spirit" make up one of these lists in Galatians 5:22-23. Paul includes nine qualities: love, joy, peace, patience, kindness, goodness, faith, gentleness, and self-control. These lists serve a great purpose by showing disciples today exactly what the Lord expects of them as his followers. They serve to direct and evaluate one's growth as a disciple. The followers of Jesus know they are growing and maturing as disciples if they are growing in their abilities to practice these traits.

The apostle Paul compiled other lists of qualities of the new life in Christ in Colossians 3:12-15 and Ephesians 4:20-32. These lists differ in the specific traits that he includes and the style he uses to present them. Likewise, Peter penned another list of Christian virtues in 2 Peter 1:5-8. Jesus himself taught a list of traits commonly known as the *beatitudes* in his Sermon on the Mount, describing life in his kingdom (Matthew 5:3-10). Even when taken together, these lists do not contain all the character qualities that disciples ought to develop as they follow Jesus. These lists are not intended to be exhaustive, nor does one list contain qualities that are somehow more important than the qualities of the other lists. Each list is a sample of character traits meant to show that discipleship is about cultivating character in the imitation of Christ. Paul explains to his readers that the purpose of discipleship, from the moment one leaves the waters of baptism, is "to clothe yourselves with Christ" (Galatians 3:26-27).

The fruit of the Spirit are attributes of our spirits that then manifest themselves in the activities of our physical lives. The level of love that distinguishes Christians has to come from within, from our spirits, where we have experienced the love of God. Joy based on spiritual reasons, peace as inner contentment, and patience in the sense of spiritual endurance are also qualities of our spirits. Kindness originates from a merciful spirit. Goodness is what is, first of all, good for our spirits and our relationships with God. Faith, too, is a quality of our spirits that manifests itself in lives of faithfulness. Gentleness, as well as self-control, has to begin with the inner life instead of being practiced as a mere physical discipline. Each of these qualities, of course, will manifest itself in our physical behaviors: in language, in actions, in the treatment of other people, and in the outward activities of worship to God. However, they must originate as qualities of our spirits. God created us to enjoy spiritual life and these qualities are the result of living a spiritual life in profound fellowship with him.

These nine qualities are fruit of the Spirit because they are the results of "keeping in step" or walking in harmony with God's Spirit (Galatians 5:25). We are not alone in our struggle to learn to practice a new way of life. God's Spirit has made us alive and provides the necessary help we need to grow consistently in these qualities. What does God expect us to do? What will he do for us through his Spirit? After we are born again, becoming spiritually alive through God's Spirit who lives in us, our responsibility is to yield ourselves to the practice of righteousness by putting off the old person and putting on the new person. Paul summarized the practice of living a transformed life in his Ephesian letter.

> You were taught, with regard to your former way of life, to put off your old self, which is being corrupted by its deceitful desires; to be made new in the attitude of your minds; and to put on the new self, created to be like God in true righteousness and holiness (Ephesians 4:22–24).

Paul uses the language of "put off" and "put on" to describe our responsibility in the process of spiritual transformation. Putting off the old person means to stop entertaining the corrupt mentality and stop practicing the destructive behavior that we used to pursue habitually. Putting on the new person means to begin to create new habits by cultivating the image of God through practice. Something that the Spirit does not do for us is suddenly and completely fill us with the qualities that we would like to possess in the image of our Father. Growth in these qualities requires the experience of consistent practice. First, practice requires a decision on our part to take what we believe about the teaching of Jesus to the level of daily application. Second, practice requires the creativity to reflect on the teachings of Jesus and imagine increasingly profound ways to practice. Third, practice requires the faith and courage to live by the teaching of Jesus even when we do not see responses that we hope to see in the behavior of others. Patient, consistent practice is our role in transformation.

Although practice is our responsibility, the Spirit does not leave us alone but graciously offers us help. He is the Advocate, called beside us to strengthen our spirits, so that we can consistently practice the character of our Father. The Spirit's help with our consistency is one way in which he empowers us to live a transformed life. In his letter to the Ephesians, Paul reassured the disciples that he was praying for them, asking the Lord to grant them essential strength to practice the transformed life: "I pray that out of his glorious riches he may strengthen you with power through his Spirit in your inner being, so that Christ may dwell in your hearts through faith" (Ephesians 3:16).

Paul's words are not poetic imagery or empty assurances. If he was praying for such help, then he must have believed the Father could answer his prayer. The problem every Christian faces is with consistency in the practice of Jesus' teachings. We face moments of distraction, challenge, or weariness that threaten to slow down or stall our progress. At times we may feel very enthusiastic about learning to love, and, in other moments, we feel tired of constantly serving in love when no one appreciates our sacrifices. We can certainly feel tired of being patient when people around us do not treat us with the same patience. In such moments we need strength in our spirits to practice love or patience consistently, despite what other people do or do not do. We make the decision to practice, but the Spirit of God can strengthen us so that we do not become tired in the practice. Later, in the chapter on self-control, we will discuss the Spirit's help in more detail.

The purpose of this book is to encourage transformation in the image of Jesus by learning to practice the qualities of his character. Remember, learning to practice these qualities is a lifetime project. Maybe there are people who believe that one evening, before going to bed, they can pray and ask God to make them more loving or more joyful, and then they will wake up in the morning perfectly loving and joyful. Perhaps they think that, during the night, God will grab a vial of love from some shelf in heaven, fill a syringe, and inject them with love so that they arise the next day full of love. In the same way, the reader should not expect to become the perfect disciple suddenly after reading this book. The book serves only to give direction toward understanding and practice. Disciples must pray for help and God will certainly bless them with wisdom and the life experiences necessary to learn to be more loving and joyful. He will bless them with strength in their inner beings. He will give them the joy of his presence as they struggle to learn. But the labor of discipleship is to learn how to practice. In harmony with Jesus' teaching, two other underlying themes of this book include the need to start with the heart and the value of challenges. Life experiences can challenge disciples to surrender preconceived ideas about these qualities and view them as Jesus did, without self-imposed limits.

With the exception of the chapters on faith and self-control, the chapters devoted to each of the fruit of the Spirit will follow the same overall approach to cultivating these qualities by emphasizing three essential steps: understanding, reflection, and practice. Disciples must first understand the meaning Jesus gave to these qualities in order to break away from preconceived notions about them. Developing these qualities also requires careful reflection about the possibility of practicing them in one's own life and the challenges one might face in practicing them. The ultimate emphasis in each chapter is on practice, presenting ideas to stimulate the reader to learn to practice each of the fruit of the Spirit. We cannot grow without spiritual practice. Disciples can use the same approach—understanding, reflection, and practice—to work on any of the qualities listed in the various passages of the New Testament.

One of the beauties of the Christian life is the ability to open ourselves up freely to the Lord Jesus so he can transform our hearts and behavior in the imitation of his life. Paul wrote, "We, who with unveiled faces all reflect the Lord's glory, are being transformed into his likeness with ever-increasing glory, which comes from the Lord, who is the Spirit" (2 Corinthians 3:18).

CHAPTER ONE

LIVING IN LOVE

"TO THEM HE GAVE THE NAME BOANERGES,
WHICH MEANS SONS OF THUNDER"
(MARK 3:17).

From "son of thunder" to "living in love"—this was the incredible transformation that happened in the life of the apostle John. Jesus gave John and his brother James the name "sons of thunder" because of the aggressive personalities they had when he first invited them to be his disciples. Then, after many years of following Jesus, learning to think and live in the image of the Father, John wrote, "God is love. Whoever lives in love lives in God, and God in him. In this way, love is made complete among us so that we will have confidence on the day of judgment, because in this world we are like him" (1 John 4:16b-17). Toward the end of his life, when he wrote his biography of the life of Christ, he referred to himself several times in the gospel as "the disciple whom Jesus loved." He had come to understand how powerful God's love is; the love of God had completely changed him. John's self-description was not arrogant boasting but a humble expression of his gratitude to the Lord, who patiently loved him even while John struggled to learn how to love others.

When Jesus selected John and James to be apostles, they were far from being perfect examples of Jesus' teaching about love. At one point during their training, they selfishly sought to be prominent above the other apostles in Christ's kingdom: "Let one of us sit at your right and the other at your left in your glory" (Mark 10:37). Then, not too long after Jesus taught them about the unconditional nature of love that should identify his disciples, the vengeful behavior of James and John made obvious the fact that they still had much to learn. When Jesus and his followers approached a Samaritan village on their way to Jerusalem, the Lord sent some of the disciples ahead to prepare for his stay in the village. But the Samaritans, many of whom shared undisguised prejudice against the Jews, refused to receive the disciples since they were on their way to Jerusalem. James and John reacted with an impulsive desire for vengeance. They asked Jesus, "Lord, do you want us to call fire down from heaven to destroy them?" (Luke 9:54)

When Jesus chose them, they were aggressive, brutish fishermen who understood little about loving others, especially their enemies. Much later, after the death and resurrection of Jesus and after John himself took on the work of teaching and training others to love like Jesus loved, he must have reflected deeply on the patient, gentle love of Jesus. Surely Jesus had loved him unconditionally. Jesus had accepted him. Jesus never gave up on him and graciously forgave John each time he failed. John understood that Jesus died for him and for the whole world so that we could understand the depth of God's love. John knew that he was someone who had genuinely experienced the Lord's love. He, above all the other apostles, needed the full extent of Jesus' love.

To feel loved by the Lord gives us such a wonderfully calm sense of security and an unwavering view of our value as human beings. Without the love of Christ, we could easily become lost in self-doubt and self-condemnation. John discovered, however, that the Lord loves us so completely, not just so we will enjoy being loved, but in order for us to learn to love, to become like him, and so to live with him. "Whoever lives in love lives in God." Using very precise language, John explained in the context of this statement that confidence in our relationships with our heavenly Father actually depends on our abilities to love others as he has loved us.

Most everyone in the world knows something about how to love others. We can learn, just from our experiences in living in this world among fellow human beings, that loving others is a good and even admirable quality. When we love others, most people will love us in return. But understanding how to love in the way that God created us to love can only come from him. The truth Jesus taught is that there is an abiding form of love that does not depend on the behavior of others. This kind of love can come to form a part of who we are in our innermost being, regardless of the behavior and reactions of others. When John declares that "God is love," he is describing the nature of God, something that does not change. God is not just loving, he *is* love. Since this degree of love does not depend on a loving response from those whom we love, it is unconditional. God revealed that he *is* love—that this degree of love forms part of his nature—when he sent his Son as a sacrifice to save us from the consequences of our sin. We could not have known that such love was true, right, or even possible without God revealing the nature of his love to us through such an incomparably loving act.

For this reason John concluded that to love one another with this kind of love is evidence that we have been born of God. Without knowing him we would not have discovered our abilities to love unconditionally,. When we seek to practice this level of love, love is no longer a passing emotion or a carefully dispensed commodity; instead, love is life, a way of existing. In the language of the Scriptures, we are "living in love." To live in love is to come as close as we can to being love as God is love.

John further reasoned that when we love one another to the degree that God loves us, he "lives in us and his love is made complete in us" (1 John 4:12). The original Greek word that John used and that is translated in English versions as *complete* here and in verse eighteen as *perfect* (NIV) means *to finish a process* or *fulfill a purpose*. Consider carefully what John is saying: when we come to live in love, loving others as God loves us, his love finishes a process or fulfills a purpose. So, although feeling so deeply loved by the Lord was very gratifying to John, he understood that the real purpose of God's love was to teach us and persuade us to love others with the same love. When we live in love, "in this world we are like him." If we are like him, then we can live in his presence: "Whoever lives in love, lives in God and God in him." Furthermore, when the purpose of God's love is perfected in us, and we come to live in love, we can be free of fear in his presence. Ultimately, the love of God realizes its highest goal by forming us into people who can live with absolute confidence in his presence. We have no fear in his presence because we are like him, living in love.

Human beings have always had the habit of creating different lists of what seem to them to be the requirements for enjoying peace with God. John clarifies and simplifies this confusion by explaining the most fundamental ground for a living relationship with God: live in love. If we are afraid for some reason to be in the presence of God, then we ought to learn to live in love until it is a persistent quality of our spirits.

UNDERSTANDING

From the very beginning of his earthly ministry, Jesus taught his disciples the most fundamental principle of life in his kingdom:

> If you love those who love you, what credit is that to you? Even "sinners" love those who love them. And if you do good to those who are good to you, what credit is that to you? Even "sinners" do that. And if you lend to those from whom you expect repayment, what credit is that to you? Even "sinners" lend to "sinners," expecting to be repaid in full. But love your enemies, do good to them, and lend to them without expecting to get anything back. Then your reward will be great, and you will be sons of the Most High, because he is kind to the ungrateful and wicked (Luke 6:32-35).

The way to become children of God was not through wearily keeping the human traditions invented by the Pharisees but by loving unconditionally, as the heavenly Father loves. The purest kind of love is given without consideration for anything in return, solely for the benefit of the one being loved. We love, not because of what we want in return but, instead, because of who we want to be. The Father does not love us because we deserve to be loved but because of who he is. He is love. Do we love like the Father loves? The only way to know the answer to this question in our personal lives is to confront the possibility of loving those who are very different from us, those from whom we can expect nothing in return, those who offend us, and even those who may want to harm us.

Jesus illustrated this principle in practice and in parable for his disciples. Consider the famous parable Luke recorded in Luke 10:25-37 of the Samaritan who helped a Jew who had been robbed and left for dead. Jesus told the parable in response to a question that "an expert in the law" had raised. "Teacher," the lawyer asked, "what must I do to inherit eternal life?" In fact, he was a lawyer whose expertise was in God's covenant, the Law of Moses, so he ought to know the answer. Jesus replied, "What is written in the Law? How do you read it?" The lawyer offered the answer that everyone acquainted with God's covenant with Israel ought to know: "'Love the Lord your God with all your heart and with all your soul and with all your strength and with all your mind'; and, 'Love your neighbor as yourself.'" He was correct; this is eternal life. Loving God with everything in us and everything we are brings us joyfully into his presence. Loving others fills us with confidence in his presence. Jesus patiently told the man, "Do this and you will live." Eternal life means to live in the Father's presence; to live in his presence we must live in love.

Jesus' statement convicted the man's heart. He must have honestly realized at that moment that he was not loving his neighbor. Maybe, like all of us, his heart was periodically filled with jealousy, selfishness, and even greed. So, "to justify himself," he asked Jesus, "And who is my neighbor?" To explain to his own conscience why he was not loving his neighbor, the lawyer suggested that he was not sure exactly who his neighbor was. Lawyers can be very precise and analytical in their thinking. If he knew the exact limits of the meaning of *neighbor*, then he could love with more focus, knowing he was fulfilling the precise requirements of the law without doing unnecessarily more than required. The reply that Jesus gave to his question was surprising and would forever illustrate the unconditional nature of Jesus' love.

To clarify the meaning of *neighbor*, Jesus told the lawyer a quite credible story that was very much within the realm of possible, practical experience. A man, presumably a Jew, while traveling from Jerusalem to Jericho, was overcome and robbed by thieves who left him stripped of his clothes and terribly beaten, nearly to the point of death. Similar events happen today. Then a priest and later a Levite (a priest's helper), presumably righteous people, passed by the scene without doing anything to help their countryman. This, unfortunately, also happens today. Our self-interests, our preoccupations, our limited focuses serve to blind us to the needs of those around us, leaving us in darkness. Then, surprisingly, a Samaritan traveling through that part of the country saw the man and felt compassion for him. That he felt compassion meant that he put himself in the place of the beaten man, imagined his suffering and immediately thought of ways to give him relief. He did not ask whether the man was deserving, whether he had a family who might take care of him, or whether he had a job to pay the Samaritan back for any expenses incurred in his care.

That a Samaritan would be the one finally to stop and help the injured man must have surprised the lawyer and whoever else might have been listening to the story. There was a long-standing prejudice between Samaritans and Jews. They normally cared nothing for each other and, in fact, held each other in abject disrespect. Jesus carries the story to an even more surprising conclusion. Not only did the Samaritan feel pity, but he then acted in response to this emotion, generously sacrificing social and financial concerns to guarantee the man's recovery. He immediately used his own resources to care for the man's wounds. The Samaritan put the man on his own donkey and took him to an inn where he could completely recover. The next day when the Samaritan had to continue his trip, he left enough of his own money for the innkeeper to care of the man. Furthermore, he told the innkeeper, "Look after him and when I return, I will reimburse you for any extra expenses." The Samaritan's care for an absolute stranger and possible enemy was unconditional and self-sacrificing.

Considering the responses of the priest, the Levite, and the Samaritan, Jesus' question for the lawyer was, "Which of these three do you think was a neighbor to the man who fell into the hands of robbers?" Although most modern versions translate the question in this way, the original Greek text more precisely states, "Which of these three do you think *became* [emphasis added] a neighbor to the man." With this language Jesus was changing the perception of who our neighbors are. The Law of Moses had also commanded, "Love your neighbor as yourself" (Leviticus 19:18). Traditionally Jews had considered all members of their nation as neighbors with special responsibilities to each other. The priest and the Levite should have considered themselves to be neighbors to the injured man who was a Jew. In fact, a neighbor is, by definition, someone who lives close-by. But instead of coming close to the man to help him, as neighbors should, they walked away from the man. The Samaritan, on the other hand, who did not live close-by, *decided* to come close to the man. Who became a neighbor to the man? The answer was unavoidable. "The one who had mercy on him," replied the lawyer. By his decision, motivated by compassionate love, the stranger became the man's neighbor. Jesus taught that traditional, cultural norms of acceptance do not determine who our neighbors are. Instead, we determine who our neighbors are by the decisions we make to come close through loving care. Jesus told the lawyer, "Go and do likewise." If the man wanted eternal life, he ought to decide to live in love, as the Samaritan did, seeking moments to become a neighbor.

The part of this principle that people easily overlook but that adds so much depth to our understanding is the phrase, "as yourself."

Had the lawyer ever imagined himself in such desperate need like the man whom the thieves brutally beat and left for dead? If he could imagine himself in such a condition, would he care enough about himself to allow a Samaritan to help him? If such a situation were conceivable, then he would have to show loving compassion to a Samaritan or other strangers for whom he felt no natural inclination. Understanding how to love himself would directly help him understand how to love his neighbor. A healthy love for ourselves would at least include caring for ourselves when we are injured and protecting ourselves from danger. Healthy love for ourselves also includes caring for ourselves emotionally and spiritually. It includes integrity or self-honesty so we do not deceive ourselves but live lives consistent with our principles and values. It involves respecting and valuing ourselves. It means having mercy and patience with ourselves when we make mistakes. Loving ourselves would also include having confidence in our abilities and humbly appreciating our positive qualities. What are the healthy desires we have for ourselves? Answering this question helps us understand how we can love our neighbors.

There is also an unhealthy love we might have for ourselves that actually prohibits us from loving our neighbors. Greed, selfish ambition, self-centeredness, and self-indulgence are certainly forms of self-love, but they are qualities that destroy relationships. Interestingly, we cannot practice unhealthy forms of self-love toward our neighbors. Take, for instance, individuals with selfish ambition who wish to progress economically without regard for whom they harm in the process. They could not consistently love themselves and their neighbors in the same way. They could not entertain a lust for their own personal advancement and, at the same time, intensively desire to promote their competitors or even their colleagues. Furthermore, loving only those who are like us or who can do something for us are manifestations of a twisted self-love that would never allow us to love strangers or enemies. Some of these forms of self-love can be deceptive, convincing us that we are genuinely loving people, when, in reality, our practice of love is far different from the way our Father created us to love. We can conclude, in fact, that our abilities to love our neighbors will depend first of all on learning to have a healthy love for ourselves.

Consider Paul's beautiful description in 1 Corinthians 13:4–7 of love in practice: "Love is patient, love is kind. It does not envy, it does not boast, it is not proud. It is not rude, it is not self-seeking, it is not easily angered, it keeps no record of wrongs. Love does not delight in evil but rejoices with the truth. It always protects, always trusts, always hopes, always perseveres." Paul provides examples of how to love our neighbors and, by implication, how to properly love ourselves. Healthy self-love is to treat ourselves and to want to be treated by others with patience and kindness instead of harshness. Boasting and inciting the envy of others are forms of destructive self-love. With a healthy love for ourselves, we would not wish that others would treat us in proud, rude, or self-seeking ways. If we respect and value ourselves as God's creation, then we would want others to protect and trust us without becoming easily angered with us or keeping a record of all our mistakes. Always hoping, being optimistic about the possibility to live in the image of our Father, never giving up on ourselves is to love ourselves. If we admit these are ways we ought to love ourselves, then we are bound to love our neighbors in the same way. To know the practical requirements of love in every situation, all we must do is reason, "How must I love others in the same way I ought to love myself?"

The principle of loving our neighbors as we love ourselves is parallel in meaning and even identical to another famous ethical principle that Jesus taught: "Do to others as you would have them do to you" (Luke 6:31). Guided by this principle, we ask ourselves how we would like people to treat us and then treat them in that very same manner. If we hope for the respect, compassion, and mercy of others, then we will treat others in this very way. According to this principle, our behavior will not be conditioned on the response of the other person. Even if the other person does not treat us as we had hoped, we will still treat them with respect, compassion, and mercy because we continue to desire to be treated in this way. Likewise, loving our neighbors as ourselves implies unconditional love since how we love ourselves, as well as how we wish to be loved, should not change depending on the behavior of others. If a healthy form of self-love includes respecting ourselves, we ought to continue to respect ourselves regardless of whether others show us respect. If respect for ourselves ought to be unconditional—and it ought to be—then respect for others will likewise be unconditional.

In practice the moral results of the two principles will be the same. In fact, we can derive all other divinely delivered moral principles from both of these two principles. Jesus taught, "So in everything, do to others what you would have them do to you, for this sums up the Law and the Prophets" (Matthew 7:12). Inspired by the Lord, Paul further wrote, "The entire law is summed up in a single command: 'Love your neighbor as yourself'" (Galatians 5:14). If we treat others the way we want them to treat us, then we will not steal, or lie, or intentionally bring injury upon another human being. If we love our neighbors as we love ourselves, the results will be the same; we will not steal, or lie, or intentionally bring injury upon another person.

The parable of the Samaritan helping the man overtaken by thieves provides us with the divine interpretation of the teaching, "Love your neighbor as yourself." There is now no room for the discussion of lawyers who might debate the limits of love. Through this parable Jesus illustrated how far the term neighbor extends and how unconditionally generous we ought to be in loving others in the same way we love ourselves. On another occasion, while having dinner in the house of a Pharisee, Jesus illustrated this principle not in a parable but in practice, further challenging preconceived ideas about loving one's neighbor.

Luke describes the moment when someone came to Jesus who had not been left for dead by thieves, but who had been brutally beaten in her spirit by the guilt of sin. A Pharisee named Simon had invited Jesus to dinner, and, while they were dining, a woman, who was recognized as a "sinner" in the town where Simon lived, entered the room. She came in and stood behind Jesus, weeping. Since Jesus was sitting on the floor at the low table with his feet behind him, her tears began to dampen his feet. She wiped the tears from his feet with her hair, respectfully, humbly kissed his feet, and then poured perfume on them. Washing feet was a necessary task in that culture but not with the tears of emotional and spiritual pain. Simon, blinded by his own destructive form of self-love, mentally criticized Jesus for allowing this "sinful" woman to touch him. What Simon did not realize was that the woman had the potential for becoming his neighbor because of her desperate need for compassion.

She was suffering from the consequences of destructive decisions. Simon, however, could not understand her suffering because, in his Pharisaic self-righteousness, he did not imagine himself to be a sinner. Just as the priest passed by the injured man, Simon passed by the woman on his way to criticize Jesus. Jesus, however, came for this precise reason: to relieve such suffering that comes from guilt. He wrapped her wounds up in the healing bandages of forgiveness and commended her for her profound love. To forgive our neighbors is to love them as we love ourselves. We love ourselves enough to want to forgive ourselves when we make mistakes and to be forgiven by those whom we have offended. If we need the forgiveness of others, then we ought to be ready to forgive them. Those who have an unhealthy love for self, in the form of a proud refusal to admit mistakes, will not be able to love their neighbors. The spiritual difference between Jesus and the woman was far greater than the cultural difference between the Samaritan and the man left for dead by the thieves, but, like the Samaritan who generously healed the injured man, Jesus freely healed the woman. In fact, Jesus would sacrifice his life so that the woman could be well.

The parable of the Samaritan and the experience of the woman who came to Jesus in Simon's house make us think about extreme examples of loving someone completely unknown to us or different from us. Ironically, loving our neighbors who are strangers may be easier than loving someone close to us. Our relationships with friends, family, or brothers and sisters in the kingdom can fill with jealousy, envy, pride, and resentment. These poisonous emotions turn the actual practice of love into something that is insincere or nonexistent. Furthermore, we can take those closest to us for granted and assume they do not need even the simplest gestures of love, like words of gratitude and encouragement. It is not unusual for people to give generously to the needs of the poor in a far distant country whom they have never personally met and at the same time not be able to maintain healthy, loving relationships with the people closest to them. The apostle Paul wrote that we need to begin to practice love toward those immediately around us and not forget to love those who are very different from us. "As we have opportunity, let us do good to all people, especially to those who belong to the family of believers" (Galatians 6:10). John is clear and adamant in the language he used to teach that our relationships with God depend on how we love our brothers (those people closest to us). "We love because he first loved us. If anyone says, 'I love God,' yet hates his brother, he is a liar. For anyone who does not love his brother, whom he has seen, cannot love God, whom he has not seen. And he has given us this command: Whoever loves God must also love his brother" (1 John 4:19-21).

The apostles of Jesus, John included, who spent so much time listening to his teachings and observing his surprising practice of love, had a difficult time learning to love each other. They were no different than we are. They struggled with pride, ambition, negativity, criticism, and other attitudes that could have threatened their relationships. But Jesus carefully, patiently taught them a new way of thinking and living, starting with their hearts. At the end, the night before Jesus died, he optimistically taught the disciples, "A new command I give you: Love one another. As I have loved you, so you must love one another. By this all men will know that you are my disciples, if you love one another" (John 13:34-35). Jesus' love for them was unconditional and self-sacrificing. They learned this lesson and it transformed them. John taught his fellow disciples that their love for each other should be very practical:

> We know that we have passed from death to life, because we love our brothers. Anyone who does not love remains in death. Anyone who hates his brother is a murderer, and you know that no murderer has eternal life in

> him. This is how we know what love is: Jesus Christ laid down his life for us. And we ought to lay down our lives for our brothers. If anyone has material possessions and sees his brother in need but has no pity on him, how can the love of God be in him? Dear children, let us not love with words or tongue but with actions and in truth (1 John 3:14–18).

In the world we often love without receiving love in return; but, among the disciples of Jesus, who are devoted to loving as Jesus taught them to love, loving one another as they love themselves, love will naturally be mutual. Thus, they create a community of people who love one another because of their mutual commitment to the principle, "love your neighbor as yourself." Even though they receive love from each other, their love is, nonetheless, unconditional. The fact that they love unconditionally makes their love persistent and uncompromising. In the first century church, loving one another meant that the rich actively loved the poor with the self-sacrificing love of Jesus, and the poor loved the rich in the same way. The master loved his servant, and the servant loved his master. Think of Paul's compassionate letter to Philemon to encourage him to forgive and accept his servant Onesimus, who had run away and then returned as a brother in Christ. The Jew learned to love the Gentile and the Gentile loved the Jew, considering each other without distinction or preference in the body of Christ. Because of their love for each other, the world knew they were disciples of Jesus. The followers of the Pharisaic rabbis were known by their multiplied rituals and rules. The disciples of famous Greek thinkers were known for their philosophical sophistication. The disciples of Jesus were known by their amazing degree of kindness, generosity, humility, and patience. Their community was evidence of the transforming power of Jesus' love.

Loving others as we love ourselves may sound simple but it is not. One of the challenges to living in love is to replace the unhealthy, destructive forms of self-love with healthy care, integrity, respect, and mercy for ourselves.

REFLECTION

The greatest form of love for self is to seek an intimate, spiritual relationship with the Creator and to be willing to sacrifice all else for this. This is the highest form of care, integrity, and respect we can have for ourselves. Imagine, however, someone arguing that if we are to love our neighbor as ourselves, what happens to love for self when we sacrifice something of ourselves to serve the good of someone else? Does this sacrifice of self mean that we no longer love self? The answer to this question is two-fold. First, if our existence were to consist solely of the material and physical, then one could make an argument that sacrificing ourselves on a material level might constitute a negation of self. But, from the standpoint of Jesus' teaching, our essence is spiritual. We are spiritual creatures, created in the spiritual image of God. The body is simply the dwelling place for the spirit at this present time, living in this material world. When we materially sacrifice our resources or ourselves for the benefit of others, we are actually loving our spirits by giving value to our spirits. Our spirits, the spirits that we are, have qualities. Mercy, gentleness, patience, kindness, humility, and love are examples of these qualities of our spirits that we express through the actions of our bodies, the instruments of our spirits. If, with our bodies, we perform humble acts of service, such as washing someone's feet, we hope that this quality comes from humility in our spirits. Our spirits must first possess the quality of humility so that we can genuinely and sincerely express it in the way we behave with our bodies. Humility involves a level of sacrifice: we sacrifice our priorities to serve the priorities of another person, we sacrifice a superior position in order to lift up someone else to a higher position, or we sacrifice the fulfillment of our physical needs to satisfy the needs of someone else. The sacrifice of humility gives value to our spirits, forming us into the creation that God wants us to be. Therefore, at the same time we are loving others by making them strong both physically and spiritually, we are loving ourselves in a spiritually healthy way by cultivating humility. Refusing the work of humility in our spirits allows pride to destroy us; this is truly self-hatred.

Remember, the question is whether we can love ourselves by sacrificing ourselves to love others. The second part of the answer to this question is that by sacrificing time, energy, or resources to practice love toward others, we have imitate fellowship with our heavenly Father. John wrote, "Dear friends, let us love one another, for love comes from God" (1 John 4:7). Remember, the goal of our transformation as followers of Jesus is to be like our heavenly Father. It is the Father's plan that we become like him. John taught that when we live in love, even sacrificing to live in love for others, we are like him, we live in him, and he lives in us. Unconditional, sacrificial love thus brings us into God's presence. In fact, when we practice other healthy qualities of our spirits, such as mercy, justice, compassion, and patience, these qualities connect us to him because they exist in their fullness in him. Enjoying living fellowship with our heavenly Father is the most spiritually healthy, loving thing we can do for ourselves.

One of the greatest moments of joy for our spirits comes when we love like the Father loves, unconditionally and sacrificially. Think about the pleasure that comes from receiving love from others whom we have loved. The pleasure is immediate and satisfying, and we interpret it as the reward for loving. We feel secure, valued, encouraged, and enthusiastic about life. Life is lovely, and we determine to continue loving so that we can feel love in return again. But, amazingly, even greater pleasure can come from loving when we receive no love in return. Many would say that there is nothing pleasurable about loving without receiving love in return or, even worse, when we receive mistreatment in return for love. One of the challenges of loving unconditionally is that the joy is not immediate and comes with time, after experience. At first when we receive nothing in return for love, we may feel empty, bothered, frustrated, or even angry. If this kind of love is new to us, our physical natures start to battle with our spirits, claiming that it does not make sense to love if people will not love us in return. The arguments against continuing to love in this way can be powerful. Why waste my time? What am I gaining from this relationship? If this person really does not understand what I am doing for them, then why should I continue? If we are convinced that by loving unconditionally we can be like our heavenly Father and have confidence in his presence, we put frustration and fear aside, making a decision to continue to love. Love at this point is a decision instead of an emotion. We do not feel like loving, but we decide to love because love brings us into God's presence. We continue to be generous with people regardless of receiving anything from them. We continue to forgive even though people repeatedly offend us. We persistently show mercy, expecting nothing in return, without being afraid that people will take advantage of our mercy.

The result is a transformation in the kind of pleasure we experience. When we finally let go of the frustration of receiving nothing in return for the love that we practice, we are free to experience a different kind of pleasure that fills our spirits. The pleasure of God living in us and us living in God is incredibly powerful as it grows and fills our spirits. We feel very close to the Creator because we know we are loving exactly the way he wants us to love, despite the fact that people are not loving us in return. Learning to love unconditionally transforms our hearts, changing us from the inside out. The challenge to love transforms us into people we enjoy being much more than the selfish, envious people we used to be. We realize, too, that our lives now have genuine meaning because our love has the power to introduce people to the love of God by showing them the beauty of a transformed life. It is not surprising that we feel this spiritual pleasure in palpable ways in our physical lives. The body is the spirit's instrument of existence in this world. The joy we feel in our spirits gives us physical energy, enthusiasm, light in our eyes, and confidence in our steps. We physically feel like nothing can conquer us because in our spirits we sense that we are truly living in his presence. At this point we become free to love as he loves and let the pleasure of his presence consume us.

This joy in our spirits comes from the consistent practice of love over time. Each time we face the costliness of love, we decide to love, even though we do not feel like loving, and we grow closer to the image of our Father. There is no doubt the process of learning to love like our Father loves can be painful. People whom we have loved change and begin to treat us in an offensive way. People to whom we have shown much compassion make wrong choices and seem to waste the compassion we have shown them. Friends cruelly criticize us, oppose us, slander us, betray us, and act as if they are our enemies. We go the second mile with people, doing much more for them than we are obligated to do, giving them many opportunities and advantages they would not otherwise have, at much expense to us. Then, finally, they do not respond the way we hoped they would. The mistakes of others cause us grief and expense that are not fair for us to suffer. We decide to be generous to someone in need, and then, afterwards, we experience financial problems and no one appears to help us. We encourage, we listen, we sympathize, we support, we give hope, and people take us for granted, acting as if we have done nothing for them. Such moments challenge us in our spirits and are the very moments when we learn to love. Before we face these challenges, when we still are simply loving because we are loved, growing in the joy of his presence is not as possible. Loving only those who love us in return or only those with whom we have some affinity or connection keeps us from the real pleasure of God's presence because we have yet to become like him. Living in love as God is love requires a determined decision to be like him when we face the costliness of love. Making this decision to love, despite the cost, is the beginning of real transformation. The Father understands the price of love and suffers with us when love is hard, when those whom we have loved take love for granted or reject us. John also wrote of Jesus, "He was in the world, and though the world was made through him, the world did not recognize him. He came to that which was his own, but his own did not receive him." (John 1:10-11).

PRACTICE

Learning to live in love is a life-long project, and the Lord Jesus wants to begin our training now. He has taught us the nature of God's love, he has shown us the way to love, and he has persuaded us to love through his own love for us. Now he will strengthen us in our spirits when love is costly, and he will fill us with the joy of his presence when we love as he loves. But unconditional, self-sacrificing love is not a concept we just roll over and over in our minds or talk about or even just read about. Love in truth is love in deed, in action. "Dear children, let us not love with words or tongue but with actions and in truth." We read and think about love, but learning to love as God loves comes through practice. Paul prayed that the Christians in Philippi would grow in their ability to love, "This is my prayer: that your love may abound more and more in knowledge and depth of insight" (Philippians 1:9).

Seeing what we have not seen before. Imagine being able to see moments to love that we never before noticed. We would be incredible instruments of God's love if we could learn to love people in a variety of circumstances and situations that we have never been aware of before. We would enjoy the knowledge and depth of insight that Paul prayed for if we could more completely lay aside self-centeredness and understand the needs of another person's heart by listening to his words, paying attention to his gestures, and observing his behavior. If we could see how to respond quickly and wisely with active love, love would become part of our nature. If we could have the freedom and abandon in our hearts to love without any consideration of the cost, simply because we want to live in love, then we would truly abound in love. The answer to this prayer, though, will come from the Lord's providential work in our lives. He will open doors for us to love others, allowing us to pass through difficult, challenging moments to learn to love. He wants to work in us and reveal the joy of his love to the world through us. To receive the answer to this prayer, we surrender ourselves to his work, opening ourselves up to love without reservation in all the moments he lays before us.

Unfortunately as human beings we seek the security of comfortable surroundings and people with whom we feel safe. We feed ourselves emotionally with friendships we can depend on. We protect ourselves from harm by avoiding people who might judge us or even reject us. We cultivate relationships that promote our sense of well-being and help us progress. The result of what we consider to be natural self-defense is isolation from people who could teach us how to love as God loves. The lesson we learn from the Samaritan is that the neighbor who can teach us to love may be someone we would more likely avoid. We reason in our hearts that we are not people persons and do not enjoy meeting or making new acquaintances. This preference for the emotional safety of isolation is a mentality that the Lord wants to remove from his disciples as he transforms them. We might say, "I know I tend to be defensive, but this is just the way I am." We would be wrong, though, in speaking this way, because the Lord created us to live in love, and that is just the way we ought to be. Our self-perceptions can be far from the truth. The Lord knows us from a different perspective because he is the one who formed us. If we are afraid to reach outside of our comfort zones, the Lord can take away the comfort zones for the sake of our training.

Learning to practice living in love, first of all, requires us to look beyond our comfortable surroundings to see the needs of people whom we would not normally even notice. Looking for someone to love whom we know, whom we respect and appreciate, who is like us, who could respond with love, we look past and ignore people who actually need our love. What we might choose to see in people is not necessarily what the Lord intends for us to see. To live in love we open our eyes to imagine how the Lord could be working in and through the lives of people whom we might consider to be far from his kingdom. Jesus addressed this problem of poor vision in a possible scenario he imagined for his disciples.

> I was hungry and you gave me nothing to eat, I was thirsty and you gave me nothing to drink, I was a stranger and you did not invite me in, I needed clothes and you did not clothe me, I was sick and in prison and you did not look after me." They also will answer, "Lord, when did we see you hungry or thirsty or a stranger or needing clothes or sick or in prison, and did not help you?' He will reply, "I tell you the truth, whatever you did not do for one of the least of these, you did not do for me" (Matthew 25:42-45).

Jesus' first disciples must have understand his intended message in these words because they were often surprised when Jesus stopped to help someone whom they would never have thought of helping. He loved Zacchaeus the tax collector, the Samaritan woman who had had several husbands, the rich man who did not want to surrender his wealth to help the poor, and the woman from Syrian Phoenicia who was a Gentile. These people were very different from Jesus, and his disciples were amazed that he stopped to offer life to such people. We read these stories today and read them again and again to the point that what Jesus did no longer surprises us. But, at the same time, we should not be surprised that he is asking us today to do precisely the same as he did.

We really do not even need to leave our comfort zones in order to leave our comfort zones. If we surrender in humility to serve those around us with whom we feel most at ease, we will see moments to love that never before entered our perception. When Jesus, the Master, tenderly washed his disciples' feet, the feet of the servants, he taught those closest to him a visible, unforgettable lesson about the humility of love. Introducing this moment in his biography of Jesus' life, John said that Jesus showed the disciples "the full extent of his love" (John 13:1). Living in love includes loving actions that might make us feel uncomfortable, although we are serving those within our comfort zones. In the home there are responsibilities and chores that a father would never consider doing because they simply do not form part of his customary role; but fulfilling such responsibilities provides a moment for him to serve with humility the ones who normally fulfill them. The mother or wife learns to love when she decides to listen with attentive consideration, even while something inside of her screams out the need to be listened to. The children learn to love when they postpone the gratification of some immediate desire and wait patiently for others to be satisfied first. The humility of love can open our eyes to see what we did not notice before.

To see what we have not seen before, we consciously set a goal for ourselves to increase in the knowledge, insight, and practice of love. At the beginning of each day, we usually set some goals that we would like to accomplish for that day, or at least we have an idea about what we would like to achieve. We are serious about some of these goals because we feel obligated to reach them due to some previous promise or some present responsibility. We probably set other goals we would like to accomplish, but we understand that not all goals are equally important. Some may be out of our reach because of the lack of time, resources, or interest on our part. Some objectives we have will not even surface to our consciousness very often because they are crowded out by other priorities and obligations. There is one obligation, however, that will always be before us and that should occupy our focus above all else as our daily goal. Paul simply wrote, "Let no debt remain outstanding, except the continuing debt to love one another, for he who loves his fellowman has fulfilled the law" (Romans 13:8). At the end of each day, we want to say that we have learned something new about the practice of love and that we have loved as God loves. Tomorrow we want to accomplish the very same goal, as the most serious and conscious priority that we set for the day. How could anything be more important if living in love brings us into God's presence?

Going where we have not gone before. Next, increasing our practice of love requires us to understand the range of loving actions in our own culture. When Paul wrote that love is the "fulfillment of the law" (Romans 13:10), he implied that every moral command that describes how we ought to behave toward others is, in its essence, a particular, specific way of living in love. Love is to speak the truth in contrast to deceiving others and making them seem like fools for believing us. Love is to speak words that respect and encourage by lifting up another person's spirit. Love is to refuse to steal, to pay our debts, to work honestly for the wage that we receive, and to keep promises we make to others. Love is to treat others with patience and mercy when they make mistakes in the same way that we will need to be patient with our own imperfections. Love is to show gratitude and appreciation to those who serve us, without ever assuming we deserve what they offer us. The key to practicing love in a variety of moments is to discipline ourselves to think in each moment what love requires and never overlook moments that seem at first to be insignificant. We can speak a gracious word to a salesman whose products we have no intention of buying, or stop to play with a child, when we are otherwise engrossed in our own seemingly important concerns.

If we find ourselves at a place in life when the amount of time we spend serving the needs of others seems to be overwhelming and we tell ourselves we do not need to look for any other moments to love people, it is time to stop and pray. We need to ask the Lord to give us wisdom to make good decisions about the management of our time and to help us understand where we can serve in the best way with the talents he has given us. At the same time, we can never become too busy lovingly serving those close to us to ignore the small gestures of attention, gratitude, and encouragement for those with whom we have the most fleeting of encounters or those with whom we share nothing in common or those who may place themselves in obstinate opposition to us. Ironically, such people are the ones who can teach us much about living in love. Living in love is looking to love in every moment.

On the other hand, we may find ourselves in a place in our lives in which we feel like we are doing well at loving everyone around us and do not feel particularly challenged by the lives we are living to grow in love. In fact, as time passes we have the tendency, often unconsciously, to surround ourselves by people who are the natural objects of our love, such as family and close friends. We eliminate from our consciousness people who need our love but who would challenge our sense of security and the comfortable routine we follow. Living in isolation from those who genuinely have the potential to teach us to love actually causes us to stagnate as disciples, while we enjoy the peace and tranquility of isolation. The surface waters of a stagnant pond are calm, but the tranquility covers deadness beneath.

What we seek in order to become alive in love and grow in love is new experiences, new acquaintances who need our love. We need to find people or let people find us. Jesus had to go out "to seek and save the lost." Some, like Zacchaeus (Luke 19:1-10), did not feel confident to come to him first. Then there were others who sought out Jesus, but Jesus needed to make himself available to them. To develop the same pure, intense desire to love the lost, the defeated, the injured, and the broken as Jesus did, we will have to seek those whom we can love. Where can we go to serve in a place where we would never have dreamed of serving before? Where can we find people who are genuinely in need of acceptance, compassion, emotional healing, and faith that will empower them to live new lives? Answering these questions takes us across borders we never imagined crossing and through doors that the Lord has wanted us to pass through for such a long time.

There is no question that, when we begin to love unconditionally those whom we had never thought about loving before, we will feel uncomfortable, afraid, or even confused about what exactly to do in order to love. Take, for instance, a disciple who has never been around people with substance addiction suddenly finding himself or herself in a situation where someone who is enslaved to drug abuse asks for help to live a new life. The disciple may not know even the first steps to take in order to support the person in the struggle to be free from the destructive power of addiction. But the desire to learn to love and live more deeply in love has the motivating power to convince the disciple to discover how to help. What begins is a long process—sometimes very frustrating and sometimes very satisfying—of learning how to love this person and bring them to transformation in Christ. There will be plenty of uncomfortable, confusing, and even heart breaking moments as the disciple learns to love unconditionally. Drug addiction is a very powerful, at times overwhelming, habit. It requires the patience of love. Addiction is destructive on many levels of life. It requires the generosity of love to support in many moments of need. Addiction to drugs drives people to behavior that is difficult to understand. Successfully helping someone overcome addiction will require the compassion and mercy of love. The pleasure that carries us through the confusion and frustration of love comes from knowing we are serving as instruments in the Lord's hands to reveal the depth of God's compassionate, patient, and forgiving love. Whether or not the person finally surrenders to the Lord and lives a new life, we know the Lord is training us to love through the experience of loving. We understand that his work is transforming us while we are trying to bring someone else to transformation, and this is pure pleasure for our spirits.

Freedom to love as we have never loved before. Our powers to practice unconditional, self-sacrificing love for others cannot be separated from practicing healthy love for ourselves. If our most fundamental interest is in protecting ourselves, our love will always have limits. We impose such limits on ourselves because we are afraid of losing a level of physical well-being and emotional security that we think is necessary for us to live. In this case we will not live in love. Living in love is ultimately a step of faith, trusting in the Lord's power and trusting in his love to bless us with joyful lives full of meaning. Without this trust we will never let go of the mechanisms we use to protect ourselves and that keep us from loving absolutely.

Christians have a peculiar problem with letting go. Sadly many believers have never yet come to understand what the gracious love of God has accomplished in their lives. Believers are sensitive to sin because they sincerely want to live a righteous life to honor their heavenly Father. But when we sin, if there is little understanding of the nature of God's forgiveness, we are more likely than unbelievers to use defense mechanisms to protect ourselves against feelings of guilt. We may be more likely to justify ourselves by speaking about all the good works we do, by ignoring our mistakes, by claiming we are victims, by criticizing the behavior of others so that we appear more righteous, or by using any number of other mechanisms to protect ourselves spiritually and emotionally.

The result, though, is that these defense mechanisms only serve to alienate us from the very people we need to love. If, for instance, we are living in guilt instead of living in love, and someone offends us, our first reactions to the offensive behavior will be resentment and destructive criticism. We use the offending behavior of the other person to prove to ourselves and to others that we are more righteous than the person who offended us. Loving the person by forgiving them does not serve our purposes. Keeping the offender in the status of being an offender serves to help us justify ourselves. The problem is that self-protection in the destructive form of self-justification will not allow us to be free to love. We honestly may ask ourselves why we cannot forgive the person, without realizing that we have a deeper problem that does not allow us to forgive: we have never fully accepted God's forgiveness for ourselves. Our failures to love and forgive others are symptoms of weaknesses in our relationships with our Father.

Freedom to love comes from fully and completely accepting God's gift of forgiveness for ourselves. We can be righteous only because of God's gracious gift of Jesus. Righteousness is not something we can maintain through our own pitiful ways of protecting ourselves from guilt. The more we understand we cannot justify ourselves and that we all, everyone one of us, no matter who we are or where we have come from, are totally dependent on the grace of God for forgiveness, the more we will be able to love. John wrote, "We love because he first loved us." Accepting his love and forgiveness is the beginning of a healthy love for ourselves. We can, without fear, lay aside all of our defense mechanisms and be free to love others fully as we have been loved. To practice love, we can determine to stop criticizing, judging, and attacking others as useless strategies to protect our own righteousness. Instead, we simply and purely accept our imperfections and ask the Lord to forgive and heal us. We need this healing so that we can be free to love.

We have discovered that loving our neighbors as we love ourselves begins with having a healthy love for ourselves based on the Lord's gift of forgiveness. The more deeply we are aware of how much he has forgiven us, the more free we are to love our neighbors. In effect, the Lord has made it possible for us to have a healthy love for ourselves that empowers us to love others freely without fear or reservation.

John was not alone in his thinking about living in love. The early disciples learned to view their lives from this perspective. Paul also wrote, "Be imitators of God, therefore, as dearly loved children and live a life of love, just as Christ loved us and gave himself up for us as a fragrant offering and sacrifice to God" (Ephesians 5:1-2). God is love. Love is his essence, the nature of his Being. The closest we can come to the imitation of his essence is to live in love.

CHAPTER TWO

CELEBRATING JOY

"I HAVE TOLD YOU THIS SO THAT MY JOY MAY BE IN YOU
AND THAT YOUR JOY MAY BE COMPLETE"
(JOHN 15:11).

Imagine the many different moments in which we feel joy and how joy feels in each of those moments. Walking through a meadow on a sunny spring day, surrounded by wildflowers and singing birds, green, wooded hills stretching off into the distance, joy feels light, airy, like being alive and energetic. Spending time relaxing with an intimate friend, sharing personal news, talking about the heart, discussing ideas that encourage and inspire, joy feels like acceptance, security, and hope. Witnessing the birth of a healthy child, watching as newborn eyes first flutter open to take in faces and images of a new world, joy feels like amazement, wonder, and gratitude. Finishing a laborious project, winning a competition, or overcoming a daunting challenge, joy feels like relief, satisfaction, enthusiasm, and confidence. Seeing a loved one after a prolonged absence, joy feels like anticipation, discovery, and renewal.

Joy is connected to so many other emotions depending on the experience in the moment and its meaning to us on a personal level. To define joy as a feeling of pleasure or happiness does not reveal much. We would then ask, what does pleasure mean? What is happiness? Instead, we describe joy by explaining all the emotions that we take pleasure in feeling and describing the different events that elicit these varied emotions in us. Furthermore, there are different levels of joy, some superficial and fleeting and others profound and enduring.

There is also a joy that is different from the all rest. It can include all the pleasurable emotions we associate with light and life. Even when we are suffering in some facets of our lives, this joy can endure on the deepest level: at the core of our beings. As it surges forth from deep within us, from our spirits, it makes us feel connected to something incredibly greater and more powerful than we can imagine.

I feel this joy of fellowship with the Father when I present a lesson from the teachings of Jesus or offer counsel about living a transformed life, and the eyes of people light up with excitement from understanding something helpful to their spirits that they never understood before. I feel it when I am in the right place at the right time, beyond any coincidental explanation, when the Lord undoubtedly has brought me together with someone to talk about the Christian life. I feel it when I am tired and predict I will not be able to think clearly to present a sermon, and yet when I begin to speak I am filled with tremendous energy and clarity to speak about the Lord. I feel it when I am alone with the Lord, reading his word, and I come to understand his heart on a deeper level. In such moments I do not know whether just to smile to myself, shout with joy, cry because of profound gratitude, or sing a song. I feel alive, excited, enthusiastic, amazed, and thankful. I feel the joy of being so very close to the Father, like an instrument in his hands, an extension of his Being. This joy is unique. It does not come to us except through our relationships with him. It feels different than any other joy. It envelopes and fills us. When he uses us as his instruments, when we pour ourselves out to him in fervent prayer, when he helps us overcome a destructive temptation, when we marvel at some aspect of his creation, when our hearts are filled with worship and praise for him, this joy rises up in us and expresses itself with surprising power. Such events and other similar moments call to the surface a joy that is always there when our spirits are connected to his. It is a fruit of the Spirit.

UNDERSTANDING

The apostle Paul includes joy second in the list of the fruit of the Spirit. Certainly, we think, love belongs at the top of the list because love comprehends all other character traits and behaviors in the Christian life. It is also clear from our own experiences that joy is the immediate result of freeing ourselves from ourselves to love unconditionally. Why, though, does Paul put joy in the second place on the list? If someone were to ask us randomly to make a list of some of the most important character qualities that ought to describe a good person, would joy occur to our minds so quickly as to occupy the second place on our list? We cannot really know for certain why Paul placed joy in this position, but what is just as impressive is the fact that joy even occupies a place on the list. We tend to think of joy as an emotion and not as a character quality on the same level as being loving, patient, kind, gentle, and so on.

The fact that joy is a fruit of the Spirit means that there is a joy that is not just an emotion, but rather a quality or condition of our spirits that does not come and go as emotions usually do. Love, gentleness, or patience, as fruit of the Spirit, are not supposed to ebb and flow; they are supposed to increase steadily in our lives as disciples while we work to cultivate them. Since joy appears on the list of the fruit of the Spirit, there must be a particular form of joy that shares the same characteristics as the other qualities. Like the other fruit of the Spirit, we can work to develop joy as an abiding condition of our spirits. When we express spiritual joy, we are not expressing a momentary feeling but a condition deep within us that was already there, before we experienced an event that brought it to the surface. Think of joy in our spirits like the fiery core of the earth. From time to time, the molten lava within breaks out through fissures in the earth's crust in the form of volcanoes. Even after the initial explosive power of the volcano, the core within still remains molten and ready to burst forth again in another moment. While everything is calm on the surface, we might forget what is inside, but it will always burst forth again, given new circumstances that release its power. The surface calm does not mean the core has cooled. In the same way, when we appear to be emotionally calm or even sad on the surface, our surface emotions do not mean that our inner cores of joy have diminished in intensity. The joy within is still just as full of enthusiasm and spiritual pleasure. Our work in cultivating this joy as a fruit of the Spirit is to practice lives that will make the core burn ever more brightly with even greater power.

Furthermore, we are correct in usually thinking of joy as an emotion that is a reaction of pleasure. There is no contradiction between saying that joy can be a condition and also an emotion. We simply need to be specific about what we are describing: an abiding quality of our spirits or the emotional expression of that quality.

Jesus also made another distinction in his teachings between two different kinds of joy based on the reasons for that joy. One of them is a joy based on temporal reasons. Temporal describes something that is material, non-spiritual, and restricted by time. This kind joy is not only limited by time but is also dependent on circumstances and can be unpredictable. The other joy, Jesus says, is "my joy" (John 15:11), the joy that he reserves for his followers, that is based on spiritual reasons, and is, therefore, an abiding condition, constant, powerful, and eternal.

The parable of the rich fool (Luke 12:13-21) best illustrates the nature of temporal joy. According to Luke's account, two brothers were disagreeing about how to divide their inheritance. One of them came to Jesus asking for counsel to solve the dispute. However, Jesus had not come to be a lawyer to solve civil conflicts. He must have surprised the man by responding, "Watch out! Be on your guard against all kinds of greed; a man's life does not consist in the abundance of his possessions." Jesus' purpose was to teach the reality and beauty of enduring, spiritual values that would replace destructive attitudes such as greed. Against the backdrop of the man's request, Jesus told the following parable:

> The ground of a certain rich man produced a good crop. He thought to himself, "What shall I do? I have no place to store my crops." Then he said, "This is what I'll do. I will tear down my barns and build bigger ones, and there I will store all my grain and my goods. And I'll say to myself, 'You have plenty of good things laid up for many years. Take life easy; eat, drink and be merry.'" But God said to him, "You fool! This very night your life will be demanded from you. Then who will get what you have prepared for yourself?" This is how it will be with anyone who stores up things for himself but is not rich toward God.

One of the truths that Jesus intended to teach by means of this parable was that the kind of joy based on material success, which the rich fool experienced, is the kind of joy that is conditional and fleeting. Since his joy depended solely on physical circumstances, losing his material possessions would not leave any remaining core of joy within him. There was no doubt that the man felt happy. Perhaps he had worked very hard during his life and had anxiously looked forward to the moment when he could stop working and start enjoying the material benefits of all his labor. He was satisfied, content, and thought he now deserved an enjoyable rest. There would be no more backbreaking work from sunrise to sunset, no more worry about drought or crop-devouring insects. Now he determined to relax and experience the joy of a materially successful life. He had not learned what Solomon had learned, "that this too is meaningless." Reality is that material success, like any other temporal source of joy, is conditioned on circumstances that could change in any moment. Jesus, in fact, called the man a fool for not investing in spiritual sources of joy that would always endure.

Feeling the emotion of joy for having worked hard and having arrived at a time of comfortable rest was not wrong. We feel a sense of well-being and pleasure for many goals that we accomplish. The mistake is in forming expectations for temporal joy that such a joy cannot fulfill. We assume that this emotion of joy will last. We hope that the joy of buying something new, of eating a delicious meal, of winning a competition, or making a new friend will last, but time makes the new become old, time dulls the taste of the food, time diminishes the enthusiasm of the win, and time and circumstance beyond our control can rob us of friendships. Then, what will remain? Temporal joy has no core that remains. When the conditions that produced the joy change or vanish, nothing of the former joy stays with us except for the mere memory.

The other kind of joy that Jesus calls "my joy" is very different. Jesus promised to give his disciples this kind of joy when he was speaking with them during the evening before his death on the cross. He knew that his disciples, especially those who had been so close to him, would face overwhelming sadness and despair at seeing him crucified. Yet, he promised them a joy that would be complete and remain with them, despite what would happen the next day. To deepen their understanding, he told them another parable, this time about a vine and its branches.

> I am the true vine, and my Father is the gardener. He cuts off every branch in me that bears no fruit, while every branch that does bear fruit he prunes so that it will be even more fruitful. You are already clean because of the word I have spoken to you. Remain in me, and I will remain in you. No branch can bear fruit by itself; it must remain in the vine. Neither can you bear fruit unless you remain in me. I am the vine; you are the branches. If a man remains in me and I in him, he will bear much fruit; apart from me you can do nothing. If anyone does not remain in me, he is like a branch that is thrown away and withers; such branches are picked up, thrown into the fire and burned. If you remain in me and my words remain in you, ask whatever you wish, and it will be given you. This is to my Father's glory, that you bear much fruit, showing yourselves to be my disciples (John 15:1–8).

This parable describes the intimate relationship between Jesus and his disciples. He is the vine. They are the branches of the vine. As long as they remain in him like branches connected to a vine, he provides all that they need for their spiritual well-being: knowledge, faith, forgiveness, peace, hope, confidence, purpose, and more. Just as it is impossible to distinguish between the vine and the branch at the point of connection between the two, it should be very difficult to distinguish between Jesus and his disciples if they truly model his teachings and live in his image. Time and circumstance cannot rob them of this relationship. They remain in the vine as long as they choose to be dependent on him. As his disciples, they should keep his words, living transformed lives according to his teachings. Just as Jesus remained in the Father's love by obeying his Father's commands, they too remain in Jesus' love by obeying his commands. Jesus sought to give them an unwavering assurance that, though they would face sadness in the coming days, nothing could rob them of their relationships with him. His message to them was simple, "Remain in me." The language Jesus used here became the language of the New Testament; to be "in Christ" characterizes the meaning of the Christ-life. To live the Christian life means to protect and nourish this intimate relationship we have with the Lord.

Jesus then explained to the disciples the reason for teaching this parable about his relationship with them: "I have told you this so that my joy may be in you and that your joy may be complete." Although Jesus certainly experienced sadness, such as the sadness he felt when he thought about how many people were like sheep without a shepherd or the sadness from witnessing the suffering of the humble, he had a joy that remained with him. His joy, the joy that he promised to give the disciples, was the joy of his relationship with the Father. No matter what would happen, he would remain in the Father, intimately connected to the Father. Remaining in the Father's love was the source of joy that Jesus had; and this joy of relationship was the joy Jesus also gave his disciples. He told them the parable of the vine and the branches to explain his relationship to them. The joy he gives us is the joy of an eternal, spiritual relationship that gives us the same joy that Jesus himself has. Our relationships with Jesus and, in the same way, with the Father, bring us, from deep within our spirits, all the healthy emotions that joy calls forth: enthusiasm, acceptance, encouragement, confidence, inspiration, energy, light, hope, relief, satisfaction, and contentment.

These emotions flow from a core of joy deep within us that remains in us as a quality or condition of our lives. We live in Christ and therefore we live in joy. The stronger our relationships to Christ become, the fuller and more complete the core of joy within our spirits becomes. The core remains even when it is not expressed; but events happen in our lives that bring it to the surface, like the molten lava that surges forth from the core of the earth, bursting through the earth's crust in brilliant eruptions. Consider the experience of Jesus himself. Jesus once sent seventy-two disciples out on a mission to preach the gospel (Luke 10:1-24). They returned with great joy because, "Lord, even the demons submit to us in your name." When Jesus heard their report and witnessed their incredible enthusiasm, he was "full of joy through the Holy Spirit." The fact that the Father had blessed his humble disciples with such great power and understanding caused Jesus to express his joy by praising the Father for his wisdom and grace. The joy of Jesus flowed from his relationship with the Father; it was joy through the Holy Spirit. Furthermore, he always had this joy. It was his. But at this moment, the successes of his disciples brought his joy to expression in his enthusiastic celebration of praise for the Father. After the disciples' enthusiasm subsided and they calmed down, joy remained within them as it did within Jesus. Their relationships with the Father produced great fruit when they preached the gospel as the Lord's instruments. After they finished this particular mission for Jesus and returned to their normal routines, their joy would remain in them because their relationships with the Lord remained alive.

In fact, that joy would be a constant source of strength, even when their mission work would not be successful and the opponents of Jesus would persecute them. In the fact the persecution that early disciples experienced revealed an intriguing truth: we can suffer on one level of our existence and feel joyous on a deeper level, in our spirits, at the same time. The apostle Peter discovered this reality: "Dear friends, do not be surprised at the painful trial you are suffering, as though something strange were happening to you. But rejoice that you participate in the sufferings of Christ, so that you may be overjoyed when his glory is revealed" (1 Peter 4:12-13). The disciples rejoiced at the same time they suffered. In this case they did not rejoice despite their suffering but because of their suffering. Persecution for living the Christian life in purity connected them with Christ, as they participated together with him in the similar treatment that he, too, received as their Lord. Their experiences deepened their relationships to him because of what they shared with him and therefore deepened their joy based on those relationships.

In a similar way, James taught, "Consider it pure joy, my brothers, whenever you face trials of many kinds, because you know that the testing of your faith develops perseverance. Perseverance must finish its work so that you may be mature and complete, not lacking anything" (James 1:2-4). James encouraged his readers to find joy in the face of trials, not despite trials but because of trials. The testing of our faith produces perseverance. When we determine to live in the image of Jesus, practicing his character despite the opposition, our faith in Christ increases, becoming more steadfast as we decide not to give up. Trials, in fact, have the potential for making us more mature in the Christian life, imitating his character with more consistency and faithfulness. Instead of separating us from Jesus, trials convince us to live even more closely to him. Trials strengthen our relationships to him and thus deepen the joy flowing from these relationships.

The fact that there are two kinds of joy, a temporal and a spiritual, should not surprise us; these two kinds of joy easily relate to the two different aspects of our nature as human beings. We are physical and temporal as well as spiritual and eternal. There is a part of us that is limited by time and will cease to exist while there is also a part of us that will continue on. Paul wrote:

> Therefore we do not lose heart. Though outwardly we are wasting away, yet inwardly we are being renewed day by day. For our light and momentary troubles are achieving for us an eternal glory that far outweighs them all. So we fix our eyes not on what is seen, but on what is unseen. For what is seen is temporary, but what is unseen is eternal. Now we know that if the earthly tent we live in is destroyed, we have a building from God, an eternal house in heaven, not built by human hands. Meanwhile we groan, longing to be clothed with our heavenly dwelling, because when we are clothed, we will not be found naked. For while we are in this tent, we groan and are burdened, because we do not wish to be unclothed but to be clothed with our heavenly dwelling, so that what is mortal may be swallowed up by life (2 Corinthians 4:17–5:4).

In this passage Paul contrasts the experience of our "outward" nature with our "inward" nature. We can be "wasting away" while we are being "renewed" every day. There is a part of us, the "tent" that we live in, that grows weak and spent. There is another part that "dwells" in this "earthly tent." The earthly tent refers to the body. Paul's use of the pronoun *we* implies that the being that we really are is that which lives in the body. Therefore the word *we* must refer to our spiritual natures, that is, our spirits. The body grows weak and decays, but the Lord constantly renews the strength and energy of our spirits. We can physically suffer and spiritually feel joy at the same time because of the way God designed us: body and spirit.

Paul indicates in this passage that our spirits can feel emotion. While we are living in our physical, earthly bodies, our spirits "groan" and feel "burdened." We physically groan when we stub our toes on a rock or struggle under a heavy burden, but groaning also represents the sort of emotion we feel when we are frustrated and despairing in our spirits. Spiritually we feel despair because of the frustrations we experience when, for instance, we fight to overcome an especially powerful temptation. We fight fierce battles to conquer temptation and live God-centered lives. The conflicts between satisfying our bodies and nourishing our spirits burden us, making self-control a constant challenge. Our spirits react emotionally to these battles and we groan deep within ourselves. It is not a groaning that comes from being physically exhausted but from being spiritually tired. Despite how much we might feel burdened, the Lord can renew the energy and enthusiasm of our spirits. Because of our relationships with him, the Lord can give our spirits strength so that joy replaces groaning. With renewed strength, determining to fight temptation, victory vanishes despair and spiritual joy surges forth again. Furthermore, even when we groan because of physical weakness and pain, this spiritual joy remains. One day he will even take away our physical groaning by clothing us with our "heavenly dwelling."

To complete our understanding of the joy we have in Christ, it is important to fully contrast temporal joy with spiritual joy. We have already seen that temporal joy is an emotional response to circumstances that can include a variety of feelings like enthusiasm, confidence, contentment, calm, relief, security, assurance, excitement, amazement, and anticipation. Eating delicious food, exercising, winning a competition, and even taking drugs can produce these feelings that we associate with the emotion of joy.

Spiritual joy, on the other hand, is a condition or quality of our spirits that comes from living, active relationships with our heavenly Father. We feel connected with him, and these connections produce some of the same emotional responses such as enthusiasm, amazement, security, calm, relief, and so on. But when we feel spiritual joy, these responses originate in our spirits. We can feel confident because of the encouraging connection we have to a close friend. But, on a deeper level of our existence, we feel confident in our spirits because of the connections we have with God. Although the emotional response of confidence is similar, the source of joy is different. We must not confuse the two kinds of joy by thinking that the joy of having a good friend is the same as the joy of being close to God. The joy of being connected with God is what the writers of the New Testament call "joy through the Holy Spirit" (Luke 10:21), "joy in the Holy Spirit" (Romans 14:17), and "joy given by the Holy Spirit" (1 Thessalonians 1:6). The touch point for this joy is not between the neurons of our brain but between spirit and Spirit. Feeling absolutely connected with God, in his presence, with full confidence and peace is an emotion that only our spirits can feel.

Since temporal joy is based on circumstances that do not last, the emotions of temporal joy do not persist. When the music stops or the effect of the drugs ceases, the joy diminishes and eventually vanishes. Spiritual joy remains because our relationships with the Father, through his grace and patient forgiveness, remain. Some Christians have developed the false idea that their relationships with God can be just as turbulent as friendships with other humans. We may have a friend with whom we have good conversations and spend fun times, followed by periods of hurt and silence, in endless cycles. Some people are afraid that they go through these same cycles with God when they make mistakes. God, however, has proven his love and his desire to forgive. Jesus taught in the parable of the vine and the branches that we can be removed from the vine for failing to bear fruit, but being cut off from the vine will depend on our decision to try to live without him.

Here, then, is another contrast between temporal joy and spiritual joy: temporal joy, since it depends on circumstances outside of our control, cannot carry a guarantee to always be present. We expect this kind of joy to always fill us, and, when it does not, we complain and act as if people or destiny has robbed us of something we deserve. Individuals who expect drugs to give them continual satisfaction become addicts to the false expectation that drugs can ultimately satisfy. In order to satisfy to this degree, drug-induced joy would have to be an abiding condition of life, but it cannot be so; instead of bringing lasting satisfaction, the use of drugs ultimately destroys. Temporal joys share in this deceit when people become addicted to their own personal, temporal pleasures, looking for complete satisfaction through these fleeting pleasures.

Spiritual joy is ultimately satisfying for the very reason that it is an abiding condition of our spirits that makes our spirits healthy and alive. Jesus promised the disciples that the joy he would give them would be "complete" (John 16:24). They would have "the full measure" of his joy within them (John 17:13). Deepening this joy by deepening our relationships with the Lord is very much in our control. Spiritual joy is, in fact, so constant and dependable that is it an anchor for our souls.

REFLECTION

The writer of the letter to the Hebrews explains that a special kind of hope serves as an anchor for our souls. What God has promised to us as his children is confirmed by the unchangeable nature of his word. When he promises to do something, he has the power and the inviolable integrity to fulfill his promise. Because it is impossible for God to lie, we can place unwavering hope in what he has promised us. This kind of hope that is founded on his promise is absolutely certain. Therefore the writer concludes, "We have this hope as an anchor for the soul, firm and secure" (Hebrews 6:13-19).

The spiritual joy that is founded on our relationships with the Lord is equally as steadfast as the hope we have and provides another anchor for our soul. The Lord is faithful to us. He is consistently patient, merciful, and forgiving. His unconditional love is unwavering. The joy that comes from our relationships with him is, therefore, constant, consistent, and powerful. It is an anchor that steadies us when life is full of storms that threaten us physically or spiritually. Taking up our anchor and deciding to drift in the middle of a storm does not make sense. Without it the storms would dash us against the rocks. The Psalmist wrote about joy in the middle of troubles, "When anxiety was great within me, your consolation brought joy to my soul" (Psalm 94:19).

Unfortunately, we do not pay much attention to the anchor until the storm comes. Herein is the reason we fail to deepen our spiritual joy. When temporal reasons bring us a certain level of pleasure in our lives, consciously or subconsciously, we do not see much purpose in paying attention to our spiritual joy. While we have food, clothing, homes, dependable jobs to pay our bills, healthy families, good friends, and time for a few enjoyable distractions, we are happy, even content. This level of joy seems so satisfying and fulfilling, at least when we face few problems. When difficulties come, we believe we can invest even more time and energy in these pleasures, and, in this way, cover over the problems or make them disappear. Though in our hearts we want to live a spiritual life, we find ourselves living to increase our temporal joy, to have better houses, higher paying jobs, and more pleasing distractions.

Sometimes, however, the difficulties that threaten our temporal joy do not disappear so easily. We lose our jobs along with the security and satisfaction we felt from our work. Our relationships with someone dear to us suffer serious conflicts or loss. We experience health problems. Because of an economic crisis or due to uncontrolled spending, bills pile up without an easy solution. A close friend betrays us. We experience failure or defeat that calls into question the value of things that we thought could make us happy. The result is a crisis of joy.

A point of crisis happens when circumstances force us to consider making a decision. A crisis of joy, when temporal joy fails, provides us the chance to evaluate what we believed could give us joy. The story of the lost son (Luke 15:11-24) precisely illustrates this valuable moment. From the viewpoint of Jesus' teaching, the crisis the young man experienced represents a crisis between temporal and spiritual joy. After the young man had spent all of the inheritance he had demanded from his father, he should have understood that the pleasures he had been seeking could not satisfy his spirit. Those pleasures could not even satisfy his body. After he had lost all of his money, he continued to hope to find joy in the country far from his father. Only when he had exhausted all the possibilities of finding temporal joy, did he finally think about the satisfaction and pleasure he used to have in his father's house. Now, finally, he thought of the joy of his relationship with his father in a different way than he had before. With the father he had an anchor of joy. He knew he could depend on what he had with his father, so he returned to find renewed joy, this time through valuing more deeply his relationship with his father. He now viewed this relationship as a reason for humble gratitude. When he returned, there was great celebration from genuine joy.

The problem is that in moments of crisis, when temporal reasons for joy fail us, we make the mistake of focusing with even more determination on the things that give us momentary pleasure, hoping that this joy will drown out the problems. It is like playing some favorite music, and, then, hearing some people near us beginning to argue, we raise the volume of the music to drown them out. Soon the volume is so loud that we can think of nothing except the loudness of the music and fail to focus on anything productive. Such an experience is similar to the solution the lost son followed at first, when he wasted all his funds and then "hired himself out to a citizen of that country." He decided to immerse himself in the life of that place.

When temporal joy continues to fail us, we may decide to do something similar to the course that the lost son followed. We return to our Father in heaven and take hold once again of the anchor of spiritual joy that we have with him, at least until everything is better. At that point we can make another mistake. Will we finally see the value of carefully investing our energies in deepening our spiritual joy, or will we treat it merely as a backup plan? Will we just resort to thinking about our spiritual joy when temporal joy fails? God cannot be our backup plan. If we run to him only when we are in trouble and only until good times return, our relationships with him will not be productive. How can we expect to cultivate deeper relationships with anyone if we only resort to them when we have problems? Consider the frustrating cycle that begins with dependence on temporal pleasures, followed by the disappointment of temporal joy, then focusing on joy with the Father until the disappointments resolve, and, ultimately, returning to a life dependent on temporal joys. Following this pattern, we will never experience the completeness, the fullness, the richness of spiritual joy with the Father. We will never give it a chance, and this is the real tragedy. The lost son, on the other hand, finally surrendered himself completely to joy with the father and broke any destructive cycle he might have experienced.

There is another kind of crisis that we feel in our spirits which has the power to finally convince us to practice deeper, living relationships with our Father. The lost son experienced this type of crisis even before he found himself so disappointed in the far country. While he was still in the father's house, before he ever left, he faced a crisis, not of temporal joy, but of something like our spiritual joy. Somehow he had come to believe that the pleasure he felt from living in his father's house was not satisfying. Perhaps he had begun to take for granted the joy of life with his father. Maybe he failed to understand everything that made him content in his life with the father. Perhaps he began to spend less and less time with the father and more time thinking about being somewhere else. For whatever reason the moment came when he thought that the joy of the far country could be greater than joy from his relationship with the father. This moment was a moment of crisis that challenged him to decide between staying with the father and leaving for the far country.

The time also comes in our lives, many times repeated, that calls us to decide which kind of joy will be the focus of our lives. We ought to feel grateful, and certainly we can feel happy, when we have health, sufficient resources, and enjoyable relationships on a temporal level. The question is, what will be the focus of our lives? Imagine putting the amount of energy and time into our relationships with our heavenly Father that we normally invest in being physically and materially happy.

We have many experiences that challenge us to evaluate the sources of our joy and demand that we make decisions about where we will invest our energies in the most satisfying way. Ironically, temporal reasons for joy can threaten to drown out our spiritual focus. When everything is going well physically and materially for us, we have the tendency not to think about the relationships we have with the Father. Enjoying the good life may actually represent a spiritual crisis for us. Imagine if the lost son had not experienced any difficult disappointments in the far country; he might have been there still! We can be thankful this life is not perfect, because if it were, we might never look for something better with the Lord.

A crisis of spiritual joy can also happen when we face suffering in some form because of our relationships with the Lord. Some examples could be the opposition of loved ones who do not believe, the loss of friends because we will not conform to their values, or conflicts with our jobs that demand practices inconsistent with the Christian life. It could be anything that deceives us into thinking that our relationships with the Lord bring us more heartache than joy. We come to this false conclusion either because we have never really understood the depth of joy we have with the Father or because we are caught up in the emotions of a temporal joy that is blinding us. We can imagine that once the lost son started thinking about the pleasures he might enjoy in the far country away from the father, those thoughts pushed out the peace, security, and acceptance he felt in the father's house. His perspective of life became seriously distorted, and he left the father.

The disciples of Jesus faced a crisis that threatened the joy of their relationships with him while his body lay in the tomb for three days. Jesus had explained the truths of the parable of the vine and the branches the night before his death so that their "joy might be complete". Then, during the same evening, he told them about people who might kill them, thinking that in so doing they would be "offering a service to God" (John 16:1-2). Sometime later, referring to his coming death and resurrection, he also told them, "In a little while you will see me no more, and then after a little while you will see me" (John 16:16). Jesus warned them that during this lapse between not seeing him and then seeing him again, "I tell you the truth, you will weep and mourn while the world rejoices" (John 16:20). The joy that they had felt for three-and-a-half years, the joy that became more thrilling, more filled with anticipation with each parable and miracle, would be snatched from them, at least so they thought, when their Master died on the cross. Their joy would seem to turn into unbearable grief and despair. But, Jesus told them, "You will grieve but your grief will turn to joy" (John 16:20). Just as a mother forgets the anguish of childbirth after her child is born, their despair would be replaced by joy that no one could take away from them.

Whatever the crisis of spiritual joy we experience, our grief will also turn to joy if we remain, no matter the cost, connected to the vine. The crisis is useful and even necessary. It has the power to teach us to focus our energies on increasing the enduring spiritual joy of life with the Father. Hopefully, we will not have to go as far as the lost son went in order to value more deeply our relationships with our Father; but, when he returned to the father, the joy he felt was different because now he was different, and, consequently, his view of his relationship with his father was different. After the crisis, the joy in our spirits becomes more settled, powerful, and no longer just a back-up but instead the light of our lives.

PRACTICE

Unfortunately, we may have to pass through a crisis of joy to convince ourselves to pay more attention to the need our spirits have for joy. Before needing to experience such difficult times, we might discover, if we honestly look at our hearts in a moment of quiet solitude, that we do not depend very much on our relationships with the Lord for joy on a daily basis. To be truthful, we might have to say that we do not think very much about the Lord during our normal days, going from one activity to another. We know that we have joy in the Lord; after all, the Scriptures say that we have joy in him. Even if we have been firm believers for years, perhaps our faith has never really brought us to the point of needing to feel spiritual joy deeply. The disposition of our hearts, from moment to moment during the day, may depend more on how we perform at work, how we get along with the people around us, what the weather is like, or whether we have to stand in long lines or wait in slow traffic on the highway. The idea that we can actually feel joy in our spirits may seem to some degree unnatural. On a deeper level of our consciousness we might even be afraid to feel the intense thrill and overwhelming wonder of knowing the Lord is present with us. Many people are afraid of showing temporal emotions; imagine what they must think of feeling spiritual emotions!

There is no need to be discouraged or embarrassed if we do not feel the joy of our relationships with the Lord in every moment; all believers experience periods in their spiritual lives when the strength of this joy wanes. Even if we have not experienced pure, intense joy since the time we felt the initial spiritual excitement coming out of the waters of baptism, we can at least evaluate our sense of joy at the present and discover what to do to accept and to nurture spiritual joy as an active, growing part of our lives. Remember that spiritual joy is a fruit of the Spirit: it shares some essential qualities with the other fruits, namely that we must practice joy order to grow in joy.

Practicing joy, of course, does not mean standing in front of the mirror rehearsing an excited smile or learning to react to discouraging circumstances with a positive attitude. Spiritual joy is a condition of our spirits that depends on our relationships with our heavenly Father. When we feel joy in our spirits, we sense our connection to the unimaginable power, the gracious love, and the eternal nature of the Father. We feel like the branch that is firmly connected to the vine, drawing life and energy from the vine and actively bearing fruit. Our joy with the Father expresses itself in enthusiasm, confidence, peace, courage, and hope. There is no need to practice in front of the mirror, but there are ways to practice joy in order to grow in joy. Since joy is a condition of our spirits and not just a passing emotion, the goal of growing in joy is to make this condition deeper, more meaningful, more constant, and more consistent in its expression. We long for the "complete joy" that Jesus promised his disciples. Because the joy Jesus called "my joy" flows from our relationships with the Father, practicing joy means to practice our relationships with him. As we become more aware of his presence in our lives and open ourselves up to the way he wants to work in our lives, joy naturally grows.

James wrote, "Come near to God and he will come near to you" (James 4:8). Maybe these words represent a spiritual platitude that no longer has the power to grab us and energize us, but they form a promise, a serious, sacred promise from the Creator of the universe. When we actively try to come closer to him, he will fill us with his presence and with the incredible of joy that comes from his presence. We know from our own experiences that sometimes we feel like a wall exists, at least from our perspectives, between ourselves and another person. We are not sure what the other person is thinking. Communication is awkward or nonexistent. But if we bravely speak with humility and do something to lovingly serve, we might discover that this person really wanted friendship with us and that no wall actually existed. We even take the first step if the relationship is very important to us. Just like the father of the lost son waited for the son to come and then ran to meet him, our heavenly Father is waiting for us to decide we want a deeper relationship with him, and then he will gladly come running. There will be celebration. Once we decide how valuable our relationships to the Father are, what can we do to deepen our consciousness of these relationships?

Pursue transformation. Living in the presence of the Lord is, first of all, a transforming experience. No one ever stood in God's presence without being transformed in some way. We are never the same afterwards. Pride turns into humility. Fear turns into confidence. Bitterness and hatred are transformed into forgiveness and love. The purpose of living in his presence and enjoying communion with him is to be transformed. At the same time that we are actively learning to love, pursuing peace, and practicing patience, he is also working to provide us opportunities to learn and strength in our spirits to empower us to grow. Paul wanted the Ephesians to know "his incomparably great power for us who believe. That power is like the working of his mighty strength, which he exerted in Christ when he raised him from the dead" (Ephesians 1:19-20). The power that God exercised when he raised Jesus from the dead is the same power that works in our lives to raise us spiritually from the dead and transform us.

During this process of transformation, there will be moments when we surprise ourselves at the changes happening in our hearts and our behavior. We never thought we could be as patient or as forgiving as we have become. If, in a given moment, we show uncharacteristic compassion in our actions toward another person, we realize that living with the Lord is really changing us. This realization of his work in our lives fills us with enthusiasm and confidence in the Christian life and a sense of closeness to the Lord that we do not otherwise feel. If we desire to deepen our relationships with our Father and allow joy to grow, we can begin by actively pursuing transformation. But our transformation must not be independent of him; it must be in cooperation with him. Whether you are a new Christian or you have been living the Christian life for many years, open yourself up to discovering new ways you can practice the character of Christ. Let the Lord open up opportunities for you. Humbly ask for the wisdom and strength he can give you in your spirit. Enjoy working with him.

Deepen your prayer life. A transformed prayer life is another way to deepen our relationships with the Father. The disciples asked Jesus to teach them how to pray (Luke 11:1). They were Jews. They knew how to pray. Nevertheless, they had undoubtedly listened to the prayers of Jesus and heard his enthusiasm, his humility, his joy, and his submissive spirit in his prayers. His prayers were not ritually repeated words but instead the communication of a heart that was open and ready to be absolutely transparent. His prayers consisted of very personal communication with his Father, in reality a new way of thinking about God. In response to their request, Jesus taught them to address God as their Father. He also gave them two illustrations about a friend asking a friend for bread and a son asking a father for fish. In these two stories, Jesus described communication that uses the language of a close relationship. Prayer was essential to the relationship he wanted them to have with the Father.

The night before he died, he wanted them to feel even more confident in prayer. He promised them, "Until now you have not asked for anything in my name. Ask and you will receive, and your joy will be complete" (John 16:24). Why would joy be complete when they received what they asked for in prayer? Did Jesus mean to say that they would be happy because they would receive exactly what they asked for? But what of the times when they would not receive what they requested? Would joy escape them? Spiritual joy in prayer does not come from receiving whatever we might request. Joy that depends on receiving what we ask for leads to a very temporal, materialistic view of prayer. The truth is that the joy of prayer comes from knowing through prayer and God's answers to our prayers, whether positive or negative, that he is working with us and in us. In the context of this promise Jesus gave the disciples about prayer, he was talking with them about their relationships to him and to the Father. Jesus' death on the cross would not diminish the intimacy they could feel. He would still be present with them. Knowing that he was present and working in their lives to transform them was the joy of prayer. To understand the joy that comes from prayer, we have to stand back and look at the bigger picture. Joy is not about a particular and positive answer to a specific prayer. Joy is about constantly communicating with confidence, knowing that he is listening and working. We celebrate enthusiastically in the moments when he answers some specific prayer, but the enduring joy of prayer is the joy of relationship, the joy of speaking from our hearts and listening and watching for his answer. To grow in joy, we can grow in the personal, intimate, and open level of communication we practice with him and learn to feel free just talking with him, pouring out our hearts, whether with tears or with the smiling laughter of gladness. To increase your joy in the Lord's presence, no matter how many years of experience you have in prayer, practice prayer on an even more personal, more open, more transparent level. Open your heart without fear. Use the language of intimate friendship and of a child communicating with a loving, forgiving father. Learn to recognize his answers, knowing that, as James says, "Every good and perfect gift is from above, coming down from the Father of the heavenly lights, who does not change like shifting shadows" (James 1:17).

Yield to the Father as his instrument. We also deepen the joy of such personal intimacy with the Father when we allow him to use us as his instruments. The apostles John and Paul both described Jesus' role in the creation of the universe using similar language. Speaking about Jesus, John wrote, "Through him all things were made; without him nothing was made that has been made" (John 1:3). Paul also wrote concerning Jesus, "For by him all things were created: things in heaven and on earth, visible and invisible, whether thrones or powers or rulers or authorities; all things were created by him and for him" (Colossians 1:16). Jesus is the reflection of the nature, character, and power of the Father and, in some way, Jesus manifested this relationship in the creation. The Father created all things "through him." He was the instrument of his Father's creative power.

In a different but very real sense, we, also, as children of God, serve as tools of his creative power. Paul invites us to be "instruments of righteousness" (Romans 6:13). The Lord gives our bodies strength and energy to practice what is right, not just for our own personal salvation and transformation but also to show others the beauty of living in the image of Christ. People can learn to understand the compassion, mercy, and forgiveness of God by the way we love them. If a person who has not known God desperately needs to discover how to live a new life, we can show him or her by our own lives that transformation is possible with the Lord. Just as Paul considered his own life to be "an example for those who would believe on him and receive eternal life" (1 Timothy 1:16) because of the incredible mercy God showed him, our lives can also serve to show others the depth of God's grace. In a very direct sense, we also serve as messengers of the good news of Jesus. Paul reasoned, "How, then, can they call on the one they have not believed in? And how can they believe in the one of whom they have not heard? And how can they hear without someone preaching to them?" (Romans 10:14). The Lord brought together Philip with the Ethiopian (Acts 8:26-39) and Ananias with Saul of Tarsus (Acts 22:2-21). God could have personally declared the gospel to both the Ethiopian and Saul, who would become Paul; yet, he sent human instruments to teach them the gospel. Despite our weaknesses and insecurities, the Lord can graciously and providentially bring us together with people who are hungry and thirsty to know him and to begin new lives. The moment you realize that God has brought someone to you so that you can tell of his love, model his mercy, and explain the possibility of living a new life is a moment of incredible joy. You know that you are in the Father's hands, that he is using you in a very significant and special way to give a gift that has eternal value. Open yourself up to being his instrument and you will feel the joy of his confidence in you. You will feel the enthusiasm that comes from being a branch that is bearing fruit because of your intimate connection to the vine. Practice being his instrument and you will be practicing intimacy with the Father that deepens joy.

Let the word of God be a revelation. Joy with the Father is also the joy of revelation. Revelation uncovers something that was previously hidden. The word can refer to the direct help the Holy Spirit gave to the apostles and early disciples when they needed to learn new truths (John 16:7-13), but it can also refer to knowledge we come to understand by means that are not so miraculous.

Learning to meditate carefully on the teachings of Jesus and learning to practice his truths promises new insights into his wisdom and reveals the beauty of living life with him. We can read and study for many years and still discover new understanding that we had never seen before. The word of God is written in a way that allows for different levels of understanding: What did the text or the teaching recorded in the text mean to the original readers and listeners? What does it mean to Christians today? What does it mean for my personal life? How can it examine and call into question my previous thinking? How can I practice the teaching in specific ways in the present moments? Then, when we come back to the text later, with more experience and understanding from practice, we will discover even more truth that will change our lives. God is speaking to us through his word. He is calling us to live closer to him, and, as we draw closer, he comes closer to us. Deeper insight from these moments of revelation, uncovering what was previously hidden to us, brings him closer. The joy that we feel is the joy of discovery, admiration, awe, anticipation, and hope. We know that without him and his patient teaching, we could never have known what we know.

John wrote, "We know that we have come to know him if we obey his commands" (1 John 2:3). Committed and surrendered obedience to the teachings of Jesus gives us a revelation of the Father that we cannot receive in any other manner. The experience of actually forgiving someone over and over and over again teaches us the cost, the grace, and the unselfish nature of God's forgiveness. After struggling to forgive someone who has repeatedly offended us, we say to ourselves, "Now I understand a little more about how God has forgiven me." We discover something about God's heart that only experience could reveal to us. The real-life practice of the character of Christ gives us a much deeper insight into God's heart than we ever could have had only by reading. Such practical revelations bring Him, who seemed so far away from us, ever closer. Intimate knowledge of another's heart always brings us closer. The gratitude and peace we feel in such moments are the expressions of the joy of a more profound relationship.

Other revelations of a similar nature come from understanding the complexity and beauty of God's natural creation. Go for a walk through a forest, a hike up to a mountain vista point, go out to the desert beyond the reach of city lights and look up to the star-filled night sky, or look into a microscope, considering the complex processes at work in a cell, and you can appreciate the mind and power of God. There must be an eternal, infinitely powerful Designer. As we struggle to conceive of a Being so powerful and yet so loving, he comes close to us. To look up at a starry sky without belief can be disconcerting, isolating, and even terrifying, but to look up with faith makes us feel part of him.

Now, read differently than you have before. Practice this joy by carefully meditating on his teachings and allowing them to interrogate your thinking and change your behavior. To consistently experience the joy of Christ, look for the Father, look for him in his word, look for him in the practice of his character, and look for him in his creation. What you discover will be cause for celebration.

Celebrate with him. The joy of living with the Father also deepens through the victories of faith we experience. We understand how sin works. Sin promises pleasure and then destroys. The letters of Paul constantly reminded Christians then and remind us now to "Watch," "Be careful," "Do not let anyone deceive you ..." Nevertheless, no Christian is absolutely exempt from the deceitfulness of sin. When temptation confronts us in its full force, the struggle to overcome can be excruciatingly difficult. By faith we know that, despite any short-term promise sin makes to us, it will destroy us in the long-run. By faith we know that the Lord will never allow us to be tempted more than we can bear. By faith we know that there is a way of escape from the temptation, and we do not have to despair. And by faith we know that the Lord will not leave us in the middle of the struggle but will strengthen our spirits. So we struggle by faith and, just as he promised, we finally overcome and finish as victors. We may stumble. We may fall. But we finish victorious. There is little joy that compares to what we feel when the struggle is over. When Satan's temptation of Jesus was over and "angels came and attended him," Jesus must have felt the joy of relief and victory. Satan would come back, but Jesus had now experienced victory and the joy of that moment would motivate him during the next battle. The moment we realize that we have stood firmly and refused to surrender, the joy we feel in our spirits is the joy of relief, peace, confidence, and hope. Our victories connect us deeply to the Father because our victories are his. He has empowered us in our weakest moments. He knew our weaknesses and has protected us from completely falling. He loved us enough, though, to let us make the decision ourselves to overcome and win. So practice the joy of victory by facing the battle and refusing to surrender, and then celebrate the victory with your heavenly Father. He will fill you with the intense joy of his presence.

There will be moments when the joy that is always there surfaces and compels us to express it, like the fire from the center of the earth that bursts through the outer crust in a volcanic eruption. When we realize the Lord really has changed us in some genuine way, when we pray without holding back any emotions, when the Lord answers our patient petitions, when we see he has used us as his instruments, when we arrive at new, illuminating understanding of his word, and when we finally overcome a powerful temptation are all moments for celebration.

Spiritual joy is a condition that expresses itself in celebration. We need to celebrate such moments when we feel the Lord's presence fill us. Paul encouraged the Christians at Philippi to "Rejoice in the Lord always. I will say it again: Rejoice!" (Philippians 4:4) Paul is so emphatic about the need to rejoice that he repeats his instruction, "I will say it again, Rejoice!" Rejoice means to celebrate. Celebration is the expression of joy. To rejoice or to celebrate recalls and reinforces the reasons why we feel joy. We celebrate anniversaries, for instance, in order to express the reasons why we are happy and thankful for special events that happen or for precious relationships we have. Without the celebration we would have the tendency to take joy for granted or even fail to appreciate what we should be thankful for. Celebrating our spiritual joy "in the Lord" is absolutely essential in order to grow in joy and make joy a real, consistent part of our lives as disciples.

Spiritual celebration moves us to express our joy openly and enthusiastically. The power of the Lord's presence can, at times, be an overwhelming experience that must burst forth in celebration. We cannot keep it to ourselves. We want to tell someone else about it. Telling people about our joy is a form of celebration. The Samaritan woman who met Jesus at the well near Sychar, after speaking with him, left her water jar next to the well and quickly returned to the town, telling everyone who would listen, "Come, see a man who told me everything I ever did. Could this be the Christ?" (John 4:29). Andrew, when he first met Jesus, went to tell his brother, Simon Peter, "We have found the Messiah" (John 1:41). The apostle John, who recorded this moment, noted that this was the "first thing Andrew did," when he met Jesus. Andrew's message to his brother was an act of celebration after having waited for the Messiah for such a long time. John is the same one who recorded the conversation Jesus had with his disciples about the parable of the vine and the branches that included Jesus' promise to give his disciples "my joy." John is very focused on showing how the joy of a relationship with Jesus affected people. He also wrote in language that still today communicates the excitement he personally felt when he was with Jesus. He wrote to share this joy with his readers so their joy could be "complete."

> That which was from the beginning, which we have heard, which we have seen with our eyes, which we have looked at and our hands have touched—this we proclaim concerning the Word of life. The life appeared; we have

seen it and testify to it, and we proclaim to you the eternal life, which was with the Father and has appeared to us. We proclaim to you what we have seen and heard, so that you also may have fellowship with us. And our fellowship is with the Father and with his Son, Jesus Christ. We write this to make our joy complete (1 John 1–4).

Giving thanks in prayer is another form of celebration which expresses our joy to the Lord himself. When the seventy-two disciples returned from their hugely successful mission to preach the gospel in the towns of Galilee, Jesus spoke to the Father about the joy that filled him through the Holy Spirit: "I praise you, Father, Lord of heaven and earth, because you have hidden these things from the wise and learned, and revealed them to little children. Yes, Father, for this was your good pleasure" (Luke 10:21). Jesus expressed thrilling joy by enthusiastically praising the Father. To praise means to tell about something good someone has done. Prayer is praise when we tell the Lord how deeply thankful we are for something he has done. Praise is more powerful when it is specific. We might say, "Thank you Lord for all the good things you have done for me." But if we were to explain exactly which things he has done are the ones that have given us particular joy, then our praise would much more genuine. We make the conscious effort to think about those precise things that fill us with joy. This form of celebration is not just for his glory but also serves to reinforce our joy.

Singing songs of praise is also an expression of joyous celebration. James wrote, "Is anyone happy? Let him sing songs of praise" (James 5:13). The potential to perceive melodious sounds and to imitate those sounds in song is a gift of God's design. We certainly have to train our ears and voices to repeat the pitch and duration of the melodies we hear, but the potential to do so to accompany the words of our hearts is a gift of God that distinguishes us from other animals. God created us to praise in song. Song, therefore, is a God-given form of celebration. We certainly sing praises during worship services with the church, but there must be other moments when the expression of praise flows from within us because of something personal. James would say in such moments, "sing songs of praise" (James 5:13). We can train ourselves to allow experiences of the Lord's presence to bring spiritual joy to the level of our consciousness and cause us to sing, even spontaneously sing, because of joy.

Paul described another form celebration that we do not commonly consider but that has a special kind of power to encourage our joy to grow. He said of the Christians in Macedonia (from Philippi, Thessalonica and Berea) that their "overflowing joy" motivated them first to give themselves to the Lord and then to give "as much as they were able, and even beyond their ability" in order to help Christians in Judea who were suffering from lack of food.

> And now, brothers, we want you to know about the grace that God has given the Macedonian churches. Out of the most severe trial, their overflowing joy and their extreme poverty welled up in rich generosity. For I testify that they gave as much as they were able, and even beyond their ability. Entirely on their own, they urgently pleaded with us for the privilege of sharing in this service to the saints. And they did not do as we expected, but they gave themselves first to the Lord and then to us in keeping with God's will........ (2 Corinthians 8:1–5).

The Macedonian Christians celebrated their incomparable joy in the Lord through making deeper a commitment to the Lord and to his people. They had spiritual joy despite their temporal poverty, and, in fact, their "extreme poverty" was transformed into acts of "rich generosity" because of joy. If we enjoy doing something, our joy can motivate us to be even more devoted to that behavior; as a result, we practice that behavior with more frequency; and then as a result of the more frequent practice, we experience more joy. This cycle with the potential for repeating itself is the special power of this form of celebration. Celebrating by making a deeper commitment produces even more joy that comes from the greater commitment.

There are certainly moments in the Christian life when we do not feel like celebrating: we make difficult sacrifices to do what is right, we suffer physically either from sickness or from abuse, we become discouraged because of opposition, we become tired from not seeing immediate results from our efforts to love. What do we do now? We celebrate, not because of the difficulty or tragedy but in spite of it. If we discipline ourselves to celebrate moments that bring our joy to the surface, then we will be more accustomed to celebration itself and more likely to think about celebrating during other moments that threaten to drown our joy. The experience of Paul and Silas while imprisoned in Philippi offers a poignant illustration of this principle (Acts 16:19-34). They had been arrested, falsely accused, severely beaten, and then thrown into an inner cell of the prison. There was no reason to celebrate these events. But neither did the events present a crisis of joy for them. Paul and Silas knew the reason for their joy. They were suffering, but the Lord had not abandoned them nor had they isolated themselves from the Lord, becoming so absorbed in discouragement that they do not even think about the him. In fact, Paul and Silas probably felt closer to the Lord because their suffering united them together with him. They could not, however, ignore the hardships of their situation. It would be nearly impossible to overlook the pain of the beating and the filth of the inner cell. Their prayers and their songs were the attempts of disciplined hearts to celebrate life with the Lord, in spite of the circumstances they were in. Their joy was an anchor for their spirits in such discouraging moments. Their joy at such a time was a powerful witness for faith in Jesus and profoundly influenced the other prisoners and even the jailer himself. Spiritual joy triumphed that night, not because it spontaneously sprung forth but because it was practiced.

We do not wake up suddenly one morning with the level of spiritual discipline that Paul and Silas had to celebrate in the middle of suffering. Such joy, as a fruit of the Spirit, is the result of practice and growth. Joy cannot be a static quality that is just simply present without increasing or decreasing. But to increase our joy, to cultivate it, to make it more consistent, deeper, and more powerful in its expression, we need to develop more profound relationships with our heavenly Father. Then, the joy that comes from these relationships will give birth to the celebration that naturally flows from it. The closer you draw to him, the more intense this celebration will be.

CHAPTER THREE

PURSUING PEACE

"WHOEVER WOULD LOVE LIFE AND SEE GOOD DAYS…
HE MUST SEEK PEACE AND PURSUE IT"
(1 PETER 3:10-11).

The town I have lived in for many years can be a violent place at times. Its location in the central part of the state creates a clashing point between youth gangs from the north and south fighting for control of territory to sell drugs. Violence has come close to home. Gang members drove through our neighborhood and shot at the house across the street from us because the young man living there, who as a child had played soccer with us in our yard, was becoming involved with the gangs. Young people I have met and worked with at the county juvenile hall face long prison terms for impulsive acts of bloodshed, that they have come to regret over and over again. Once, before leaving on a trip to work abroad, I met with Carlos, a sixteen-year-old who was seriously thinking about dropping out of the gang he belonged to. We promised to speak together when I returned from the trip. When I returned he was dead, shot in the stomach in an ambush, as retribution for brutality that he had committed.

Why? On the surface the fighting appears to be a turf war over drug sales. At the same time, gang members themselves create myths to recruit new young members by explaining their violence as a necessary means to protect their ethnic group, despite the fact that opposing gang members share the same ethnic background. One youth was most honest when he confided to me that there are things he wanted to have, like a certain make of car with a rocking stereo system and shiny chrome wheels. The quickest way for him to get what he wanted, he explained, was by selling drugs. Desire leads to greed and greed inflames desire to the point that violence seems to be a very reasonable means to eliminate any obstacles that might block the satisfaction of those desires.

Unfulfilled and out-of-control desires not only cause conflicts on the streets, but also in the home, between family members, and among friends. Violence on the streets and arguments in the home often share a common source. James precisely expressed this truth when he explained that conflicts between us come from conflicts within us. "What causes the fights and quarrels among you? Don't they come from your desires that battle within in?" (James 4:1) The real battle is in our hearts, where conflicting desires rob us of peace. The pursuit of peace must begin with our own hearts.

UNDERSTANDING

Peace is a condition that is immediately recognizable by what it lacks: there is no conflict, no argument, no disturbance, no confusion. We suddenly, dramatically sense peace when the loud, crushing, crashing music becomes silent, the yelling ceases, the arguments resolve, the harsh wind goes still, and the running, rushing, roaring turmoil of everyday life in the city is shut out by the quiet solitude of a place apart. Peace is also full of calm, the tranquility of order and harmony. Peace is productive. Peace happens when all the parts work together the way they are supposed to, when all the pieces fit together to produce something complete, and when people cooperate to achieve the same goal. The Greek word for peace shares a root in common with the word for join. Peace joins together in harmony. Paul wrote about the religious divisions between Jews and Gentiles, explaining that Jesus is our peace, "who has made the two one and has destroyed the barrier, the dividing wall of hostility" (Ephesians 2:14). Jesus is our peace because, on the most fundamental level, he joins us together.

Where there is peace, other emotions also prevail. The harmony and order of peace provide a sense of security and confidence. Things work as they should, and we can predict the results. We do not have to worry or be afraid because the storm has ceased. There are, of course, moments that unexpected peace makes us worry, such as when the children playing in another room suddenly become quiet, but generally peace removes fear. Furthermore, contentment and happiness inevitably accompany the presence of peace. As human beings it is natural for us to feel most happy when we are at peace. As individuals, though, we differ in how much order we require in our lives or how much disorder we are willing to suffer. But even those who seem to live with disorder actually do seek order on some level in their lives, just not the same order others seek. A person's room may be a disaster of disorder while he spends time meticulously organizing the tedious steps of a computer program. Organizing data gives him a satisfying sense of accomplishment, contentment, and peace; the condition of the room is outside of his consciousness.

Why do human beings prefer peace? Our deep desire for peace should not surprise us. We form part of a natural universe, created by a God who is, as Paul wrote, "not a God of disorder but of peace"

(1 Corinthians 14:33). From the subatomic level to the massively explosive power of stars in the universe, God created physical laws and relationships that are ordered and harmonious. Even when certain physical systems in the universe seem to be random, we discover, upon looking more closely with more sophisticated tools, that order is always present. Where there is order, there is peace. In the same way, the teachings Jesus, revealed to us from the Creator, have the purpose of bringing peace and order to our lives. Compassion, mercy, generosity, and self-sacrificing love bring people together. When we come to practice these qualities, as well as others that Jesus taught, we sense completeness, contentment, and confidence that are companions of peace.

Interestingly enough, although we were created to feel content when we are at peace, the promise of fleeting pleasure deceives us, and we practice behavior that ultimately leads to confusion and turmoil. Sin, in fact, introduces disorder into our world, into our homes, and into our own hearts. For instance, the result of selfishness is disorder in our spirits and in our relationships. Instead of unselfishly seeking the benefit of others, we decide to protect our own interests and take advantage of people, thinking that we will only be happy when we finally have what we want. We convince ourselves that we will only be content when we fulfill our desires, no matter the cost to others. But we never find contentment and we destroy our relationships. Self-centeredness produces confusion, strife, and war. Remember the words of James, that the fights and quarrels among us come from the battles within us.

Understanding peace includes seeing how fundamentally necessary peace is to our existence, realizing that our lives will never be satisfying until we have peace. God made us for peace. Even the most violent youth on the street, when he has a quiet moment alone in his room, longs for peace. To someone he trusts, he will admit that he would like to have a family someday, a wife and children to help him enjoy peaceful relationships in a tranquil home. He is tired of constantly worrying about looking over his shoulder to prepare for unseen threats. On some level the desire for peace battles the desire to have what others have and, thus, to feel important, respected, and powerful.

Our willingness to pursue peace will depend on how precious peace is to us. Trying to remove guns from the streets will not diminish the violence, nor will endless sessions of counseling resolve family conflicts until the desire for peace is more powerful than the deceptive desire to satisfy self before others. Peace must be most precious to people.

REFLECTION

The first step we might want to take to create peace in our lives would be somehow to escape from all the people who really cause us problems: the people who express their own opinions too much, who have nasty habits, who love to argue, all the critical people, all the people who never want to do what we want to do, all the ones who never help us with our work, and who seem to always have something negative to say about us, all the people who...well now...not too many friends left! In fact, left all alone in this world, we would still not have peace. Peace does not begin by eliminating all the conflicts we have with people around us. Peace begins within our own hearts.

The reality is that we need peace on three different levels and the first does not have to do with the people around us. Before we can have peace in our relationships with family members, friends, and even our enemies, we first need to have peace with ourselves in our hearts. Remember, when we speak about our hearts in this context, we are referring to the desires and emotions that motivate us to do what we do. The battles within our hearts boil up and overflow into conflicts in our relationships. The battle within our hearts that James refers to is a battle due to unsatisfied desires. There are things that we eagerly want to possess, experiences that we would like to participate in, and friends whose company we would like to enjoy. When we do not have what we want, a battle begins in our hearts. We rationalize why we deserve it and accuse ourselves of being powerless to obtain it, fighting with depression for not having it.

The battle of self against self, the part of self that accuses and the part of self that defends, can come in waves of despair, then hope, and then despair again. When we encounter someone who has what we want, the battle inside turns to envy and jealousy on the outside, creating conflict with that person. In the extreme case, James says that, "You want something but don't get it. You kill and covet, but you cannot have what you want. You quarrel and fight ..." (James 4:2). The other person may wonder why we act so aggressively or critically toward her since she has no idea of the fight inside our heart. If, at the same time, we do not want to have a conflict with this person, we will struggle to maintain a healthy relationship with her. But our negative emotions toward the person will continue to threaten our peace until we first resolve the overpowering desire in our hearts to possess what we do not have.

The battle within us, that boils over into conflicts with others, emanates from self-centeredness. Human beings have the natural tendency to protect themselves from danger and conserve their lives. Even the Lord teaches us not to abuse our bodies since they are instruments to serve him and the means for him to manifest his life through us. But, left uncontrolled, the desire for self-protection grows into a fierce protection of our self-interests. We put ourselves, at least in our own thinking, at the center of our world, expecting people to conform to our needs and wishes. What matters the most is confirming our importance and worth as people. Others must give way to us and listen carefully to our problems. We serve others only when it is convenient for us or when we can expect some favor in return.

A battle rages among our different emotions because we are confronted by the needs of others, sometimes the desperate needs of people whom we could help if we had the inclination to do so. To keep ourselves at the center of our world, we have to argue with ourselves to justify why our needs are more important and why the other person does not deserve our help. Then, when people deny us what we expect from them or do not conform as we wish, the battle is on with them. The issue at hand can lose perspective because what is at stake is self-importance. "Wash the dishes? Are you kidding? I have my own work to do!" "What do you mean 'your' needs? I have my own needs!" "Please don't bother me with your petty complaints! Can't you see that I am busy?" We wonder why we cannot have peaceful relationships with people. "What's wrong with them?" "Don't they care?" The problem, though, is the conflict in our own hearts.

Pride represents another battle within ourselves. The negative, destructive form of pride is the feeling that we are right, we do not make mistakes, at least not as many as the next person, and that we are better, more righteous, and more deserving of honor. Pride develops as a deceptive defense mechanism to protect us against self-criticism and a lack of self-confidence. The problem, to which we are oblivious at times, is that we do make mistakes and we are often wrong. When there is conflict in our minds between who we are and who we think we should be, that conflict will boil over into criticizing others for not being who we think they ought to be.

We cannot suffer self-criticism very easily simply because self-criticism represents conflict within us, robbing us of inner peace. We have to avoid conflict, especially conflict on such an intimate level within ourselves. To elude this inner confusion, we tend to focus on the shortcomings of others. The inner emotion of pride now manifests itself externally in our relationships. Instead of just trying to convince ourselves that we are better, we also try to convince others, pointing out their mistakes and emphasizing our superiority. Distracted by their mistakes, we do not have to think about our own. Pride also manifests itself in the language of self-justification and condemnation of others. In Jesus' parable of the two men praying, the Pharisee demonstrated this destructive behavior when he said, "God, I thank you that I am not like other men—robbers, evildoers, adulterers—or even like this tax collector" (Luke 18:11). Of course, as we increasingly criticize spouses, children, friends, or enemies, conflicts with these people increase. Even if they do not take our criticisms personally and try to ignore the conflicts, we have to continue the battles, at least in our imaginations, in order to keep our minds from thinking about our own mistakes. If we understand we must resolve our conflicts with these people, we will first have to resolve our own problem of pride.

The battle in our hearts may still take another form related to pride: the fight against feelings of insecurity. Pride is one symptom of the deeper problem of insecurity. To feel insecure is natural for us as human beings. It is a natural emotion that we ought to feel, understanding our limited powers as mortals. Fear is certainly healthy at times. But events constantly happen that remind us we are not absolutely powerful, and we cannot control everything and everyone whom we would like to control. Insecurity also manifests itself as a lack of confidence about our abilities or our value as people and can result in a persistent feeling of low self-esteem. One inner voice says we are worth nothing and another inner voice argues that we are obviously better than the next person. Although some degree of insecurity is natural, the way we deal with it is problematic. When the conflicts in our hearts concerning our personal worth reach a certain level of disturbance, we can react aggressively to anyone who challenges our ideas or who threatens to diminish our control. We exaggerate any perceived attempt to criticize our value. On the other hand, we may feel such little self-worth that we passively surrender to the manipulation of others until, finally, we are filled with resentment at the way they control us. Trying to resolve conflicts with such people will be unsuccessful until we first resolve the inner battles with unhealthy feelings of insecurity.

Guilt can take the battle to an even higher level. There is no inner peace where there is unresolved guilt. Guilt is self telling self, "You have really failed, you cannot ignore the great error that you committed, you sinned and you must face it." We know we are not perfect. No one is perfect. But facing real guilt in the wrong way can rob us of whatever confidence or self-worth we might have thought we had. To protect ourselves against self-accusation, we offer ourselves explanations for what we did and justifications to relieve us of responsibility. We fight to feel good about ourselves. We struggle to convince ourselves that we are not the sinful people we know we are.

Then, while this battle is going on inside of us, if someone points out some mistakes in us or presumes to correct us for some errors, the battle is on with them. We surprise them with the ferocity of our self-defense in exaggerated reactions to their corrections. They had not seen the intense struggles that were already going on in our hearts.

What is surprising is the level to which these battles can rise. Very sadly, there are some quite miserable people in the world who are angry, constantly angry, angry with nearly everyone. What is the source of their intense bitterness? What are they fighting against? Perhaps they have been hurt or damaged in some terrible way, but the fact is that there are many other people in the world who have been hurt in the very same way but do not have the same bitterness. Why do some people react with such incredible anger toward everyone, not just toward the people who hurt them? And why do some people hold on to anger for so long against others who hurt them, without being able to forgive completely? The answer may be that there are battles going on inside that are robbing them of inner peace and making it impossible for them to deal with other people in a reasonable, peaceful way. They will have to discover first what these battles are that rage inside and then seek to resolve them to find peace in their souls.

Peace that is ultimately satisfying and complete is a peace on three levels. We normally focus on trying to have peace with others because the conflicts we have with people are most visible and real to our experience. We are in the physical company of people, listening to their words and observing their gestures. Now we understand that peace with others cannot come until we resolve the conflicts in our own hearts and have inner peace. But an abiding, secure peace with ourselves will not come until we have peace with God. Peace with God is the beginning. Peace with the Creator is the first level. He created a thirst in our spirits for his presence in our lives that cannot be quenched by anything else. He is the God of peace and order. He created the need in us to have harmony and fellowship with him; and, until we are at rest and feel confident in his presence, we will have battles on the other two levels. Furthermore, not only has he provided the means to have peace with him, he has also given us the tools to resolve conflicts on the other levels.

Sin separates us from him. Sin is a decision to act in a way that contradicts the way he created us to live. He created us to love and when we choose to hate, we experience the confusion and disorder that comes from living apart from him. If we are dishonest with others, if we slander other people, if we steal or cheat others for our personal gains, if we fail to be generous with others whom we can help, if we lose control and angrily lash out against others, our consciences accuse us. The resulting discord in ourselves between who we are and who we believe we should be leaves us in turmoil, without peace. The more profound result of such destructive behavior is that we lose harmony with the Creator. We cannot walk with him who is in the light while we are in darkness.

Yet, he has lovingly and graciously provided what we need to have peace with him. He took the first step, even when it was not his to take, to reconcile himself to us. Paul wrote, "Therefore, if anyone is in Christ, he is a new creation; the old has gone, the new has come! All this is from God, who reconciled us to himself through Christ and gave us the ministry of reconciliation: that God was reconciling the world to himself in Christ, not counting men's sins against them" (2 Corinthians 5:17-19). The Greek term translated here as *reconcile* means *to change* or *exchange status*, in this case, from enemies to friends and from separation to harmony and unity. The word implies a joining together, to make peace between two parties who have been separated. He sent his Son to suffer on the cross the separation that we deserved to suffer. Now we have the chance to be born again, to become spiritually alive again, and renew our relationships with him. Peace has a beginning point where the One who created us to live in peace can give us peace again, bringing us back to himself.

Once we surrender ourselves to the Lord, heart, soul, mind, and strength, he begins to transform us from the inside out, resolving the conflicts in our hearts and then empowering us to resolve conflicts in our relationships. First, he deals with our guilt through his forgiveness. By his grace he accepts us as his children when we are born again, treating us as if we had never left him. He knows we will not be perfect and continues to forgive us as we struggle to live new lives. This struggle is an enjoyable one because it brings us ever closer to his image. While we grow, practicing the life Jesus teaches us, the Father continues to forgive us and lifts us up when we fall. What happens to the guilt that was once one of the battles in our hearts? He releases us from it, not freeing us from responsibility to do what is right, but freeing us from the fear of failing, knowing that when we do make mistakes, he will still accept us. Our consciences still warn us and help us see our errors, but now we can face them, accept them, and then let him forgive us. The answer to the battle with guilt is not to refuse to face our mistakes or deny them, but to accept them and then lay them down before his mercy and love.

What happens to the battle with insecurity? First, he gives us a profound sense of worth, knowing that we belong to him and that he is working in us to make us new creations in the image of his Son. Our self-worth is no longer grounded in what we have, how we look, or some other physical, material value. Instead, our lives have value because of the people he is teaching us to be in our spirits, in love, compassion, mercy, patience, and gentleness. Then we serve him as his instruments to show others the beauty of a life surrendered to him. His power fills our lives. We become lights that can bring light to the lives of others and bring honor to him as our Father. Furthermore, knowing he is present with us and his power is working in our lives, we can give our fears and worries to him. Paul wrote, "Do not be anxious about anything, but in everything, by prayer and petition, with thanksgiving, present your requests to God. And the peace of God, which transcends all understanding, will guard your hearts and your minds in Christ Jesus" (Philippians 4:6-7). Imagine how many times the writers of the four Gospels recorded Jesus' words to the disciples, "Don't be afraid." They understood and remembered the power of these words when he spoke them. He takes away our insecurities because we know we can depend on him, even when others fail us.

What happens to destructive pride? Now that we understand he is the one who forgives us and empowers us to live new lives, thanksgiving and humility replace pride. His unending, inexhaustible mercy and patience fill us with a profound sense of gratitude. We know we would have been worthless without him and that our lives were meaningless and on the road to destruction. Then he saved us. Can we brag? Of course not. We can only give thanks. There is no longer a need to justify ourselves; in fact, we know that we can never justify ourselves enough. We can only ask for forgiveness. At the same time, we can be confident, knowing that he empowers us to live a new life and is present with us to take away our fears. But our confidence does not come from within us and is not based on our own successes and accomplishments. Instead, confidence and security depend on him, his presence and his power working in our lives. The confidence that solves the battle of pride is a humble confidence, understanding our absolute dependence on him. We step out the door to walk in the light every day, not because we are strong in ourselves by ourselves, but because we have peace in his presence and power from his providential care for us.

What happens to the self-centeredness that battled in our hearts? One aspect of the incredible transformation he makes in us is to teach us to be other-centered. When we rest our confidence and security in him, we do not have to be afraid to give ourselves to others, to love unconditionally just as he loved us unconditionally. Our lives depend on his unconditional love for us. Experiencing the beauty of his love moves us to love with the same freedom with which he loves us. Why should we be so worried about protecting our interests and our own welfare when we know that his love and power will never abandon us as we love just as he has loved us? In fact, loving like he loves assures us of peace in his presence. Remember, John wrote, "And so we know and rely on the love God has for us. God is love. Whoever lives in love lives in God, and God in him. In this way, love is made complete among us so that we will have confidence on the day of judgment, because in this world we are like him" (1 John 4:16-17).

What happens to materialism and greed, the battles that James described? The Lord has made us alive spiritually. Now we can put material possessions, accomplishments and experiences in their correct perspective, understanding that such things cannot bring us lasting contentment. Peace with God fills our spirits. Being his instruments to manifest his love and righteousness gives us satisfaction and purpose. Jesus promised, "whoever loses his life for me will find it" (Matthew 16:25). Losing our lives means surrendering the values that once pushed us to run after what could never really make us happy. Now our priority is letting the Lord transform us into his image from the inside out.

These battles do not disappear easily. Habits take time to form and time to break. The most difficult part of the battle, ironically, is to know our own hearts. Sometimes we build so many barriers to avoid having to see ourselves that we do not know which battles we are fighting or whom we are really fighting against. Even when there are trusted people in our lives who could help us see ourselves, they may still not know the secrets of our hearts.

The conflicts, though, in our souls bear symptoms in our lives. If we criticize the behavior of others, comparing ourselves to them, struggling to convince ourselves that we are more righteous, a battle of self-criticism within is boiling over into condemnation of others. If we spend a lot of time justifying ourselves to others, guilt may be producing a battle in our hearts. If fear overpowers us or if we constantly call into question our value and the meaning of our lives, then the conflict in our hearts could be insecurity. If we struggle to win arguments, trying to prove we are right, stronger, or smarter, then the battle may be pride. If we are worried about having our way, what we might lose, what we need, what we want, what we deserve, then the battle spilling out in the form of resentment toward others might be self-centeredness within. If we are preoccupied by thoughts of what we would like to possess and jealous of those who have what we do not, and if contentment escapes us, then materialism is the cause of the battle inside we must solve before solving conflicts with others. Taking the time to carefully question the thinking that dominates our conflicts is worthwhile because these symptoms in our relationships will tell us about the battles in our hearts.

Peace begins with our relationships with our Creator. Peace with our heavenly Father then provides us the tools to solve the battles inside of us. Once we have peace with ourselves, then we can move to have peace on the third level, in our relationships with others. The Lord, of course, empowers us on this level, too. Remember that, as the Creator, he is the source of peace. He knows how the infinite pieces of the universe, the complex systems, and all the natural laws governing existence fit together to work in harmony. "In him all things hold together," wrote Paul (Colossians 1:17). He certainly also knows how we can live with peace in our relationships. Jesus promised that we would have the right to be called children of God if we are peacemakers (Matthew 5:9). By making the effort to have peace, we become like our Father, the ultimate Peacemaker. There are some vital lessons to be learned from the Creator of peace.

Be first to seek peace. One of the lessons we learn from him is to be the first to seek peace, without waiting for the other person to move toward peace. Imagine the condition we were in when the Father sought peace with us! Paul wrote, "You see, at just the right time, when we were still powerless, Christ died for the ungodly. Very rarely will anyone die for a righteous man, though for a good man someone might possibly dare to die. But God demonstrates his own love for us in this: While we were still sinners, Christ died for us" (Romans 5:6-8). We were his enemies, defeated and powerless enemies, without anything to offer for peace, when he sent his Son as the price for peace. We were the ones who should have paid for peace, but we had nothing to give

Furthermore, he did not wait for us to come to him. Instead, he drew us to himself when we were still a long, crushing distance from him. We were powerless to live productive lives, powerless to solve the battles within, powerless to build healthy relationships. He did for us what we could not do for ourselves.

The question that conflicts always raise is who will be the one to be humble, loving, and noble enough to take the first step toward peace? Who will be the first one to convince the others that peace is necessary? Who will take the initiative and have the determination to find a way to make peace? Who will be the first to sacrifice to have peace? We can translate this principle to our own experiences and be first to listen, first to admit mistakes, first to change inappropriate behavior, and first to be willing to compromise and agree.

Mercy is the key. Another lesson we learn from the Peacemaker is that mercy is the key to making peace. With the statement, "While we were sinners, Christ died for us," Paul defined mercy. Mercy is offering relief from suffering especially when relief is not deserved. Often in human conflicts one side of the conflict is not satisfied and open for peace until after completely destroying the opposition. But such a peace, brokered after complete destruction, does not provide for a constructive, healthy relationship of trust between victor and vanquished. The Lord did not destroy us first and then offer peace because he wanted to cultivate a loving, trusting relationship with us.

Likewise, in many human conflicts, one party hurts or offends another party. Our sense of justice convinces us that the guilty party needs to pay before peace is possible. For this very reason, people feel justified to harbor unrelinquished resentment against others who have offended them. The mercy of God is the opposite of retaliation and full of grace. He forgives debts and forgets offenses without payment from us. Instead of keeping us at a distance, he draws us close to him. Imagine what Paul must have been feeling when he wrote those words to the Romans, remembering how he had offended God and how merciful God had been to him. He once wrote, "Even though I was once a blasphemer and a persecutor and a violent man, I was shown mercy" (1 Timothy 1:13). The Peacemaker teaches us that making peace ought not to depend on making someone pay back for the wrong they have committed. Instead of seeking to destroy others, we learn to practice gracious mercy. In fact, to be like our Father, we do more than we are obligated to do to have peace because peace is worth the price.

Peace is worth a great price. The Father also teaches us that peace with others is worth a great price. Usually the price associated with peace is the compensation or punishment we demand of the person who caused the conflict or is guilty of the offensive, damaging behavior. The consequence of sin is separation from God. This spiritual separation is what constitutes spiritual death. But we did not pay this price, Jesus did. The price the Lord paid was not his to pay. We were the offenders who needed forgiveness. Jesus had no conflict with the Father. He was the Word of God. He perfectly reflected the Father, yet the price he paid was separation from the Father. The cost he bore on the cross was not just physical death, as agonizing as crucifixion was, but spiritual death. The Father had to abandon him on the cross, if only for a moment, as the price of peace, paying the consequence that we deserved to pay. Jesus felt the incredibly heavy weight of spiritual death when he cried out on the cross, "My God, my God, why have you forsaken me!" (Matthew 27:46)

In our personal relationships we have no problems in exacting payments from the ones who offend us. If they cannot pay for what they have done, then we make them suffer our resentment, ridicule, and rejection. Of course, this kind of treatment resolves nothing and makes peace impossible. Instead, we learn from the Father to forgive, completely and freely. Genuine forgiveness will require the forgiver to swallow the cost of the offense and treat the offender as if nothing had happened. At the same time, in humility, the forgiver looks into his own heart to admit any contribution he made to the conflict and asks forgiveness from the offender. This step is not something the Lord in his perfection had to do, but corresponds to us who are sinners without exception. An added consideration worthy of noticing about the price of peace is that there are many moments in which to "go the second mile" to make peace with those with whom we disagree. We can be ready to take more responsibility for solving disagreements, pay more than our share of the cost when we disagree about prices for things, carry more burdens than correspond to us, agree whenever we can agree without regard for winning arguments, all because peace is worth the price. Peace is a priority for the Creator of peace.

Renewal of relationships. What else do we learn from our Father? We discover that peace means renewed relationships. Paul continued to write in Romans 5:10, "For if, when we were God's enemies, we were reconciled to him through the death of his Son, how much more, having been reconciled, shall we be saved through his life!" If the Creator wanted peace in the universe, he could have easily wiped out all human life completely and refused to start over again. But he wants a relationship with us, free, uncompelled, from our choice. So he draws us to him through his offer of peace and a new relationship with him as his children. Peace does not mean to simply stop being enemies but, instead, to become friends. We could certainly say to someone who offends us, "I forgive you but I don't want anything more to do with you!" This level of forgiveness, however, is not the forgiveness that the Father practices. He has not only forgiven us, but made us his children, given our lives purpose, empowered us to live transformed lives, and promised to let us live with him always. The least we can do for people, as we restore peace with them, is to actively develop relationships of trust and confidence. The original Peacemaker teaches us lessons that are difficult to learn, but we are the ones who benefit from his own practice of these very principles. Our lives depend on the kind peace that he has offered us.

PRACTICE

If we take these lessons to heart and let them consistently inform and guide our practice of peace, we will be on the road toward following the counsel of Paul when he wrote, "If it is possible, as far as it depends on you, live at peace with everyone" (Romans 12:18). The writers of the New Testament clearly understood the priority of peacemaking and peace-maintaining in the character and life of the disciples. The writer of Hebrews said, "Make every effort to live in peace with all men" (Hebrews 12:14). Peter wrote that if a person would love life, he or she ought to "seek peace and pursue it" (1 Peter 3:11). Peace is a full-time pursuit that occupies our perspectives, intentions, purposes, plans, and our daily practice of discipleship.

Peace is the ultimate arbitrator, deciding which choices we will make and what courses we will take. After listing many of the character qualities that disciples ought to develop in their lives in the imitation of Jesus, Paul wrote, "Let the peace of Christ rule in your hearts, since as members of one body you were called to peace" (Colossians 3:15). The word translated here as *rule* is from a word that means *to arbitrate, to decide* or *determine*, like a referee in a sports competition who makes the final decision to resolve a question. Surrendering to the rule of peace in our everyday lives begins with *thinking peace*.

We have choices to make about how we will view the world and our relationships. Some people, unfortunately, because of a series of disappointing experiences, have come to view the world with doubt and distrust. Because people have broken promises with them in the past, they assume that other people will deceive or betray them in the future. They constantly look for what they interpret as the signs of deceit in the behavior of others. They convince themselves that they are only being careful in their relationships and avoiding being naive. But their views of life are very pessimistic only because they have decided to view relationships with the assumption of doubt.

Likewise, people may have experienced so much conflict in their lives that conflict has become a way of life to them. They assume that relationships are filled with conflict and that they have the responsibility to defend their personal rights in every disagreement; if they do not defend themselves, then people will take advantage of them. They come to a discussion ready with all their arguments but not necessarily ready to listen carefully. They are ready to defend themselves but have little desire to understand other people. They calculate what they have to do or say to win. But assuming there will be conflicts easily turns into looking for conflicts to protect and confirm one's own rights.

Peacemakers on the other hand develop a view of the world that makes peace possible. Thinking peace means to develop a mind that sees the possibility for peace and is focused on pursuing peace. We have the choice, without worrying about being naive or being exploited, to look at the world from the priority of pursuing peace. This choice depends on how we view peace itself, how we view others with whom we need to live in peace, and, ultimately, how we view ourselves. What do we think about peace? How important is it?

Without realizing it, we can come to the point in our lives when we assume that discussions, arguments, and even verbal and physical violence are simply part of normal existence, like people in a war zone who become accustomed to hearing the sound of gunfire. If we fight enough among ourselves, we assume that fighting is just part of life; the possibility of living without constant fighting does not even occur to us. Peace does not seem as valuable as winning conflicts, having our way, and satisfying our personal desires. In fact, some people even prefer conflicts because the conflicts serve them in some way, like a bully on the playground at school, who is constantly trying to fight someone to prove himself.

For a child of the Creator of peace, peace is a necessary priority. We make every effort, as much as depends on us, to pursue peace because the Lord created us to live in peace and we are like him when we value it as much as he does. If we were to ask ourselves, though, how much we, in reality, value it, answering this question might be more difficult than we imagine. We persuade ourselves to think that we are trying our best to have peace when in reality protecting our emotions and rights is more important. We tend to think, "I want peace, but ... they won't listen, they don't understand, they won't do as I ask." Peace, though, is an extremely valuable way of life and peace should be the very thing that we protect. What do we really think about peace?

And what do we think about the possibility of peace? Just as much as some people look for conflict, we ought always to look for the possibility of peace. Despite our efforts, peace is not guaranteed simply because we have relationships, whether momentary or lasting, with people who prefer jealousy, pride, or self-centeredness over peace. Therefore, when we think peace by looking for peace, we are looking for all the possible choices we can make to establish and maintain peace regardless of the choices other people make. The question is, what is within our power to do?

When the temptation to pessimism occurs, thinking that peace is possible is a decision of faith because we may not feel like we have the energy to seek peace. In moments when we face people who seem uncompromisingly combative, the strength to seek peace comes from faith in the teachings of Jesus, believing his way is the right way because he is Lord. He teaches us to, "Do to others as you would have them do to you" (Luke 6:31). We practice peace because we want peace, not because others give us the chance to have peace. According to this principle, seeking peace is unconditionally based on the desire for peace. The conduct of the other person cannot change our desires for peace.

Thinking that peace is possible with difficult people is also a matter of believing in the power of God, with whom all things are possible. He has the power to renew our hearts to be humble and compassionate. By surrendering to him, he can take away any bitterness and anger that battles in our hearts. He can give us wisdom to look for the right solutions. His providence can also work on the heart of the other person. So, believing that peace is possible is not a romantic dream, but a matter of faith in the power and love of the Lord.

Developing a view of the world that focuses on the possibility of peace also depends on how we think about people, especially those with whom we have conflicts. Forming negative perceptions of people who oppose us is so common that it can seem normal. During conflicts, our desire to defend ourselves causes us to create images of our opponents that help us think we are right. We may even focus on some bothersome habits they have, that really have nothing to do with the conflicts at hand, and exaggerate these "disgusting" traits to confirm that we are right. "Not only that....but they don't pick up their clothes, they can't sit still, all they care about are their jobs, and they leave the cap off the toothpaste tube." When Paul wrote, "Get rid of all bitterness, rage and anger, brawling and slander, along with every form of malice" (Ephesians 4:31), he implied that we must simply let go of all the negative emotions that color our views of people.

Once we form negative views of people, we also use this mental framework to interpret what each person does in an unfavorable, critical way. We begin by making assumptions about their motives, believing we can adequately evaluate the thoughts of their hearts without honestly listening to understand. Then our preconceptions filter what we hear and see in them so that whatever they do, good or bad, confirms the negative view that we already have. As a result, we fall into faultfinding although we do not recognize it as such. We just think that they have lots of faults we never noticed before.

Paul explained that we simply need to "get rid of" or let go of these preconceived images. Truly letting them go requires replacing them with something. For this reason Paul wrote, "Be kind and compassionate to one another, forgiving each other, just as in Christ God forgave you" (Ephesians 4:32). Compassion, for instance, requires that we understand another person, understand what they may be suffering and work to relieve the suffering as we have the power to do so. To understand their lives from their perspectives calls for listening without any preconceived ideas, without forming assumptions. Even if we think we understand, we must listen again, wanting to know what they feel without judging what they feel, disciplining ourselves to avoid preconceived ideas. We can ask questions to clarify our understanding and assure the person we are paying attention. This level of listening demands a tremendous amount of self-control, but it is the beginning of peace because thinking more compassionately leads to thinking peace.

Thinking peace also calls for having healthier views of ourselves that are founded on humility. The New Testament defines humility in several aspects: "Do not think of yourself more highly than you ought (Romans 12:3); "Consider others better than yourselves" (Philippians 2:3); "Each of you should look not only to your own interests, but also to the interests of others" (Philippians 2:4); "Each one should use whatever gift he has received to serve others" (1 Peter 4:10). Humility empowers us to put away the pride, self-righteous anger, and the self-centeredness that creates and exaggerates conflicts. Humility lets go. In humility we can better understand that we could be wrong. We accept our need for the grace of God because we know we have been sinners, guilty of creating battles and alienating people unnecessarily. Humility takes the logs out of our own eyes before we try to take the splinters out of someone else's eye. Humility allows us to avoid the need to defend ourselves and, instead, trust in the Lord's forgiveness and mercy. Humility slows down our rush to claim our rights. In humility we desire to serve generously and lovingly instead of being served. We do all of this to seek peace.

Humility sometimes comes the hard way. Jesus gave us the choice of either humbling ourselves or being humbled (Luke 18:14). (Where you read, "Be humbled," think, "humiliated.") Finally discovering in the middle of a serious conflict that we were wrong, that we actually can be wrong, may be difficult to suffer. We feel surprised, defeated, guilty, discouraged, and weak. After all the effort we expended in proving that we were right or that we were guiltless, now our former images of ourselves are completely deflated and empty.

This is good. We need to feel empty so the Lord can fill us with the desire for peace.

Thinking peace now transforms into *living in peace.* An overriding desire to do everything we can to live in peace begins to rule our practice of discipleship. We return to the words of Paul: "If it is possible, as far as it depends on you, live at peace with everyone." Not everyone wants peace because of their own inner conflicts or because other emotions and choices are more important to them than peace. The moral responsibility that this principle presents to us as believers is to do everything that we can to make peace with us possible. What can we do to live our lives in ways that make it easy for people to have peace with us and for us to have peace with them? How can we know if we are doing everything that depends on us to have peace?

What follows is a checklist for examining ourselves to find the answers to these questions. When considering the practice of these steps to live in peace, it is essential to remember that the moments that challenge our practice of peace are also the moments that enable us to grow in peace.

First, resolve the battles within through peace with God. We have already discussed the nature of these inner conflicts and how to surrender them to God to have peace with him and in turn have peace with ourselves. Living at peace has to begin with this step. Knowing whether our problems on the outside in our relationships are due to conflicts on the inside is sometimes hard to determine. We may need the help of wise, trusted, fellow disciples of Jesus who can help us look for the symptoms of inner battles in our outward conduct. Such people would have to understand the value of peace and the reality of inner battles. But we have to be able to trust such people with complete confidence so that we have no fear in admitting the sources of our conflicts. Discovery and surrender, though, can provide such relief and calm in our spirits that the reward is worth the struggle. The rest is easy by comparison.

Second, walk by faith in the Lord, trusting in his power and love. Trying to accomplish on our own what we cannot do by ourselves leaves us frustrated, without peace. We try to control circumstances we cannot control. We try to manage the decisions of other people when we cannot. We try to solve problems using our own wisdom instead of humbly and faithfully submitting to the wisdom of Jesus. If we are believers, there are two things we know with certainty about God: he is powerful, and he is loving. Letting go is difficult because we are not sure of the result, but the result is in the hands of our all-powerful and absolutely loving Father. We cannot see what he sees. We cannot do what he can do. We cannot love like he loves. In prayer we give our anxieties to him and something incredible happens. Paul wrote, undoubtedly reflecting on his own experiences, "Do not be anxious about anything, but in everything, by prayer and petition, with thanksgiving, present your requests to God. And the peace of God, which transcends all understanding, will guard your hearts and your minds in Christ Jesus" (Philippians 4:6-7). Surrendering our battles to the Lord, truly relinquishing control to him, frees our hearts. An incredible peace comes over us that makes us sigh a breath of relief in our spirits. The peace of God guards our hearts against further threats just like soldiers guarding a castle from any seen or unseen enemy.

Third, agree with reality and admit when you are wrong. Living the fantasy that we are the victims and that others are the causes of our conflicts only robs us of the very peace we eagerly desire. The root of our constant conflicts could simply be that we are unwilling to admit when we are wrong. Of course, we all believe that we do admit we are wrong, when we are wrong, but the truth as we see it is that we are not wrong as often as other people. Children of the Creator of peace should have no problem with confessing mistakes because we can trust absolutely in his forgiveness. John wrote, "If we claim to be without sin, we deceive ourselves and the truth is not in us. If we confess our sins, he is faithful and just and will forgive us our sins and purify us from all unrighteousness" (1 John 1:7-8). The Greek word translated *confession* in the New Testament means *to say the same thing* or *agree*. Confession implies that we agree with what the Lord already understands about us, or that we agree with what others already see in us. Confession can be as simple as the words of the tax collector in the parable of Jesus who said, "God, have mercy on me, a sinner" (Luke 18:13). "I erred." "I made a mistake." "I am sorry for the problems I caused." Simple. No excuse. No self-justification.

Our faith in God's gracious acceptance and his patience with us takes away our fear of admitting wrong and replaces it with relief, peace, and confidence. He is faithful, John says, to forgive us and completely purify us. We know he will treat us in the same way the father in Jesus' parable treated his son whom he had lost to sin. He put a robe on his shoulders, sandals on his feet, a ring on his hand, and celebrated because his son who had been lost was found. He immediately restored him to be whole again.

Our problem with confession is that we are afraid people might react to our admissions the way the lost son's brother reacted to his confession, with bitter criticism and cynicism. It happens. Then we have another decision to make. Will we adamantly refuse to admit wrong and consequently suffer more conflicts on the inside and outside, or will we let the Lord give us peace on the inside and trust him to empower us to continue to be humble, despite the criticisms of others? After all, the inability of others to accept us may be due to inner conflicts they are fighting. Our worth depends on what the Creator thinks about us, and we can confidently trust that he patiently and graciously forgives us.

Fourth, know when to hold on to priorities and when to be flexible. Peace is not about appeasing people. Parents are sometimes tempted to indulge the whims of their children just to have peace. If a child complains about washing the dishes, wearing down with whining an already wearied parent, the parent might finally shout with exasperation, "Okay, forget it! I will wash them myself!" Peace? Not really. We know that as parents we have to establish certain priorities with our children. Some things are negotiable and some things are not. We cannot surrender to their whims, but we also have to choose our battles. There will be some battles that we cannot avoid simply because we want to teach them their responsibilities in the peace process. On the other hand, if we were to decide to fight every battle, whether important or not, just to maintain our control, the price we would pay would be the loss of peace.

The same truth is evident in our other relationships. We have moral convictions that we cannot surrender because they involve questions of right and wrong. But we also have preferences that involve choices we can make without violating any moral principle. Among the innumerable categories of preferences we have from how to spend our money, how much time to spend on certain activities to what to eat for dinner and what color of socks to wear, we have to decide which ones have priority and which ones are more flexible. When Paul addressed a disagreement in the early church about whether to eat meat or not, he wrote, "But food does not bring us near to God; we are no worse if we do not eat, and no better if we do" (1 Corinthians 8:8). Conflicts come when our personal priorities clash with the priorities of people with whom we share our lives. Inflexibility guarantees constant conflict. Some issues have no real value, although we would like to think so. Peace needs to rule by being the referee in such cases. What does peace require? Which preferences can we sacrifice for the sake of peace? Peace is the real priority.

Fifth, slow down to listen, to pray for wisdom, and to control emotions. Living in peace requires taking the time to slow down. We rush to find the answer, to react quickly, to take control before we lose something, to draw conclusions that lack sufficient reason, and to express our opinions before we have carefully thought them through. But life is not on our timetables. We cannot force others to follow our schedules. We should not even follow the impossible schedules we sometimes set for ourselves. The urgency we place on our decisions only leads to impulsiveness, mistaken reactions and choices, and, ultimately, to conflicts. James' counsel to slow down is invaluable, "Everyone should be quick to listen, slow to speak and slow to become angry" (James 1:19).

James also advised us to take the time to ask for wisdom. "If any of you lacks wisdom, he should ask God, who gives generously to all without finding fault, and it will be given to him" (James 1:5). James did not view wisdom from a theoretical or philosophical perspective as the Greeks did. Wisdom is practical knowledge that leads us to act in ways that are in harmony with God's heart. He defined wisdom as doing what is "peace-loving, considerate, submissive, full of mercy and good fruit, impartial and sincere" (James 3:17).

But even the wisest person will not act wisely if emotions rule, because emotions can overrule wisdom's counsel. Unfortunately, some people take plenty of time, but they use the time to review and replay some offense, to grow more bitter, and to plan some form of retaliation. Out-of-control emotions never bring peace but only serve to increase the conflict. If peace is truly the priority, then time is better spent carefully listening, praying for wisdom, and letting go of damaging emotions.

Sixth, serve in humility, living an other-centered life. Since so many conflicts originate from self-centeredness, focusing on the welfare of others will make it easier for them to have peace with us. When his disciples argued about who was the greatest among them (Luke 22:24), Jesus taught them in a most profound way to resolve their self-serving conflicts by serving each other with humility. He, the Master, washed their feet (John 13:1-17). If they could learn to serve each other humbly, they would stop arguing about who deserved the best position among them. A key to living in peace is the humble heart we have when we serve.

Jesus was the one who suffered to serve. In Philippians 2:5 Paul wrote that our "attitude should be the same as that of Christ Jesus." He sacrificed what he had with the Father to live among us to serve us by showing the way to the Father. By his personal example, the Lord taught us to live an other-centered instead of self-centered life. Respecting the interests of others above our own interests, sacrificing our time or resources to help even though others do not help us, taking care of responsibilities that really do not correspond to us help us imitate the mind of Jesus to seek peace.

To be certain, as we are learning to practice this principle of peace, we undoubtedly serve in many moments when we feel resentment because others do not appreciate what we are doing for them or because others are not doing their part. We feel the nagging fear again that others will take advantage of us. In such moments when the requirements of peace are difficult to bear, we have the chance to grow in our abilities to practice peace. We must decide that developing humility and practicing peace are more important than whether or not others appreciate us or whether others are doing their fair share of the work. Making this decision empowers us, the next time we are faced with a similar challenge, to make the same decision again, and then again, growing each time as a peacemaker in the humility of Jesus.

Seventh, communicate to build up, benefiting those who listen. How many battles begin with words! Learning to live in peace requires paying special attention to our words. When James wrote that "no man can tame the tongue" (James 3:8), he wanted us to understand that we have to pay constant attention to what we say and how we say it. Some animals can be domesticated so that the humans who care for them do not have to worry about their behavior. Leaving a trained dog in our house while we are gone should not worry us because we can trust that, while we are away, not paying immediate attention to its behavior, the dog will not destroy the house. Our tongues are different, James teaches. We cannot come to the point in our Christian lives when we can simply assume that everything we say will be appropriate, gracious, and encouraging. Maintaining peaceful relationships requires that we constantly think carefully about what we will say. Conflicts arise in unguarded times when we fail to pay attention, caught up in the emotions of the moment.

Although we are barely conscious sometimes of what we are saying during an emotional discussion, we have the added burden of evaluating our words even before we say them. Controlling and evaluating what we say before we say it is a tough task. Furthermore, after expressing ourselves, the tendency is to evaluate what we said in terms of what we intended to say. Did I say what I intended to say in the way I intended to say it? This perspective is actually focused on self and not on the person who is listening.

The apostle Paul instead taught that communication should be "helpful for building others up according to their needs, that it may benefit those who listen" (Ephesians 4:29). This principle puts the focus properly on the perception of the other person. As we carry on discussions with other people, those people come to the conversations from entirely different emotional contexts than we do. We may have had a good day previous to the discussion and they may have been under a lot stress. How they listen and understand our words depends on their context, not on ours.

We may satisfy ourselves, thinking that we have said what we intended to say, but the real question is whether the other people heard what we intended to say. What they hear depends not on what we are feeling, but what they are feeling. When Paul says that healthy communication should benefit those who listen, the focus shifts from benefiting the speaker to benefiting the listener. By first asking questions and coming to understand the listener's context, we can better assure ourselves of knowing what to say and how to say it so that the listener hears what we intended to say. Remember that peace means joining people together. Communication that builds the listener up, from the listener's perspective, joins us together.

Eighth, follow a plan to resolve conflicts. Making peace calls for the time and self-control to solve conflicts in an orderly, calm manner. Rushing out the door to work or school in the morning and arguing along the way is not the appropriate time to solve serious problems. People are distracted, thinking about other responsibilities like crossing the street without being run over by a car. Sitting down together in a calm moment but carrying on a monologue, dominated by one person, will not bring peaceful solutions either. Reconciliation involves at least two parties, so the process of peace must be a dialogue. Resolving conflicts is more effective when we can follow some fairly intuitive steps for communicating well. Here are some to consider that form the acronym, LADDERS:

Listen with your eyes, with attentive body language, with gestures of recognition and understanding, and with your heart. Listen with your mouth closed and your mind open. Without interrupting or thinking ahead to decide how you will answer, listen and then repeat back what you heard, summarizing to check your understanding.

Ask questions to understand the facts. Ask questions to clarify the issue without questioning the person's feelings, keeping the discussion focused. Avoid sarcasm, interrogation and negativity. Say, "I am sorry I didn't understand something you said. Could you please explain what you meant when you said…" Give the person time and attention to answer the questions. The result of the questions should be mutual clarity about the issue.

Determine if you really disagree. After being informed and clear about the issue, decide exactly what you agree and disagree about. Agree where you can agree. Separate the issue of disagreement from the person who disagrees so that the person does not become the issue. Even if a person has offended you, separate the offensive behavior itself from the person. What was said was offensive. The person was not offensive. Then isolate the issue you actually disagree about.

Decide if the issue is important. Remember that some issues involve moral convictions about right and wrong and are therefore non-negotiable. Other issues are preferences that call for flexibility when possible. Is the matter just an opinion? Does the question involve behavior that is dangerous or unhealthy? Will the issue make a difference tomorrow?

Earn credibility. To have credibility means to be believed and trusted by another person. Credibility is earned by consistently practicing the good behavior that you expect from others, avoiding hypocrisy. Know what you are talking about instead of just talking. If you do not have all the necessary information, postpone the discussion until you are better informed. Show the other person you care about her instead of just caring about winning a conflict.

React with the right words. Refuse to use any language that is demeaning, disrespectful, judging, or condemning, considering how the other person is listening to what you say. Use language that is merciful, calm, gentle, open, and constructive. Communicate understanding, patience, and compassion.

Solve the conflict. Prepare yourself to resolve the problem through sincere prayer to the Father, asking for wisdom. Select the right time to discuss solutions when there is calm and the opportunity to concentrate. Carefully define the problem to focus on it and not on another problem or a mountain of other problems. Admit your contribution to any misunderstandings and humbly ask for forgiveness. Determine the needs and desires of each person involved. Raise possible solutions based on the needs of each person, negotiating when possible. Decide what is the correct or appropriate solution.

Ninth, be patient when the other person does not want peace. When Paul wrote, "If it is possible, as far as it depends on you, live at peace with everyone," he then added immediately afterwards, "Do not take revenge, my friends, but leave room for God's wrath, for it is written: 'It is mine to avenge; I will repay,' says the Lord. On the contrary: 'If your enemy is hungry, feed him; if he is thirsty, give him something to drink. In doing this, you will heap burning coals on his head.' Do not be overcome by evil, but overcome evil with good" (Romans 12:18-21). Even after we have done all we can do to have peace with certain people, peace still escapes us sometimes because some people persistently want to consider themselves as our opponents.

After we have done all that depends on us, what more can we do? Do we finally stop trying to make peace? No, we cannot. We are peacemakers. This is who we are. We cannot stop providing circumstances that make peace possible. Retaliation belongs to the Lord because he alone can judge hearts and know motives. We can never see the future, nor can we see the entire picture. For these reasons we cannot know if a person will finally respond to our overtures of peace. So we patiently continue to serve. Just as love is unconditional even toward our enemies, so are our efforts to make peace. Perhaps there are battles within other people that we cannot see. When the time is right, when their hearts are open, they may finally understand the inner conflicts that cause their animosity toward us. Then we will be able to have peace. If we were to retaliate, we would shut the door on this possibility.

Tenth, keep hoping for peace. The confidence we have is that peace with God and with ourselves is certain. The Lord paid such an incredible price because he profoundly desires peace with his creation to a degree beyond our imagination. All we have to do is decide to come to him for peace. And when we surrender our anxieties, insecurities, and guilt to him, an incredible peace comes to our spirits that illuminates our lives. This is certain. We just have to give up fighting.

What is not so certain is peace from day to day in our relationships. When disagreements turn into arguments, arguments into struggles and struggles into battles, discouragement threatens to overwhelm us. These moments challenge our optimism about peace. Pessimism is an easy escape because it does not require anything of us. Surrendering to bitterness and retaliation seems to give us rest momentarily, but we soon notice that peace leaves our spirits. Negativity and bitterness cut deeply into us. Something in us dies, including the spiritual energy we felt in our relationships with the Lord.

But we do not have to give up hoping that the love of God can work even in the most violent spirit because we have faith in God's power and love to change hearts. Peter wrote, "Praise be to the God and Father of our Lord Jesus Christ! In his great mercy he has given us new birth into a living hope through the resurrection of Jesus Christ from the dead" (1 Peter 1:3). The resurrection of Jesus confirmed God's power to give life. This same power works in us to transform us. Paul wrote that God's "incomparably great power for us who believe" is "like the working of his mighty strength which he exerted in Christ when he raised him from the dead" (Ephesians 1:19-20). We have little idea in our feeble imaginations of what the Lord can do through his providence and through his Spirit to help the most hostile person seek peace. We never need to lose hope.

Why is hope so important? The children of the Peacemaker are the ones who can give people the hope for peace. The priority we place on peace convinces people that peace is possible. If we give up, there is no one to communicate hope.

The peace that begins with the Lord, then fills our spirits, and finally transforms our relationships is truly a fruit of the Spirit. It depends on our relationships with the Father and the strength his Spirit gives us. It is not just a condition that surrounds us, but it is a quality that must be embedded deeply within us. It becomes who we are. It is first a quality of our spirits that then reveals itself in our behavior. First we seek to be at peace and then live in peace. It grows as we live spiritual lives dedicated to the imitation of the Lord. He was the first Peacemaker and we follow in his steps.

CHAPTER FOUR

PRACTICING PATIENCE

"THOSE WHO HOPE IN THE LORD
WILL RENEW THEIR STRENGTH"
(ISAIAH 40:31).

We are preparing to attend to an important appointment and we cannot afford to be late, but we must wait on someone who will accompany us. That person is slowly preparing to leave, seemingly unaware of the late hour, paying attention to trivial details of clothing and appearance, looking for one thing and then another to accomplish before leaving. We feel nervous, desperate, anxious, and try to refrain from expressing the growing frustration we feel.

We have been carefully trying to help a loved one recover from a destructive addiction. When he expresses remorse and the desire to change, we readily help with resources so he has the chance to change. But we helplessly watch his repetitive cycle of remorse, followed by his promises to change, requests for help, his acceptance of our help, a period of freedom from the habit, and then another fall. His self-destruction elicits a variety of emotions from us over time. We feel sympathy for his suffering, guilt that we might have contributed to his behavior, desire to do whatever we can to support him, doubts about unlocking the secret to his addiction, frustration that he abuses our love, and anger that he seems intent on destroying his life. How long can we stand this struggle?

Our daughter went out with some friends for the evening and has not returned home at the agreed upon curfew. We call her cell phone to find out where she is, but there is no answer. Ten, fifteen, twenty minutes pass and feelings of uneasiness turn into worry. What could have happened? Why doesn't she answer her cell phone? We run through different possibilities in our minds: she just lost track of time, her cell phone ran out of battery or she lost it, she had to stop to put gas in the car, she lost her way, she had a flat tire, she had an accident.... Then worry turns into fear and fear into obsession. When she finally arrives home an hour late, she casually explains that the event she attended lasted longer than she thought it would, she forgot to call, and there was too much noise to hear the phone ring. Worry and fear flash into anger.

Although we are trying very hard to live the Christian life, there are people, even some very close to us, who look for opportunities to criticize our behavior and reject us for being something they themselves do not want to be. When we are around them, we feel absolutely insecure and afraid to say or do something that will evoke more negativity. We become preoccupied with self-defense, mentally reviewing over and over again the reasons why we think we are good people, trying to do our best. Sometimes we react by defending ourselves, explaining what we believe; sometimes we choose to suffer silently their unjust attacks. But when their words are too sharp or when they catch us in moments of frustration or exhaustion, we find holding back retaliation very difficult, maybe even undesirable. Resentment takes control over our hearts, creating an edge of bitterness that colors our communication with them.

We have jobs to do. We need to finish them. There are so many other more pleasant things we could be doing. The day is beautiful. Why do we have to be working? People are depending on us to finish, but they are not working like we are. Tired, bored but compelled by responsibility to do something, we are frustrated with the demands people make on us. We need a break, another break.

We know everyone has temptations, but the battles we face must be fiercer than problems other people face. We struggle daily not to give into thoughts that would lead us to fall. We determine to stay away from people or circumstances that would make giving in easy. We try to fill up our time with activities that distract us from thinking about temptation. Fearing that in an unguarded moment the desire of temptation may surprise us, we start thinking that falling back into sin is inevitable. Convinced we are weak, too tired for the struggle, we set ourselves up for defeat.

What do these scenarios have in common? All of them require patience in some form in order to maintain calm and peace in our hearts and to react in appropriate, successful ways to moments that challenge our character. Most people would probably first think of patience as anger control since anger is such an aggressively expressed and, thus, visibly evident emotion. But patience actually refers to the control of a wide variety of emotions.

UNDERSTANDING

The New Testament, originally written in Greek, actually uses three Greek words to name the wide variety of abilities that the English word *patience* encompasses. One of these terms, *makrothumia*, is the word Paul uses in Galatians 5:22 in the list of the fruit of the Spirit.

This term means *to suffer long* and describes the ability to wait in circumstances when waiting produces an unusual amount anxiety or discomfort. Makrothumia is slow to react with a negative response to stressful or frustrating situations. Makrothumia continues to hope instead of being discouraged and trusts in the possibility that circumstances will change for the better. James uses this word to describe the farmer who continues to work hard to produce a crop, waiting for the rains to come without being overly anxious or giving up. James also characterizes the behavior of the Israelite prophets before the time of Christ with this term. These men of God suffered persecution from their own people without surrendering their faith or reacting with retaliation. "Be patient, then, brothers, until the Lord's coming. See how the farmer waits for the land to yield its valuable crop and how patient he is for the autumn and spring rains....Brothers, as an example of patience in the face of suffering, take the prophets who spoke in the name of the Lord" (James 5:7,10). The key idea of makrothumia is that patience enables us to wait and suffer long.

The New Testament writers also used the word *anoche* to describe another aspect of patience: the ability to hold back impulsive, negative, or destructive reactions to people or events that trouble us in some way. Although "patience" is an adequate translation for this word, some English versions of the New Testament translate anoche using more precise terms. The NIV, for instance, translates anoche as "bearing with someone" (Colossians 3:13; Ephesians 4:2) and also as "endure" (2 Thessalonians 1:4; 1 Corinthians 4:12). Anoche puts up with people and events that are frustrating or stressful without surrendering to evil and reacting in negative, destructive ways. When people are angry, anoche is calm. When confronted by temptation, anoche does nothing impulsive but thinks carefully about how to escape the temptation, reacting wisely. Anoche listens, thinks, considers, and then reacts judiciously. The key idea is to hold back.

The third term used by the New Testament writers to convey another aspect of patience is *hupomone*, which precisely means *to endure, to stick with something and not give up*. The NIV translates hupomone not only as "patience" in Romans 12:12, where Paul describes people who are "patient in affliction," but also as "persistence" when he writes of God's people who are "persistent in doing good" (Romans 2:7). Furthermore, the NIV translates hupomone as "perseverance" where the writer of Hebrews says, "Let us run with perseverance the race marked out for us" (Hebrews 12:1). Imagine losing energy while running a long race as the course stretches on. You are tired, hot, and breathing heavily. You begin to doubt you will finish or at least doubt that your run will be respectable. To have hupomone means to stay focused on the goal, continue to run as fast as possible, and finish as strong as you can. Hupomone does not give up on the possibility of change or progress, does not give up on doing what is right, no matter the consequences, and does not give up on the goal. The key concept of hupomone is to endure.

The three terms are to some degree interchangeable. For example, anoche and hupomone can both express endurance. Anoche and makrothumia can both suggest calmly waiting without becoming overly anxious or frustrated. At the same time, the words can be used together to express different aspects of patience in the same context. In Ephesians 4:2 Paul wrote, "Be completely humble and gentle; be patient (makrothumia), bearing with (anoche) one another in love." Likewise in 2 Thessalonians 1:4 he wrote, "Therefore, among God's churches we boast about your perseverance (hupomone) and faith in all the persecutions and trials you are enduring (anoche)."

The three words sometimes make distinctions and sometimes overlap in meaning but together they give us a more complete picture of patience. Patience includes waiting and suffering long, holding back, and enduring. We are more likely in everyday English to use the single word *patience* to describe all of the abilities these words encompass, but the New Testament usage of the three terms implies careful attention to this range of emotions and behaviors. The New Testament authors are writing about character transformation, with the objective of clarifying the many moments in life that require some form of patience. While the requirements of patience are slightly different for the farmer who waits for the harvest, the frustrated father who restrains his emotions when disciplining his children, and the runner who runs with all his effort to win the race, there are some aspects of patience that these cases share in common too. The farmer, the father, and the runner have all chosen to respond to decisive moments in life without surrendering the principles and values they treasure and live by. They made decisions to channel their emotions to positive, constructive ends. Although the word translated *patience* that appears in the list of the fruit of the Spirit is makrothumia, we proceed in this study about practicing patience by emphasizing the complete picture of patience that the teachings of Jesus present to us. Patience is, above all, a manner of responding to people and events by waiting, holding back, and enduring.

REFLECTION

Have you ever been very nervous or worried about something and you tried to unwind by relaxing your body? You lie down and carefully, methodically, start with the muscles in your toes and feet, consciously relieving the physical tension, mentally moving up your body, trying to relax each part all the way to your shoulders, neck, jaw, and forehead. Sometimes it may work, especially if we have more stress than worry. But if worry, anger, or some other focused emotion is the problem, you may have discovered that after you tried to relax your body, you could not turn off your thoughts. You still experienced the emotions that produced the physical tension in the first place. If you do not manage the underlying emotions that fill your thoughts, the physical stress, of course, returns.

When we are anxious or afraid, we may first feel these emotions through changes in our physical hearts. The beating of our hearts begins to flutter or increase in speed. Sometimes, because of the physical nature of our circulatory systems, we actually feel as if our hearts have risen closer to our throats or that they have sunken down to our stomachs, depending on the emotions we experience. Because of the ways in which our physical hearts respond to emotions, we should not be surprised by the fact that the word *heart* has come to represent the desires and emotions we feel, whether negative or positive. To cultivate patience we have to begin with managing our emotions, that is, we begin with the heart.

We may think of a patient person as someone who can stand in a long line without complaining, someone who can pay attention to a long, detailed story without becoming bored, someone who can listen calmly, without fear, to an angry person's rage, or someone who can suffer a loss without giving up. These visible, physical signs are evidence of something deeper, more primary; they indicate a patient heart with emotions that are under control. Patience has to begin with the heart, learning to control the emotions and desires that leave us agitated in our spirits, before we try to relax our bodies.

Hearts that are out of control turn worries into anxieties, obsessions, and fears that dominate our constant thoughts, prohibiting us from focusing on anything else with any degree of concentration. A discouraging moment with an uncontrolled heart can lead to disillusionment, depression, and defeat. A series of frustrating events can turn annoyance into raging anger. When someone reacts with sudden anger to an experience that seems to have little importance in reality, we wonder why such an insignificant problem could produce such a burst of fury. All of a sudden, out of nowhere, the person screams irritation or spits out a ridiculing remark that seems to have little to do with any immediate problem. What happened? We could not see the heart and so we did not see the increasingly powerful emotions that had been building up over time. Like a train that begins slowly, gradually gaining speed, and then finally rockets down the mountain out of control, emotions, once they begin to escalate, can run out of control, reacting in an explosion of anger that we did not expect. The problem was that we could not see the train until it suddenly came speeding down the tracks toward us. Up to a certain level, emotions can be invisible, without external symptoms in a person's behavior. We cannot see a person's heart, and the person who loses control may not even be aware of his or her rising emotions. The sudden burst of anger, though, is a sign that the heart was out of control.

We say that emotions are out of control in such cases but, ironically, in another way they are in control. They are controlling and overriding our reasoning abilities. The struggle to overcome impatience is really a battle between emotions and reason to determine which will rule. Different parts of our brains are dedicated to reason and emotion. Despite the fact that those parts that produce emotional reactions in us are much smaller than the areas of the brain that process logical responses, emotions can hijack our reason and cause us to respond without clear thinking.

There are, however, moments when emotions need to overcome reason. As a survival mechanism, God created us with the ability to react to certain circumstances without much thinking. When we are afraid of an imminent danger, fear causes us to run without thinking. This is good. If we are walking on the sidewalk near the street and an approaching car appears to be coming too close, we should not spend much time thinking about whether to jump out of the way; the best reaction would be to throw ourselves out of the way of the car and then, afterwards, think about what happened. In this situation, allowing reason to take its time to think, making us patiently wait to see what might happen, could be deadly.

But there are other times when emotions ought not to rule. Imagine one driver cuts off another on the highway, and the offended driver feels enraged. The enraged driver speeds up to catch the careless one who cut him off, with the intention of running him off the road. Such road-rage not only endangers the drivers directly involved in the dispute, but other drivers and their passengers on the highway. Yet the driver who cut off the other one may have changed lanes safely. The offended driver reacted simply because his pride was hurt; he wanted to be the fastest driver on the road, without anyone deterring his flight. Pride, offended by an innocent action, produced out-of-control emotions that, in turn, subdued reason. There was no careful thinking, only impulsive rage.

A frequent example of emotion controlling reason is the tendency we have of forming preconceived ideas about someone. Imagine someone who, over a period of time, annoys you in various ways and who you "know" has opposed you behind your back at work. All the irritating instances of his behavior accumulate in your mind and form a kind of filter through which you view, from a negative perspective, everything he does or says. You do not really think about the possible context of the person's remarks, whether he really intends good or bad; instead, you just assume his intentions must be bad. The more you interpret his behavior in a negative way, the more you confirm that your idea of him is accurate, and the more certain you are that he is trying to destroy you. Now you become impatient with his "attitude" and your frustration with him colors your communication and actions. Emotions are out of control because they are conquering reason. Instead of thinking in a healthy, logical way about reality, you just react to what you interpret as meanness. But if you could step back from the situation and carefully, without prejudice, analyze the possible neutral or even good intentions the person might have, you might discover that your preconceived ideas are based on pure assumptions and not reality. Patience waits, holds back, thinks, and considers.

Patient behavior is a response that requires a patient heart. A patient heart submits to reason first. Of course, we have heard since we were children, "think before you act." But we also need to think before we think, letting reason control our thinking. Waiting, holding back, restraining ourselves, and being persistent all provide time to think. Calm responses to irritating people always come from careful thinking, even after we develop the habit of patience. Reason helps us put a person's annoying or offensive behavior in its proper context and then think of a response that is adequate and justified in the particular moment. Only after we have carefully thought about and discovered what is true and right, can we then justify anger. Anger can be a valid emotion, but only after reason has taken control and evaluated the circumstances to determine, in light of the truth, whether anger is justified and what the right expression of anger should be. A patient heart surrenders to reason.

Surrender is, in fact, an essential aspect of a patient heart; however, before considering the step of surrender more deeply, we first need to understand something more about holding back and waiting. Holding back an uncontrolled heart is a lot like grabbing the reins of a wild horse and trying to restrain and calm its erratic, untamed behavior. Holding back our emotions requires a lot of strength and fearless concentration. When people offend us, one of the first ways we may react is to tell others what happened so that they might sympathize with us, confirming the hurt that we feel. Feeling this sympathy from others motivates us to tell our stories over and over again to as many people as will listen. Repeating the stories actually hurts much more than helps because each time we retell them, our emotions only increase. With each person who says to us, "How horrible! What they did to you is not right!" our hurt grows deeper and our anger grows more powerful. Ironically, by our own reactions to the offense, we hurt ourselves by increasing our states of emotional agitation. Instead of holding back, we get on the horse and ride it wildly through the fields. There is no benefit, only harm, in retelling our stories so many times without a healthy purpose.

Actually, we also retell the stories to ourselves, rehearsing them over and over again in our minds. Each time we replay them mentally, the details become exaggerated and the hurt becomes more painful. After a while, if we are honest with ourselves, we would have to admit that we can no longer accurately remember what happened. The facts have mixed together with emotions to muddle our memories.

Holding back means to stop this replaying of events, not only in our conversations with others but also in our own minds. If we need to tell the stories, then we can tell them to the Lord in prayer, asking for his guidance, or tell them to another person whom we trust to give us good counsel about controlling our emotions. A patient heart holds back emotions by doing nothing to allow them to intensify or run wild.

Holding back anger keeps it from turning into destructive verbal abuse or physical violence. Holding back worry keeps it from becoming an obsession. Holding back nervous feelings and frustration prohibits them from developing into desperation. Holding back fear or insecurity stops us from reacting impulsively, doing things that we would later regret. To hold back, though, we must know our own hearts. Personal awareness of what we feel and the ability to evaluate honestly the level of our emotions enables us to know when and how to hold back before it is too late. Physically separating ourselves from the troublesome situations gives us room to reconsider our reactions. Talking with other people whom we trust to help us genuinely evaluate our feelings and put the issues in perspective also serves to settle our emotions. The key at this point in maintaining a patient heart is to hold back emotions and take the time to decide what the reality is. What do I feel? Is there sufficient reason to feel it? Am I exaggerating the importance of what happened?

A patient heart also knows how to wait. The problem is that we want the answer now. We want satisfaction now. We want the reward for our efforts now. We want the question solved now. The rest of the world, however, is not on our schedule. We do not just wait in lines, wait for traffic, and wait for the doctor to see us, we also have to wait to find out all the facts, wait for people to change, wait for our efforts to produce fruit, wait to earn trust and build confidence, and wait for troubles to pass and for people to calm down. While we wait, we fight the temptation to do something or say something that might be inappropriate or simply wrong. Taking the time to think dispassionately about the problem and, then, either to find the solution or to allow events to follow their course at their own pace, can be quite tiresome.

One of the most famous stories in the Bible about the difficulty of waiting and holding back is the story of Job. The New Testament writer James refers to Job as an example of patient waiting: "As you know, we consider blessed those who have persevered. You have heard of Job's perseverance and have seen what the Lord finally brought about. The Lord is full of compassion and mercy" (James 5:11). The central theme of the book of Job answers the question of whether it is possible for humans to serve God from a decision of free will. But the book is also about patiently waiting on the Lord.

Job was a righteous man who was very faithful to God and whom God had greatly blessed. Satan, however, accused Job of serving God only because God had blessed him and put a wall around him of protection against tragedy and failure. Job, Satan claimed, did not choose to serve God from a completely free decision but, instead, felt compelled to serve God because of the rewards God gave him. Job's motives were not pure, according to Satan, and he would prove this view to be the case if God were to allow him to take away everything Job held dear to him. To defend the possibility that humans can genuinely serve God from pure motives, God allowed Satan to proceed with his experiment. So, in a moment, Job lost everything. He lost his family, his possessions, and finally his health. He suffered in horrible ways but did not deny or curse God.

Several friends came to Job trying to explain to him that the reason why he was suffering was due to sin that he had committed. Their explanation reflected the unfortunately common view that people suffer because God is punishing them for their sins. This human explanation was not correct in Job's case and only left him wondering what he had done to deserve such suffering. Job had to wait, agonizingly wait, while listening to the prolonged discourses of his friends who supposed that they understood God's purpose. He was waiting to discover the truth, hoping God would reveal the answer to him. While he waited, he continued to faithfully worship God. He waited, he held back any desire to turn away from God, and endured, surrendering in faith to God's justice and wisdom. When God finally did speak to Job, he did not explain to him what really happened in terms of Satan's challenge; instead, he rewarded Job for his perseverance.

Now consider the role of surrender in the process of learning patience. While holding back destructive emotions, waiting to discover the truth, and persevering, patience also requires a specific kind of surrender. Think again of the wild horse. If you were to take the reins and try to restrain the jumping, thrashing, and kicking of this powerful animal, you would soon tire. You would quickly become exhausted because the animal is too strong and full of energy. To be able to control and tame the beast, you would have to hand over the reins to someone more powerful and who knows more about horses than you do. You cannot surrender to the animal but must decide to surrender the reins to someone more capable. In the same way, to control our emotions we must not surrender to them but surrender them to our heavenly Father who is more powerful and wiser than we are.

In times of worry, anger, and even in moments of depression, emotions are full of energy that we have to redirect rather than allow it to agitate our hearts. Without channeling this energy in another direction that will absorb it or dissipate it, emotions can easily overcome us. In this regard we hear of people saying that we must "Let go and let God," but what does this language specifically mean? In practice how do we surrender to God? Are these just words that sound comforting or do they have practical value? There are in fact several ways we can give the reins over to the Lord in moments of emotional turmoil, depending on the nature of the problem that tests our patience.

Take, for instance, tragedy, suffering, or opposition that we face in living Christian lives. The Lord does not protect his children from every possible trial or evil, just like he did not protect Job, because challenges work to our benefit to purify and increase our faith. Peter wrote, "In this you greatly rejoice, though now for a little while you may have had to suffer grief in all kinds of trials. These have come so that your faith—of greater worth than gold, which perishes even though refined by fire—may be proved genuine and may result in praise, glory and honor when Jesus Christ is revealed" (1 Peter 1:6-7). Each time we decide with determination that we will follow Jesus' teaching no matter the opposition or disillusionment we might be experiencing, faith increases. The strength of each decision makes the next one even more resolute. The lasting result of discipleship will be nothing less than transformation, since this is the great work the Lord is doing in us. He is developing faith, compassion, humility, kindness, forgiveness, and love in us through the challenges he allows us to face. The people who offend us are also teaching us to love and forgive. The people who take from us are also teaching us generosity. The people who are angry with us are teaching us how to make peace. Life with disappointments and tragedies is teaching us to have faith, to trust in the Lord's providence. We can go on complaining and bickering, kicking and screaming through these experiences, allowing them to keep us in constant states of agitation or we can recognize the work of God and humbly let him transform us. When someone offends us and we retaliate, the Lord's work stops dead, in that moment, until we decide to let Jesus' teachings guide us. Patient hearts surrender to the work the Lord is doing in us and, through conscious, deliberate perseverance, learn to practice the character of Christ.

Emotions rob our hearts of tranquility as we anxiously absorb ourselves in thinking about how we will solve problems and find the answers we need by our own efforts. But the Lord is active. He opens doors for us, provides the resources we need, grants us wisdom, and strengthens us in our inner beings while we pass through the experiences that teach us. We do what we can do within our powers, but we also surrender to what the Lord decides to do, what he alone can do as he works with us. Let go and let God work. Committing ourselves to the transformation that he is producing in us implies surrender to his wisdom and power as he provides what is necessary to live new lives in him.

The results of true surrender are surprising because of the incomparable calm that comes over us. Remember the words of Paul, "Do not be anxious about anything, but in everything, by prayer and petition, with thanksgiving, present your requests to God. And the peace of God, which transcends all understanding, will guard your hearts and your minds in Christ Jesus" (Philippians 4:6-7). An indescribable peace comes through surrendering our anxieties to him. Peter also wrote, "Cast all your anxiety on him because he cares for you" (1 Peter 5:7). While we wait, we surrender. To discover this peace that brings calm back to our hearts, we trust in the Lord's providence, his power, and his wisdom. He is the Creator. He is able to intervene in his creation. He really is able to answer our prayers. But his answers reflect his love and wisdom as our Father. Surrender means to actually give the problems to him in prayer and accept the answers he gives us. We seek him in prayer and if we ever feel that we want to take the anxiety back, we seek him again in prayer.

A patient heart also surrenders to God's grace. Cultivating more patience usually makes us think of times when we need more patience with other people, but there are plenty of moments when we need to be patient with ourselves. The fact is that the lack of patience with others may be a symptom of a lack of patience with ourselves. We have weaknesses and faults. We make mistakes. We become discouraged at what we see as personal failings. Holding back emotions is difficult as they run wild, threatening to paralyze us into inaction. Frustrated and feeling guilty or without worth, we may transfer these emotions to other people, engaging in destructive criticism, ready to point out their imperfections. The praying Pharisee in the parable of Jesus (Luke 18:9-14) was following this very tactic to free himself of guilt by randomly condemning a tax collector who was praying nearby. Jesus taught that the correct response to guilt is to humble ourselves before God, admitting our imperfections to him because he can lift us up. We can be patient with ourselves and consequently patient with others because God patiently forgives us when we are willing to acknowledge our need for his mercy. He does not wait until we are perfect to forgive us but, instead, saves us by his grace, his undeserved mercy. In the same way that he accepts us, we ought to accept ourselves without waiting until we are perfect. As we more deeply appreciate his grace in forgiving us, we feel moved to be much more gracious toward others too. In the powerful work of transformation that the Lord is doing in us as disciples of Jesus, we continue to need his gracious forgiveness as he takes us step by step to maturity. Paul wrote,

> ... because of his great love for us, God, who is rich in mercy, made us alive with Christ even when we were dead in transgressions—it is by grace you have been saved. And God raised us up with Christ and seated us with him in the heavenly realms in Christ Jesus, in order that in the coming ages he might show the incomparable riches of his grace, expressed in his kindness to us in Christ Jesus. For it is by grace you have been saved, through faith—and this not from yourselves, it is the gift of God— not by works, so that no one can boast. For we are God's workmanship, created in Christ Jesus to do good works, which God prepared in advance for us to do (Ephesians 2:4-10).

Surrendering to the Lord's grace means to accept who we are with our imperfections and let the Lord continue to take us forward, lifting us up, enabling us to grow more like his Son and do the good he has prepared for us to do. We give the reins of our wild emotions over to him and he calms us down, telling us that he forgives us and wants to create something beautiful in us through his rule in our lives.

When we try to do what we cannot do, our hearts inevitably grow impatient. The frustration and vexation we feel are the natural consequences of trying to do by ourselves what is only possible with God. God alone can judge hearts. He alone knows all the reasons why people behave the way they do and understands the influences and forces that come to bear on their lives. He has a heart of perfect mercy and justice. There is a reason why we leave vengeance to him, as the

Scripture says: he knows when it is time for mercy and when it is time for judgment.

Yet, our hearts run wild, sometimes trying to imagine the reasons for someone's hurtful behavior. Suffering repeated offenses from loved ones fills us with feelings of resentment and vengeance, barely under control. We cannot imagine why friends do not give up destructive habits and continue to waste their lives. It is time for them to change, now! Frustration and anxiety threaten to overtake us. These are times to surrender to the Lord's understanding of another person's heart, letting him decide how many opportunities a person needs in order to change, leaving discipline to him if judgment is necessary. Meanwhile, we do not simply stand by, idly waiting for God to exercise vengeance like Jonah who camped outside of Nineveh. Jonah was waiting for the fire he hoped would fall from heaven to destroy the city, satisfying his own personal loathing for its inhabitants, despite the fact that they had repented. But even he understood that the Lord was "a gracious and compassionate God, slow to anger and abounding in love, a God who relents from sending calamity" (Jonah 4:2). So, instead of just waiting for God to work, we surrender to the Lord by persevering. We continue to do the work he wants us to do: encouraging, forgiving, showing compassion, counseling, providing people with opportunities to change, and loving unconditionally. When we have doubts about whether we ought to continue to show mercy, we can make the decision to trust in the Lord's understanding of people. He knows their hearts. So we continue to practice mercy while surrendering to the Lord's mercy and his providential work in the person's life.

Ultimately, surrender depends on trusting the Lord. Have you ever participated in the exercise of trust where one person stands in an elevated position several feet above a group of friends, back turned toward them, and then, with arms crossed, falls backward into the arms of the friends? Free falling in this way can either produce a rush of fear that takes one's breath away or a sense of relaxed peace, depending on how strong and trustworthy the friends are. A patient heart trusts in the act of surrender. If surrender is difficult, then the problem is trust. Remember David wrote, "One thing God has spoken, two things have I heard: that you, O God, are strong, and that you, O Lord, are loving" (Psalm 62:11-12). To trust in a group of friends who promise to catch us if we fall into their arms, they must be both strong and loving. These two qualities are precisely what the Lord possesses in infinite degrees, promising that surrender will be a calming experience. Complaining and bitterness disappear through understanding that the Lord knows precisely where we are, what we are experiencing, and what we feel. At the same time, he is loving and strong enough to provide what we need. What follows patient surrender is a profound sense of gratitude and contentment, bringing peace to an anxious heart. A patient heart, then, holds back, waits, and surrenders while persevering. Patience of this sort transforms lives.

PRACTICE

We have been discussing the active role the Lord has in our lives that gives our hearts rest, but now what must we do? Transformation comes through practice. There was not much Job could have done while his body was covered with painful, debilitating sores except remain faithful to God. But there was much Jonah could have done besides waiting under the shade of a vine, hoping for the Lord to punish Nineveh. He could have continued preaching and when the people repented, he could have led them on to higher and holier lives with God. But Jonah did not want what the Lord wanted.

The goal of transformation is to make patience a habitual way of living, especially during experiences that previously would have filled us with anxiety, frustration, or anger. The Lord is working with us. He empowers us, but we use this power to practice, consciously, patience. In one way patience is a gracious gift from God because he provides the experiences and strength needed to grow more patient. But, at the same time, we make the deliberate decision to respond with patience in a wide variety of situations. The key to practice is learning the response of patience in these different settings from the view point of Jesus' teaching. Practicing patience in such different circumstances is what Paul would call, "clothing ourselves with patience" (Colossians 3:12-13).

Patience with ourselves. The practice of patience begins by learning to be patient with ourselves. As we have seen, frustration or disappointment we feel about ourselves unfortunately translates into impatience with others. If, at the end of the day, we feel pressure for not having completed the work we should have finished, we leave ourselves emotionally vulnerable, either to criticism from others or the temptation to criticize others. In some cases people who received heavy amounts of criticism and negativity when they were growing up become just as impatient with themselves as others were. Their impatience with themselves can manifest itself in the inability to stick with a project and see it through to its finish or through persistent self-criticism and self-doubt.

The struggle to be patient with ourselves is due also to the habit of comparing ourselves to all the expectations people have of us, whether those expectations are valid or not. Parents expect their children to be financially successful or to excel in a sport or to be the "perfect" child who does not make messes. Young people feel the expectations of friends whose acceptance they seek. They feel the need to dress in the latest fashion, have all the right elements of "beauty," and possess all the right toys. Husbands and wives whose love is self-centered put emotionally unhealthy expectations on each other. Employees feel stressed because of the unjustified expectations of their superiors. What can we do to deal with the anxiety that all of these expectations create in us?

We cannot always escape the words and behavior of people who threaten to make us feel disappointed in ourselves; but we can consciously replace those self-critical thoughts with a different kind of thinking, viewing ourselves the way the Lord truly sees us.

The Lord is infinitely wiser than the people who surround us. His hopes for us are much more reasonable and valuable. You may have read in the New Testament something about being "perfect." The Lord, however, does not expect us to be perfect in the sense of being without mistakes or errors. In fact, when Jesus said, "Be perfect, therefore, as your heavenly Father is perfect" (Matthew 5:48), he used the Greek word *telios* which means *complete* and, in some contexts, means *brought to completion* or *maturity*. In the work of transformation, the Lord is bringing us to completion or maturity. His hope for us is that we can cultivate all the qualities that he possesses as our Father, such as compassion, kindness, grace, mercy, forgiveness and, above all, unconditional love, in their complete form. In the context of this passage in the gospel of Matthew, Jesus was talking about the degree of love that shows love even for enemies. This is a complete love, and as we develop this degree of love, we are becoming complete as our heavenly Father is complete.

The frustration we experience with other humans is that they expect things from us that we cannot fulfill. Being financially successful or possessing all the accepted tokens of beauty may be, of course, beyond our powers. But developing the character that the Lord desires of us is possible. He never asks us to be something we cannot be. Furthermore, he treats us as a work in progress. He is always in the process of bringing us to maturity. He does not expect us to behave as completely mature adults, with all the right character qualities in any given moment during our lives, because we will always be developing and maturing. The Lord is also graciously ready to forgive us when we fail, unlike others around us who constantly remind us of our shortcomings. To have patience with ourselves we will have to practice, consciously, replacing the false expectations that other humans have of us with the hopes the Lord has for us. Whenever we catch ourselves defending ourselves, whether mentally or verbally, we stop and remember what is true and just about who we ought to be. We are children of the Father, and his hopes for us are the only ones that matter.

Interestingly, as we focus on who our Father wants us to be instead of being anxious over people's expectations, we become more patient, merciful, and compassionate in our relationships, learning to deal in gentle ways with the demandingly critical people in our lives. We discover that their demands do not fill us with so much stress and we can hold back negative emotions because of the peace and confidence we feel from knowing who are becoming in the Lord. When disciples of Jesus truly focus on learning to live transformed lives, the usual social expectations they face no longer have any power to create anxiety. The joy of a transformed life replaces the constant dread of disappointing people.

At the same time, we can make many practical changes in our lives to lessen impatience with ourselves. These changes make holding back and waiting easier. Paul gave some very productive counsel concerning patience when he said, "Do not think of yourself more highly than you ought, but rather think of yourself with sober judgment" (Romans 12:3). To be "sober" in this context means to make decisions that are grounded in reality, serious, and reasonable. The tendency to form goals and make plans that are more idealistic than realistic inevitably leads to frustration when such goals remain out of reach. A teenage boy who decides he wants to become a professional football player or a teenage girl who decides she wants to be a high-powered model will face a lot of frustration in the process of trying to make the ideal something real. Adults face the same emotional battles when expending themselves to find the ideal job or buy the ideal house. For the disciples of Jesus, choosing to have realistic goals means deciding to look around, close by, and see whom they can serve in love and compassion, just as Jesus would.

Furthermore, simple decisions, like getting enough rest, not taking on more work than we can actually finish, using good time management principles, removing ourselves from situations that unnecessarily distract us from what is healthy and productive, protect us from disappointment in ourselves. The purpose of these and other changes we can make in our daily routines and habits make managing our emotions easier. By carefully evaluating our lives, we can recognize what circumstances can leave us vulnerable to emotional turmoil. If there are some changes we can make in our activities and relationships to lessen unnecessary anxiety or stress, then the resulting peace is worthy of the effort to make the changes. The disciples of Jesus feel compelled to make such changes because, for disciples, to be patient is not a preference but rather a requirement of following Jesus. Disciples of Jesus are patient because their Lord is patient.

The Lord is full of mercy toward us; let's be merciful to ourselves! We change what we can change to help us focus on following Jesus without so much emotional drama. On the other hand, there are circumstances and relationships that we cannot alter even though they challenge our emotional peace. These are the situations that teach us patience. Remember the practice of patience depends on learning how to respond to the challenges.

Patience with idiosyncrasies. Because idiosyncrasies represent what should be insignificant differences between people, they should require less patience than any other aspect of behavior; yet, sometimes these peculiarities in the behavior of people drive us crazy. The different ways we laugh, the patterns we follow for organizing ourselves, habits of eating, distinct hand gestures or facial expressions when we speak, whether we like to go out and be around people or spend the evening engrossed in books, the manner in which we make decisions (quickly, impulsively or with exaggerated deliberation), or the way we walk down the street while talking to an invisible friend on a cell phone are examples of the slightly strange customs we all have that make us individuals. *Idiosyncrasy* is an interesting word because the meaning of its Latin root is something like *private mixture*. These aspects of behavior are the individual mixture of qualities that make every person distinct. They are characteristics that are neither right or wrong in themselves but represent the freedoms of behavior that we can choose for ourselves. The origin of a particular idiosyncrasy may be physical, cultural, or simply learned habit.

For some reason, however, we react to the peculiarities of another person as if they are an invasion into our territory. To the person pacing in front of us, we say, "Will you please sit down, you are making me nervous." To the one whose hand gestures are a bit wild, we say, "Put your hands in your pockets if you want me to listen to you!" The obvious truth is that God did not design us as clones of each other. He uses each of us with our peculiarities to be special, individual instruments for him. Paul was not like Barnabas, and Peter was much different from John. Their individual, special qualities did not give one person more value over another but, instead, made them unique instruments in God's hands for special purposes.

Patience moves us to accept each other with our idiosyncrasies, holding back criticism and judgment, bearing with each other without complaining, relaxing to appreciate the differences that make us unique. Without them life would be boring indeed.

Patience to grow. Although as disciples of Jesus we share the purpose of spiritual transformation, this profound change in heart and soul does not look exactly the same in everyone at any single moment. We share faith in the Lord and follow him as the Teacher who gives us new life. Our common goal is to cultivate compassion, humility, kindness, patience, generosity, unconditional love, and many other qualities of our spirits. Yet, we are at different levels of learning about this character and knowing how to practice it. For instance, learning to be humble can be difficult for some and very easy for others, depending on their understanding of humility, their social positions, their accomplishments in life, family relationships that they had while growing up, how long they have been living the Christian life, the sorts of challenges they have had in the practice of humility, or a myriad of other factors. Since no one's experiences are exactly the same, learning humility will be a different process for everyone. This reality is also true about every other aspect of the character of Christ.

We grow at different rates. Just as in a physical family parents ought not to have the same expectations of a five-year-old child as they do of a teenager, neither should we have exactly the same expectations of each other as disciples in terms of degrees of character transformation or commitment. What we can hope for is growth. Parents hope that the five-year-old, as well as the teenager, continues to grow. The Lord hopes that the new Christian, as well as the Christian who has been following Jesus for many years, continues to grow.

Character formation requires patience just like farming. The farmer plants the seed, tends the soil, waters, treats the weeds, and waits for the plant to grow, mature, and bear a harvest. The teaching of Jesus is planted in the heart, and continued learning, experiences, challenges, and choices bring character to maturity and a harvest of holiness. Meanwhile, as one's character develops, those who have the power to participate in the process patiently contribute what is needed. They give time and space for growth. They hold back unnecessary criticism and judgment, they give counsel, they encourage, and they provide a safe environment for growth. Patiently they wait, never giving up and always staying close. It is a tragedy when someone takes the courageous step of being born again and beginning the Christian life, and then those who first fervently declared the gospel to him abandon him, leaving him to learn on his own. It would be like a plant that rises from the soil with the promise of bearing beautiful fruit and then withers for lack of water and nutrients. When Paul left his previous life of persecuting Christians, the disciples did not believe that he had become a Christian until Barnabas came to support Paul, convincing the others that Paul was truly converted. Barnabas' support and encouragement was crucial to Paul's early development (Acts 9:26-28). When John Mark returned home in the middle of a missionary journey, apparently for reasons of weakness, Barnabas was the one who later gave him another chance to participate in the challenge of preaching in distant and dangerous cities (Acts 13:13; 15:37-39). Barnabas was a patient brother in Christ and would have been a great farmer.

Patience with the mistakes of others. As we are growing in character, it is inevitable that we make mistakes. The habits of the people we once were have a tendency to creep back in while we are struggling to practice our new character. Often in the process of change, we fight over and over again to put off a destructive habit that has plagued us for many years. If we are honest, we know it happens to us and, of course, happens to others. We know in our hearts the problem is not a lack of desire to change but, instead, the need for more self-discipline to control thoughts or a better understanding of how to practice new habits. We would like people to be patient and merciful with us—but this is precisely what other people need from us.

In fact, James uses more direct language when he states, "Judgment without mercy will be shown to anyone who has not been merciful. Mercy triumphs over judgment!" (James 2:13). The Lord has been gracious to us, and, as we have seen, his grace ought to motivate us to be merciful to ourselves; but the mercy we have received should also move us to be very gracious to others when they make mistakes. Patience is merciful, holding back judgment and providing encouragement to do what is right.

Patience is also compassionate. Remember that compassion means to suffer with someone and help relieve his or her suffering. If a child trips and falls while running, and then starts crying from the pain of a skinned knee, a parent who stands by, yelling, "Why did you fall?" is not helpful and relieves nothing. The need in the moment is to alleviate the pain and then lift them up to help them run again. We may also remove some obstacles from their paths that might have caused them to trip. We give them some counsel about how to run more safely. If the child continues to run in a dangerous manner, then we might have to take them out of the situation or give them stricter limits for running. People who are honestly trying to follow Jesus suffer in their hearts when they fail. Our role as their brothers and sisters is not to pile up suffering upon suffering until we crush them, but to help them overcome the pain of guilt and show them the way to live safer lives.

The New Testament teaches a number of different ways to help someone who has fallen back to former habits that represent graduated degrees of mercy from gentleness to severity. The answer is never to ignore the sin, but instead to deal with it in the appropriately patient manner. For instance, in the case of someone who has been surprised by sin, Paul says, "If someone is caught in a sin, you who are spiritual should restore him gently" (Galatians 6:1). In other cases when someone continues in sin, Jesus taught first one brother, then two or three should go to the person and urge a change in behavior. If these first stages do not result in change, then the local body of believers should go to the individual to warn him or her to change (Matthew 18:15-17). Only after the person stubbornly refuses to change should the brothers and sisters separate themselves from the individual, for the purpose of demonstrating the seriousness of the issue and provoking repentance. Patience does not ignore sin because, of course, it is sin that keeps us from living transformed lives. But when sin happens, patience holds back anger and resentment while lovingly, carefully following through with teaching and warning at the appropriate moment with the appropriate level of seriousness.

Patience when hurt. Having patience with the mistakes of other people is more difficult when those mistakes hurt us personally. People who are struggling to put off the habit of lying not only lie, but they lie to us. Disciples who fight the battle to control anger, become angry not just with others but with us too. When their behavior harms us, we take it personally, and then we label it as offensive, feeling betrayed, disrespected, and resentful. As a result emotions run wild. But patience holds back destructive emotions, surrendering them to the Lord, and waits for change. Patience perseveres, sticking with the person, forgiving, supporting, and encouraging him to change. Jesus said, "If your brother sins, rebuke him, and if he repents, forgive him. If he sins against you seven times in a day, and seven times comes back to you and says, 'I repent,' forgive him" (Luke 17:3-4). Patience is continued forgiveness without giving up or giving in to the wild emotions that destroy relationships.

When people say something that offends us, we have the tendency to think that they understood exactly what they said and that they intentionally meant to hurt us. We deceive ourselves into thinking that we know their hearts. When they repeat the same behavior, we are even more certain that their intentions are to hurt. We might even say to ourselves, "I know them and I know how they are!" Patience, however, responds differently, holding back assumptions about motives of the heart. Remember that God alone knows our hearts. The offensive person may not even understand why he said what he did. His words may have been impulsive without much reason. Perhaps he was upset with someone else or nervous about some other situation and he expressed these emotions in his anger toward us, when we were not actually the sufficient cause of the anger. Perhaps he was just tired and lacked the energy for self-discipline. Maybe he is simply evil to the core but most likely not. Patience can wait for an explanation if one is forthcoming, but meanwhile patience looks beyond the personal aspect of offensive behavior and continues to treat the person with the same regard and respect as always, surrendering the motives to the One who can see motives. Is it naive to assume the best about people until clearly proven otherwise? No, it is patient.

Patience in the face of challenges. As disciples we face many more kinds of trials besides the offensive behavior of a brother or sister still struggling to put off the old person. First of all and most importantly, we deal with our own personal temptations that often continue to assault us without relief. In the deepest part of our hearts, we love the life the Lord is creating in us, but we have to fight because temptation does not cease. We also face financial crises, serious health problems, family turmoil, frustrations at work, people who are difficult to deal with, and opposition to the Christian life in many forms. From a positive side, we also set spiritual and material goals for ourselves that are worthy of our efforts but require constant focus and work to achieve. In such moments we may feel tired, abandoned, frustrated, or worried, and emotions again threaten to run wild.

In fact, any goal, whether to overcome temptation, solve financial problems, recover health, or grow in some character quality as a disciple of Jesus, requires patience in the form of holding back the discouraging emotions and persevering to achieve the desired end. Perseverance is actually more like a process than simply an attitude, a process that involves four elements: a goal, desire, a crisis, and the finished work.

Clearly, to cultivate patience we have to have goals that challenge us enough to create the need for patience. But there is something to remember about our goals in the Christian life: they have to be realistic and right if we expect to build patience. Goals such as working enough hours and earning enough money to buy our "dream house" or working jobs where we have no problems or conflicts with anyone may not be realistic goals given our circumstances and the direction the Lord is taking us. Everyone, though, can grow in humility, compassion, kindness, and forgiveness,.

Given a realistic goal, we also need a sufficient desire to attain the goal, enough passion to move us to put all of our effort into finding satisfaction. Paul compares the Christian life to participating in the Olympic games. As part of this analogy, he wrote, "Run in such a way as to get the prize. Everyone who competes in the games goes into strict training." (1 Corinthians 9:24-25). The word Paul used that is translated "competes" in this passage comes from a Greek word that is the origin of the English word *agonize*. Running the Christian race involves running with the intense effort of one who competes to the point of agony to win. Having clear, worthy goals means we will not run aimlessly, but we also must have a passionate desire to reach those goals. The struggle to put off the old person and put on the character of Christ is much more demanding than we may think. Desire must match the challenge presented by the goal. If certain sins are still enjoyable to us to some degree, our desires to overcome will be diluted by some lingering pleasure; and then, when the struggles to overcome the destructive habits become great, we will not have the strength to persevere. Perseverance depends on the worthiness of the goals and on the passion of our desires.

Another key element of practicing perseverance is crisis. Perseverance, in fact, would not be necessary if there were no crisis. The crisis is the moment when the goal becomes difficult or costly to achieve. Imagine a runner easily gliding along, feeling confident with his pace, running for some distance, and then suddenly needing to run up a steep hill, against a strong wind. This challenge is the moment that tests patience. The runner cannot say that he or she has perseverance when running easily, no matter how long the distance might be. The real challenge that the hill and the wind present requires stamina and produces perseverance. Continually running against such challenges increases the runner's strength and endurance. In the same way, James states, "Consider it pure joy, my brothers, whenever you face trials of many kinds, because you know that the testing of your faith develops perseverance" (James 1:2-3). The "testing" is the moment of crisis. The result of the testing is perseverance.

In times of crises when we have doubts, when we are exhausted and feel overwhelmed, or when we are distracted from our goals, we have to make decisions to either keep going or stop. If our desires are deep enough, we will continue. To evaluate our desires, we think about the goals, how much they mean to us and whether they are worth so much agony. For this reason, in his comparison between the Christian life and a race, Paul emphasizes to his readers that we are running for a crown that will last forever, a life with God. The crisis forces us to ask, "Shall we keep going or give up?" Can I realistically achieve the goal?" "Am I doing all I can do?" In such moments a well-trained, disciplined runner will not stop running unless he is injured. Even if he sees that he cannot win, he will at least finish simply to avoid the humiliation of quitting. In the case of the Christian life, quitting the race that leads to spiritual transformation is too costly. The alternative is spiritual death. Winning is always possible.

On the other hand, some disciples decide that aggressive expressions of anger represent such an ingrained habit that achieving self-control is not possible. "This is just the way I am. I cannot change who I am." But with God all things truly are possible, even anger control. He designed and created us. He knows what is possible for us. He did not create us with anger problems so we cannot say, "This is just the way I am.' Such a person may lack knowledge about how to control anger or may lack a sufficiently passionate desire to change, especially if the anger rewards her in some way (she always has her way with people when she becomes angry). But she may also lack perseverance in general. Perseverance only comes, however, through persevering.

James adds the fourth element of perseverance when he says, "Perseverance must finish its work so that you may be mature and complete, not lacking anything" (James 1:4). Enduring through the crisis without giving up finishes the work, bringing to completion the project. Without crises we would never have to struggle to reach goals and without struggles we would never discover our true potentials. Not until we pass through crises has perseverance really helped us reach farther than we have before.

Compare this truth to weight lifting as exercise. Imagine lifting a certain amount of weight a number of times and discovering that this amount of weight is fairly easy for you to lift, so you continue lifting the weight, ten, twenty, fifty times. After lifting it the fiftieth time your muscles feel good and you feel satisfied that you have exercised well. But the fact is you did not reach a crisis, and perseverance could not finish its work. Instead, lift enough weight so that you have some real difficulty lifting it ten times. Rest for a moment and lift for another ten times. Rest again and try lifting another ten times. If the weight is heavy enough, you should be able to barely lift it the last ten times and your muscles should start to twitch and shake. In the moment they begin to twitch, they are coming to the point of crisis. In this moment some people might throw the weight down and exclaim that it is too heavy. Others will persevere, agonizing to lift it the final few times as their muscles shudder. During these moments when the muscles are struggling, the fibers of the muscles are microscopically tearing and when they heal, more muscle mass will form, increasing strength. Perseverance completes its work, producing more strength by passing through the crisis.

Cultivating the character of Christ is no different. If we avoid crises in our spiritual lives or if we stop in the middle of crises and do not see them through, we will not grow to our potentials and will never know how capable we are. Whatever the quality may be, whether love, kindness, generosity, humility, or some other trait that Jesus taught and exemplified, there will always be crises; passing through them is the only way to bring the work of transformation to completion.

Paul gives powerful assurance in Galatians 6:9 where he wrote, "Let us not become weary in doing good, for at the proper time we will reap a harvest if we do not give up." Patience is perseverance. There are without a doubt other kinds of circumstances in our lives as disciples of Jesus that require patience. What all of these moments share in common is the need for us to hold back destructive and impulsive reactions, surrender our negative, destructive emotions to the Lord, wait for the Lord to do his work, continue to practice mercy and compassion while waiting, and then, when the crisis comes, endure so perseverance can finish its work. The result will be transformation!

CHAPTER FIVE

KINDNESS SHINING IN THE DARKNESS

"LOVE IS KIND"

(1 CORINTHIANS 13:4).

A group of them came from the city to the little village in the remote hills looking for members of another gang. Extorting money by threatening and killing humble, hardworking members of the community in the nearest town did not satisfy their desire for power and violence. The surrounding villages, open and vulnerable without any police force, offered more opportunities. When they heard that another gang already had begun to infiltrate these villages, they wasted no time piling into a dilapidated pickup truck to hunt down members of the opposing group. When they came to the first village, they saw no one bearing the colors and tattoos of their competition. They did find a young man in his late teens, returning from the city, walking down the dirt road. He had just graduated from school and was planning university studies to become a teacher. When they saw him, they quickly decided he would satisfy, for now, their thirst for cruelty. They stopped him and demanded money. Of course, he had none so they beat him and beat him, until he was just another broken, bloody body. Then they stabbed him repeatedly, making sure he was beyond dead. He would be their warning to everyone in the village that now their group was in control.

This particular village had seen a lot of violence in its recent history. During the civil war, guerrillas killed any adult male they thought might support the government and kidnapped young boys to force them to fight for the cause. Learning to fight was learning how to butcher and maim. When the civil war was over and some degree of peace returned, people in the village were still left with emotional and moral scars from the violence. They no longer valued life or even the needs of their neighbors like they once did. A farmer could plow and plant his field, carefully cultivate his crop, and, when harvest time arrived, wake up one morning to discover that a thief, one of his neighbors, had come in the night to steal the fruit of his labors.

So when the intruders brutally murdered the young man, people reacted to his death as a story they could report to each other but not as reason to show compassion for his family or as motivation to protect the village from violence. Cruelty was already an accepted part of their lives.

This village is not so unusual, really. Cruelty and its cousins, malice, abuse, and neglect are present in nearly every corner of the world and, at times, make it a very dark place in which to live. Even the possibility of genocide still exists in some countries. Closer at home, angry parents shake babies into unconsciousness, spouses batter each other, elders suffer from neglect, and perverted adults abuse children. The rich exploit the poor and the poor steal from each other. People without homes die in the cold. How do we react? Do we count acts of cruelty as topics of conversation, simply news reports that we can retell with a measured degree of shock and protest?

To actually fight against cruelty in this world, we have to be absolutely convinced of our powers to make a difference in the lives of people who suffer. There are plenty of idealists who talk and dream about solving problems and then do nothing significant. And there are lots of pessimists who think they are realists, denying that anything can be done and accepting cruelty as a norm for human behavior. But Jesus calls his disciples to respond by shining as lights in the world of darkness with the conviction that they can live lives that actually banish darkness.

The adversary of cruelty is kindness, an active, consistent, committed form of kindness. The Scriptures repeatedly list kindness among the principle qualities that ought to characterize the lives of the disciples of Jesus. It is one of the fruit of the Spirit as well as a part of the spiritual clothing of disciples (Colossians 3:12). Kindness is one of the traits of the heart that make the disciples of Jesus like their heavenly Father. Paul wrote that God has saved us from lives of malice and hatred through his kindness and love (Titus 3:4). Jesus taught that when we are unconditionally kind our "reward will be great, and you will be sons of the Most High, because he is kind to the ungrateful and wicked" (Luke 6:35). The kindness of our heavenly Father is powerful enough to drive out the darkness, turn his enemies into his children, and transform even heartless gang members into powerful messengers of his mercy. He invites us to be like him.

UNDERSTANDING

A variety of images come to our minds when we think of the practice of kindness: to help someone carry a load, to share a meal with someone who is hungry, to bandage up a scrape when a child falls, to let someone go ahead of us in line, to help a friend pay his rent when he loses his job, or to listen patiently to the stories of an elderly shut-in. One aspect that all of these images share in common is that they make the life of another person pleasant. The Greek word *chrestotes*, translated *kindness* in the New Testament, means to do what is pleasing for other people, to make their lives pleasant. Kindness seeks to remove the harshness, pain, and suffering of life and refuses to cause harm.

Jesus promised his disciples, "my yoke is easy and my burden is light" (Matthew 11:30). Jesus compared his teachings to the yoke that a farmer uses to join two oxen together to pull a load. The kind farmer should shape the yoke so that it perfectly fits the animals' shoulders, making any burden easy to bear. The word translated *easy* in this passage is the same word translated in other passages as *kind*. Jesus' teachings make our lives pleasant. He gives our lives purpose, he provides us with spiritual contentment that no one else can give us, and he fills us with hope. The Pharisees, who were the opponents of Jesus, had invented a multitude of traditions that made life miserable in the name of religion. He told them, "you experts in the law, woe to you, because you load people down with burdens they can hardly carry, and you yourselves will not lift one finger to help them" (Luke 11:46). The endless rules of the Pharisees were not easy on people. On the other hand, Jesus, the Son of the Creator, understands the true pleasure of a life lived in the presence of the Father. He knows the pleasure we can discover, living in love, practicing peace, and keeping our hearts pure.

The Master's teachings are kind to us, and, at the same time, point us toward the practice of kindness. From his miracles we learn that kindness means to bring healing. He came to lift up the fallen, relieve suffering, heal, and restore. How can we possibly describe the joy that his healing touch brought to a man born blind, a leper whose flesh was deformed by disease, a paralyzed man who had never walked, the daughter of a Greek woman who was possessed by evil, and a Samaritan woman whose decisions in life had left her thirsting for salvation? Jesus continues to heal us, giving us the power to leave behind lives of sin that abused and destroyed us.

His followers can live lives that bring healing too. Consider Jesus' teachings from the Sermon on the Mount (Matthew 5-7). He teaches us the practical meaning of loving our neighbors as ourselves, of replacing greed with generosity, of resolving conflicts quickly, of going the second mile in serving others, of showing mercy even when mercy may not be deserved, of controlling our anger, of not putting stumbling blocks in the paths of others that might cause them to fall, of not making false promises, of freely forgiving those who offend us, and of abstaining from hypocritically judging others. Notice, the end result of these teachings is to live a life of kindness that brings healing, making the lives of those around us as pleasant as possible, at least as much as depends on us.

This level of kindness will only develop from living a spiritual life, and, for this reason, kindness is a fruit of the Spirit. A life focused on material existence will not allow for acts of kindness that require material sacrifice. Material priorities convince us to protect what we possess and jealously guard our personal comforts. When we live for things, kindness is possible, but only when it does not deny us what we believe we need for our personal pleasure. A worldly ambitious person can be generous only when acts of generosity do not conflict with the aims of ambition. If we experience genuine, material needs, if we are hungry or in pain, we may find kindness difficult to practice because in the moment of such personal need we take our attention off of what others need. Such moments challenge our kindness but, at the same time, call us to a purer form of kindness. In such circumstances kindness will have to come from our spirits, deep within us, as a quality that satisfies our spirits more than food satisfies our bodies. When the satisfaction of showing kindness is stronger than the satisfaction of a full stomach, then kindness is a fruit of the Spirit.

Kindness of the degree that Jesus taught also depends on how we view others. Humans become capable of brutal violence when they view other humans as things to be manipulated and exploited for their own good. If humans are just things, living things, but just things, then why seek to bring pleasure to another human's life? Through the persistent presence of selfishness and violence, when one human no longer values the life of another human, kindness makes no sense and becomes simply a waste of time. If a human being is no different than a cabbage, then quarter it, shred it, throw it away and nothing is lost. Jesus, on the other hand, taught that the value of a person is the soul, the spirit created in the image of the Creator. Jesus underlined the incomparable value of the human spirit when he said, "What can a man give in exchange for his soul?" (Matthew 16:26) Kindness depends on valuing the spiritual lives of others. Nothing in the creation comes closer to the Creator than the human spirit. The reality that we are, in our essence, spirits gives us the possibility of being children of God who is Spirit. To heal the human spirit is to give pleasure to the Creator of the spirit.

Furthermore, kindness begins with the motives of our hearts, just like the other fruit of the Spirit. Being kind to others when we expect kindness in return or when we are first looking for some favor from others is relatively easy. We want something, and we are willing to give something in order to receive something. But, the practice of kindness that is a fruit of the Spirit is unconditional. It cannot depend on what we receive or do not receive. And when we receive nothing in return for being kind, kindness will have to come from a deep desire in our hearts to be like our Father. Jesus said our heavenly Father, is "kind to the ungrateful and wicked." Jesus promised that this level of unreserved, unconditional kindness from our hearts makes us children of our Father.

Kindness is related in usage to another Greek word, *charis*, which is common in the New Testament. This word refers to favor, something that gives joy and pleasure. It is frequently translated as *grace*. In Ephesians 2:7 Paul wrote that God showed "the incomparable riches of his grace, expressed in his kindness to us in Christ Jesus." The Father's desire to show us grace was incredibly deep. Paul explained that he showed us such profound favor through the kindness of sending his Son to give his life for us. Jesus suffered cruelty so that we could enjoy kindness, the undeserved kindness of being forgiven and experiencing new lives. This degree of kindness is incomparable and motivates us to show kindness from our hearts even to those who we think do not deserve it.

REFLECTION

Showing kindness when we cannot expect any kindness in return or when the person to whom we are kind has made our lives unpleasant is an example of a moment when kindness has the possibility of growing as a quality of our spirits. The fruit of the Spirit grow to become deeper, more consistent qualities when we face challenges in practicing them. In such moments when kindness must be unconditional or when the practice of kindness may be very costly, we have to examine our motives for being kind and make decisions to take kindness to a deeper level. These decisions result in spiritual growth. We become kinder in our spirits.

Imagine a person whom you work with every day who makes your life miserable. This person gives you work to do that is not your responsibility. He criticizes much of what you do, trying to find fault with even the smallest details. He opposes every suggestion you make and pays little attention when you express an idea. The truth is that he does not even carry his share of the workload. Nonetheless, you decide that if you try your best to show kindness, eventually this person will have a change of attitude. You speak graciously and courteously. You smile and listen to the unjust criticism. You offer to do extra work in order to be helpful to him. You speak well of him when with fellow workers. In short, you go out of your way to make his job easier and his life at work more pleasant, just as you would do for anyone else. Unfortunately, after some time there is no change in attitude. The offensive behavior continues. Now you must decide why you are being kind. You ask yourself, "What's the use? Why continue to treat the person well? He is not going to change!" Why be kind?

This question has the power to examine your heart. If you are practicing kindness ultimately to make your life easier and more pleasant by changing the other person's attitude through your kindness, then you will stop being kind when the other person does not change. Why be kind? As we have seen, disciples of Jesus desire to be kind because their heavenly Father is kind, and he has graciously given them new life to live in kindness toward others. We want this quality to be part of our spirits regardless of how others treat us. When such a challenge presents itself, we will have the chance to examine our hearts and decide why we want to be kind. In such moments kindness will either deepen and become more consistent or we will disregard it as impossible. Imagine how much it would grow if we decided to be kind to people who have caused some real tragedy in our lives or who have offended us in a deeply hurtful way. In order to continue to be kind, we will have to stop asking the question of whether or not people deserve our kindness. Of course, they do not deserve kindness. Neither did we deserve the kindness of our heavenly Father when he sent his Son by his grace to suffer in our place. He was kind because that is how he is in his essence. Only our heavenly Father has the power to create such kindness in our hearts. The powerful influence of his grace to transform our hearts is beyond comparison with any other spiritual teaching ever known in this world.

Kindness, without regard for what is deserved, is powerful in another way in our relationships. It bridges the gap between us and people whom we consider to be *other*. By "other" we mean people who are different and from whom we feel some sort of alienation, perhaps emotionally, culturally, or socially. Showing kindness to people who are close to us, who are like us, who have something in common with us, feels natural and easy. We feel we owe them kindness because of our relationships with them. Even in such close relationships, we cannot take for granted that we are as kind as we ought to be. We may tend to take these relationships for granted and not bother with growing in the practice of kindness toward those closest to us. Even less do we think about showing kindness to people who are other. We feel we do not owe these people anything, not that we would consciously do them any harm, but we simply do not feel any obligation to do anything for them. We are busy enough trying to be kind to families and friends.

But those people who are other are the world to whom Jesus said we are to be a light. As disciples of Jesus, we have the great work of showing the world the beauty of life with the Father in his kingdom. In the days of Jesus, the Samaritans, as well as all other Gentiles in general, were the "others" to the Jews. There is no mistake in the fact that all the gospel writers, Matthew, Mark, Luke, and John, are careful to include in their accounts the acts of kindness Jesus showed to people who were other. John tells the story of the conversation Jesus had with the Samaritan woman at the well in Sychar. The Jews traditionally had nothing to do with Samaritans whom they considered to be barbaric and spiritually ignorant. Jesus, however, stopped and spoke with the woman, patiently answered her questions about worship, and promised her living water. She was thrilled with the kind understanding he showed her and came to believe that Jesus must be the Messiah. Matthew and Mark both report about a Gentile woman from Syrian Phoenicia who begged Jesus to heal her daughter. Jesus healed the daughter and spoke of the great faith that her mother had. Luke retells the story that Jesus told of a Samaritan who kindly helped a Jewish man who had been robbed by thieves and left for dead. Jesus wanted to bring down the walls of separation between people and remove the otherness.

The tool for this work is kindness. To show kindness to a person who is very different from us has the power to bring him or her instantly closer to us. You can see the wall disappear by the way the person's face and posture change from showing suspicion or indifference to indicating pleasure and acceptance. Even a violent gang member may respond to genuine kindness because it is the very element that he has always been denied and that could make him feel like a human being.

Kindness is transforming. Kindness is the leading edge of the gospel, the first thing that can touch people and get their attention to consider the beauty of living the Christian life. Kindness brings people close enough to listen to the gospel. The kindness of Christians shows people who are other that the followers of Jesus care about people, whoever they are and from wherever they come, that they care about their needs, both physical and spiritual. Jesus did not come to feed people physically, but he did feed people, miraculously. By feeding them he proved what a loving, kind Savior he is. After feeding them, he had the credibility to teach them about the spiritual blessings in the kingdom of God and offer them spiritual food and drink. The gang member, the drug addict, the person from a different culture with a different language, and those from a different level in society with problems we never dreamed of having ourselves, will have to feel some respect, acceptance, generosity, in short, some kindness in order to believe that we care about the salvation of their souls. Kindness has the power to convince people to listen.

Kindness must be persistent. Not all people respond to kindness. Some build higher walls to protect themselves from our acts of kindness. Will we continue to forgive, to accept, to support, to be generous? In such cases continuing to show kindness will require more sacrifice of time, energy, and money. The cost of kindness again raises questions about why we ought to practice kindness to this degree and what we hope to accomplish. Being kind will have to be more important than being comfortable. It will have this deeper value in our lives when we know how close kindness makes us feel to our heavenly Father. We are as he is, as he created us to be. In addition, our willingness to bear the cost of kindness makes our message about the gospel believable and gives us credibility as messengers of kindness.

To be a light in the darkness, disciples must come to be known for consistent kindness that does not surrender. The Lord does not surrender. A light can never allow the darkness to extinguish it. His kindness is patient and, therefore, has the power to finally convince us to change our minds about living in the darkness. Paul described the "riches of his kindness, tolerance and patience" that can lead us to repentance, the change of mind that makes us turn from darkness to the light (Romans 2:4). His children have learned from his persistent kindness to wait patiently for others to change. How can we give up if the Lord has not given up on us? So, the Lord's people commit themselves to small deeds of kindness as well as sacrificial acts of kindness. They involve themselves as a community of people to serve the needy, no matter who they are or where they are from. They work to make life pleasant for acquaintances and for strangers. Then, even those who have built walls may let them fall and come to believe the message.

Indifference is the enemy of persistence. Understandably, members of a village or community who have witnessed much violence may come to accept the existence of cruelty without feeling much compassion for those who directly suffer. Violence becomes part of life. Nonetheless, even in places where violence is an everyday occurrence, kindness finds its place in the hearts of people who understand its power to relieve pain or loss with even the smallest gestures of sympathy and support. Indifference is more of a problem for people who, consciously or unconsciously, isolate themselves from cruelty and suffering. The media has an interesting role in this isolation. The television news brings the violence of the world into our living rooms. By watching the news, we feel that we are part of the world, being aware of what is happening in distant places. Yet, simply watching the news puts no moral demands on us to act. We can feel involved without really being involved. We can witness suffering and even feel emotionally moved to some degree, yet without believing we have any moral obligations to react to relieve the suffering.

Of course, we think that if the people who are suffering live far from us in a different land and different culture, then there may be little opportunity to do something. We see a need someone has, but we do not believe we have obligations to fill the need. Repeatedly witnessing a need without feeling obligated to do anything to relieve it creates a mental and emotional wall between seeing and acting. The result is a mentality of indifference. Without a doubt there are moments when we are not physically able to show any kindness, though we think that we might want to do something. We lack the necessary resources or abilities to help. And there are moments when we have justifiable reasons for believing that the need is not legitimate. The person asking for money may very likely be a drug addict and will use the money to buy drugs.

Allowing for this separation between seeing a need and responding with kindness unfortunately can become our way of viewing the world, blinding us to real opportunities in which we could practice kindness. We are too ready to claim that there is nothing we can do to help. "I am in a hurry." "I have a lot to worry about already." "The person is probably not sincere." "They should have helped themselves." "There are other people I am already trying to help." "This person is suffering from bad decisions and deserves to suffer."

When we see someone in pain or carrying some burden, if turning our eyes away is too easy, then indifference is a problem. At the heart of indifference is self-centeredness. First, we protect and satisfy ourselves, and then, if there is any emotional and physical energy left, we might think about being kind, especially if kindness is not too costly. But there is nothing significant or especially powerful about this level of kindness.

The solution is compassion. The solution to indifference and its companion, self-centeredness, is the practice of compassion. The apostle Paul lists compassion right before kindness in Colossians 3:12 as part of the spiritual clothing we put on when we become children of God. He does not list compassion as a fruit of the Spirit in Galatians 5:22-23, perhaps because the list of fruit of the Spirit is just a sample of qualities comprising Christian character or perhaps because compassion is intimately connected with kindness. Kindness requires compassion. The word *compassion* literally means *to suffer with* someone. It implies the need first to understand the suffering of another person and then to feel motivated to relieve the suffering. Compassion requires understanding and understanding requires patient listening without prejudgment. We attempt to put ourselves in the position of the other person, viewing the world from her eyes, and understand why an act of kindness from us would make her life easier or more pleasant.

The lack of compassion causes us to form too many mistaken assumptions about what the other person feels or needs without really knowing her heart. Maybe the person is not a drug addict. Maybe the person is an addict and our act of kindness could be the right act in the right moment finally to cause a change in her heart. The only way to know her heart is to listen. If people are too far away from us to listen to them personally, as in the case of someone living in a foreign land, we can still carefully inform ourselves about the need, instead of summarily dismissing it. Then we ask, sincerely ask, unselfishly ask, what can we do?

PRACTICE

Thinking about the fruit of the Spirit must always lead us to this most important question, "What can I do?" Remember that Jesus said the wise man who built his house upon the rock was the one who "hears these words of mine and puts them into practice" (Matthew 7:24). Kindness, to be a light in the darkness, must be consistent, deliberate, and planned practice. To grow in kindness requires practicing kindness in more increasingly difficult circumstances.

Some years ago a popular, cultural movement began promoting the idea of practicing "random acts of kindness." Books, websites, bumper stickers, buttons, and a host of other promotional tools spread the concept of showing kindness in small, unexpected, spontaneous ways. Pay the toll for the car behind you. Send flowers to your favorite elementary school teacher. Leave an inspiring poem or book on the seat when you get off the bus. Share your umbrella with a stranger who does not have one. Pick up some trash. Tape the exact coins necessary to a soda machine so the next person can have a free drink. This movement undoubtedly woke up many people to the joy of simple gestures that could give someone a smile and make her day a little more pleasant. Kindness does not have to involve earth-shaking acts of stunning generosity.

Remember the simple things. Jesus reminded the disciples of the importance of giving "a cup of cold water to these little ones" (Matthew 10:42). What can you do? We cannot forget the simple things. Take over a chore from someone so he can relax. Respond to a discouraging remark with a positive point of view. Spend time playing sports with a young person. Send a thank-you or note of appreciation to someone who has done something commendable. Take time to read to someone. Spend time with your parents or grandparents. Give up your seat in a waiting room. Ask someone how he or she is and then really listen. Volunteer at a seniors' center. Clean up some graffiti. Send a friend a book that they might be interested in reading. Take clothes to a homeless shelter. Buy groceries for a friend out of work. Purchase a toy or book for a sick child. Refrain from criticism or negative remarks and replace them with compliments. Take care of someone's children and give the parents a voucher for their favorite restaurant. Give another person plenty of room to pass your car on the highway. Wash someone's car. When children are selling candy or having a bake sale for their school or club, buy something for their cause even though you may not eat what you are buying (give it to someone else). Stop the gossip. Sweep a neighbor's walk. Give blood. Give somebody a ride. Help out your child's teacher with chores in the classroom. Cook a meal for someone who is returning from the hospital. Be considerate and listen to a telemarketer, admittedly a sacrificial act of kindness, but he needs the encouragement!

The goal in our lives as disciples of Jesus is to make the random common and the spontaneous planned. To avoid indifference and conquer self-centeredness, kindness has to become a mentality and a way of life. At the same time, there are some special areas of human life in which kindness is most important. If we pay special attention to these aspects of our lives, we will have opportunities to be more thoughtful in the ways we practice kindness. Consider what you can do.

Help the helpless. Human beings are dependent creatures. We cannot live without help, especially help from the Lord. There are times we find ourselves absolutely helpless in the sense that we cannot find the solutions or answers that we desperately need. In such moments we feel alone and lost. Losing a job, experiencing a debilitating sickness, facing a failure, or falling into a depression with little strength to carry on, remind us how dependent we are. Passing through these or similar experiences of helplessness humbles us, teaching us that we should not be so ready to judge others for not helping themselves. To be more consistent with kindness, we have to avoid assumptions about what people have or have not done for themselves. We just need to remember that in any moment we might feel helpless and have to depend on the kindness of others and, most of all, kindness from the Lord.

James taught a very important principle when he wrote, "Religion that God our Father accepts as pure and faultless is this: to look after orphans and widows in their distress and to keep oneself from being polluted by the world" (James 1:27). The orphans and widows represent people who are helpless. True religion, that is true worship of God, consists of practicing kindness toward the helpless. We honor God when we care for our fellow human beings who are in need of kindness. They are his creation. When his kindness toward us motivates us to show kindness to others, our lives honor him. By imitating his heart we show that he is our Creator. Concluding that people are helpless and honoring God by helping them is a much better choice than assuming people should help themselves and, thereby, missing an opportunity to glorify him.

Looking after the physical, emotional, and spiritual needs of widows and orphans is one way to help the helpless. But we are surrounded by needs that no one else may be filling. There are elders who are sick or disabled. There are children who need foster or adoptive parents. There are brothers and sisters in Christ who lose their jobs. There are young people who need role models. They need big brothers and big sisters to show interest in them, pointing them in the direction of living healthy, productive lives. There are active children who need someone to coach them on an athletic team, a coach who will also teach them the character and social skills that only a Christian could teach them. There are students who need mentors and tutors to help them face the challenges of being successful in school. There are community and school programs that need volunteers who will humbly, unselfishly, and joyfully serve because of who they are as disciples of Christ.

Kindness ought to be kind. Remember that acts of kindness are supposed to make a person's life more pleasant. When we practice kindness, we ought to practice kindness in a pleasant way. Paul once wrote that, "God loves a cheerful giver" (2 Corinthians 9:7). If we help someone who is helpless, but through our gestures, tones of voice, or disinterested, impatient attitudes, we communicate to the person that we do not enjoy being kind to them, kindness is no longer kind. Receiving help from someone who is not interested in helping is not a pleasant experience.

Carry burdens. While some people find themselves in circumstances in which they cannot help themselves, others simply need help carrying a burden—even emotional and spiritual burdens—that they have trouble carrying by themselves. Helping to lighten their loads provides great relief. Paul wrote, "Carry each other's burdens, and in this way you will fulfill the law of Christ" (Galatians 6:2). The law of Christ is that we love one another. Love is kind. Burdens make us feel weak, tired and discouraged, as if we will not be able to reach our goals under their weight. Help with our burdens makes the road easier to travel and makes joy along the way possible. The author of Hebrews wrote, "Therefore, strengthen your feeble arms and weak knees. Make level paths for your feet, so that the lame may not be disabled, but rather healed" (Hebrews 12:12-13).

Walking a level, straight, even path that others can follow is an essential act of kindness that has the power to make another person's life much easier. Our children and our brothers and sisters in Christ will especially enjoy an easier life if we make consistent, transparent decisions that make the path to Christ and the Christian life very clear. Kindness is refusing to do anything that might cause someone to stumble and fall or become confused about the direction in which to go. Kindness means being careful how we walk.

In the same way, undue stress can also make the road tiring. We all feel stress because of the pressures of time, expenses, conflicts, and the usual frustrations of normal, everyday life. Critical, negative attitudes or unjust expectations that we place on people add to stress that they may already feel and robs them of joy. When our spouses have had difficult days at work or problems dealing with responsibilities at home, taking care not to create additional stress by piling on demands is another way of carrying a burden for them. Kindness means to relieve stress and to refuse to add to someone's burdens.

Bearing a burden for another person refers to any load that we can help them carry. They have worries that we can listen to and pray about with them. There are parents who want kind advice about how to encourage and direct rebellious children. There are single parents whose children need adoptive aunts and uncles. There are fellow disciples who are trying to overcome destructive habits and need counsel and support. They face temptations and think that no one will understand what they are going through. They need someone who will kindly help them find victories and give them continued support to remain victorious. There are friends who deal with insecurities, doubts, and fears; they need assurance and confidence from someone whom they trust. There are people close to us who experience financial problems and who would trust us enough to ask for help learning how to manage their budgets. There are poor people–there will always be the poor–who need, often desperately need, kindness from those who have received so much kindness.

We understand we cannot help with every burden, but our desire is to have hearts as open as possible to the needs of others. At the same time, other people who have burdens may not ask for help because they feel afraid of imposing on us. By their discouraged voices or their stressed behavior we know we should ask them how we can help. An offer of help from a humble, gracious heart is itself an act of kindness. We can pray for wisdom to know when to offer help, when to help, and when to let others help.

Bring healing. Beyond helping the helpless and bearing each other's burdens, there are other moments when kindness makes life livable. One such moment follows physical, emotional, or spiritual injuries we experience as part of living in a world damaged by sin's corruption. Jesus described his mission in the words of the prophet Isaiah, "The Spirit of the Lord is on me, because he has anointed me to preach good news to the poor. He has sent me to proclaim freedom for the prisoners and recovery of sight for the blind, to release the oppressed...." (Luke 4:18). Jesus, of course, healed many people of physical infirmities. There is also a role for us in physical healing without having to be doctors. Recovery happens more quickly with the help of a kind person who is ready to serve by cooking a meal, cleaning the house, caring for the children, giving a ride, bandaging wounds, providing companionship, and taking care of the tasks that no one else will gladly do.

But Jesus came primarily to heal people spiritually and emotionally. The physical healing that he brought was evidence that he could heal us spiritually. Giving physical sight to a blind man meant that he could heal our spiritual blindness. There is also an essential role the disciples of Jesus play in bringing the healing of Jesus to people who are spiritually and emotionally injured.

Life has been brutal to many people. They have been beaten up by criticism and negativity, leaving them without confidence or self-esteem. They have suffered rejection that left them feeling alone and afraid to trust. Their dreams and plans have become unattainable. They have lost friends or loved ones on whom they depended. They have suffered long emotional abuses in relationships from which they felt they could not escape. They have come to hate themselves for having caused injury to others. Sin has enslaved them and the guilt from sin has brutalized their consciences. They are discouraged, disillusioned, and despair of living satisfying, meaningful lives. They need the healing of Jesus. We can bring them to the healing Savior.

The Lord is first of all rich in mercy. Hurting people need mercy and not more punishment. Mercy forgives. Mercy waits and remains patient. Mercy treats the injured with tenderness and compassion instead of further injuring. Mercy gives another chance. Remember the words of James: "Mercy triumphs over judgment!" We bring healing to people as we communicate the Lord's mercy. When people feel remorse and understand the gravity of a mistake they have committed, there is no need to assault them with more reproach. "Why didn't you listen to me!" "What do you think you were doing?" "Can't you do anything right?" The Lord mercifully offers us the chance not to look back continuously at past mistakes but to look ahead to how he transforms us into new people. The Lord turned the aggressive, impatient apostle John into the messenger of God's love, and he turned the wavering, impulsive apostle Peter into a rock of faith. (Compare John in Luke 9:54 with John in 1 John 4:12 and compare Peter in Matthew 26:69-75 with Peter in 1 Peter 1:6-9.) Kindness helps people see who they can be instead of reminding them who they used to be.

As the Lord transforms us, he gives our lives value and meaning. Practicing the teachings of Jesus for everyday living teaches us how to love, how to show compassion, how to humble ourselves, how to be patient and disciplined, how to be generous, and how to be at peace with ourselves and with others. Cultivating these qualities in our character gives our lives a deeper, more abiding value than any possession or material accomplishment can provide us. Through understanding and growing in the Christian life, people can rebuild their confidence and self-esteem based on who they are in their hearts, something no one can rob them of. We serve as the Lord's instruments of kindness by helping people see the value and meaning their lives can have by following Jesus. The Lord would never knock us down and pummel us with the stones of destructive criticism and negativity. He mercifully lifts us up and makes us stand after others have tried to destroy us. His disciples help to heal when they do the same.

Jesus makes us feel secure and safe. He is the Good Shepherd who cares for each member of his flock, protecting them from danger, giving his life for the sheep. The disciples of Jesus show the beauty of kindness by providing an environment of safety for people who have suffered mistreatment and abuse. Jesus, in fact, designed the church as a body of people who could offer emotional and spiritual refuge to those who had suffered. In the first-century church, slaves, tax collectors, prostitutes, and the poor could come together with those who owned houses and lands, intellectuals and professionals, all sharing the same heart and expecting to find acceptance and genuine love. Jesus meant the church to be a community of kindness with open arms welcoming those who need healing. In the church those who were hurting discovered they could begin life again and could belong to a family of spiritual brothers and sisters who would accept them and help them grow in their new lives. Being with trustworthy people builds trust. Being with encouraging people builds self-confidence. Being with optimistic people rebuilds hope.

Jesus was also a friend. He gave his life for his friends. Hurting people need the kindness of solid friendship. Rejection and isolation have the potential for causing such great harm because the Lord created us as social beings to need and to enjoy friendship. Something profound inside of us is lost when we lose a friend. Yet society, suffering from the stain of sin, often seems bent on making people feel excluded, isolated, and rejected. Cliques form in school. Ambition in the work place causes people who were once friends to betray each other. One race or class demeans another. One culture stands in judgment over another. People feel isolated in their neighborhoods, among their circles of friends, and in their own homes. It is possible to feel alone even when standing in the middle of a crowd of people. The kindness of loyal, patient, accepting friendship has so much power to heal because it helps people see that their lives matter, that they are not alone, and that people care.

Those who have felt life's brutality have the potential for understanding more deeply the healing that Jesus brought and have more sympathy for others who need kindness. Yet, there are people who have suffered and jealously guard whatever they have regained of their lives, unwilling to show kindness for fear of losing something.

They still need the spiritual healing that only Jesus can perform so they once again will feel free to give.

Is kindness always possible? One final question about kindness might have already occurred to you and is necessary to raise. Is kindness always possible or appropriate? Imagine competing with someone, playing a game or participating in an athletic contest. Think of an intense game of basketball that determines a championship. The players invest all of their concentration and energies on the goal of winning the game. One team will win and one will lose. Losing is not a pleasant experience. So is it possible to play to win, cause the other team to lose, and still be kind? The answer is yes, because kindness and competition are not mutually exclusive. Competition, even when intense, can still be kind. Playing by the rules, eliminating unnecessary aggressiveness, helping up a competitor when he falls, replacing "trash talk" with praise for the competition, and playing with graciousness instead of being confrontational or quarrelsome make competition and even losing as pleasant as possible.

The writer of Hebrews describes another example of experiences that are potentially unpleasant. The author explains why the Lord disciplines us by allowing us to experience hardships. He observes that, "No discipline seems pleasant at the time, but painful. Later on, however, it produces a harvest of righteousness and peace for those who have been trained by it." The word translated *pleasant* in this passage is the same word translated in other places as *kindness*. Suffering is not enjoyable. Losing what we have, feeling physical and emotional pain, and facing opposition, prejudice, or hatred are experiences we would like to avoid but cannot. Hardship in this form has the power to increase our faith and make us more focused in our Christian lives. Suffering trains us to be more dedicated to living righteous lives by teaching us what we really ought to value. In fact, the writer of this text is actually providing reasons why discipline from the Lord is encouraging because "the Lord disciplines those he loves" (Hebrews 12:6) just as human fathers respectfully discipline the children they love. He also writes, "God disciplines us for our good, that we may share in his holiness" (Hebrews 12:10). Although in the moment discipline is not pleasant, the result makes our lives more enjoyable because we have a stronger faith and more power to resist distractions and temptations. Before we judge the Lord as unkind for allowing his children to suffer difficulties, we ought to remember the end result and the Lord's loving purposes.

The Lord's consistent kindness has the power to convince us to change our minds about trying to live without him, and, instead, come to him in complete surrender to live as he created us to live. Remember the words of Paul as he encourages us to appreciate the "riches of his kindness, tolerance and patience" which, he says, "leads you toward repentance." Only if we were to finally reject his kindness and determine to live away from him, would he have to separate us from his presence, a decision that Paul describes as the "sternness" of God that replaces his kindness (Romans 11:22). Choosing to face God's sternness instead of enjoying his unfailing kindness, of course, makes no sense, but the decision is ours.

We should see some signs in our behavior that indicate to us that we are cultivating kindness in the image of our Father. We should have increased intuition for knowing who needs help, less interest in selfish goals, more genuine practice of kindness without regard for what we might gain, less worry about how people will react to our kindness, simply being kind because kindness flows from our relationships with our Father. The kindness of the children of God must be distinctive enough so that it is neither random nor rare, but thoughtful and persistent. It should reach the "other" as well as those closest to us. It should be light in the darkness for the most despairing addict or violent gang member.

CHAPTER SIX

GOODNESS: LIVING THE BENEFICIAL LIFE

"THE GOOD MAN BRINGS GOOD THINGS OUT OF THE GOOD STORED UP IN HIS HEART"

(LUKE 6:45).

As the young boy went out the door for school, his mother reminded him, "Be good!" She said it to him nearly every day as he left for school, and he had become so used to her words that they really did not register in his mind. If he did stop and think about being good, he would understand that his mother was reminding him to pay attention to the teacher, speak respectfully, quietly do his work, and not play roughly at recess. She had told him about all of these things before.

After the first six months at his new job, the man's boss came to him at the end of one day and told him, "You are doing a good job with the company. I am glad we have you on board!" He did not know what his boss thought was good about his work (maybe his successful sales figures, maybe his disciplined work ethic, perhaps his ideas for cost-cutting), but he was glad his boss was pleased.

She knew her neighbor needed a good friend, someone to talk to, confide in, and depend on, and she was happy to be a support for her. The woman living next-door was a young mother with three small children who needed the wise counsel of a caring friend.

What do we mean when we say that someone or something is good? What makes a boy a good boy, an employee a good employee, or a friend a good friend? The word *good* usually stands for all the qualities that we admire and honor with respect to a specific category of people or a particular kind of thing. Of course, people may differ about the qualities they expect to see in someone they label as "good." Maybe for some parents a good boy robotically follows orders, never speaks unless spoken to, and easily blends into the woodwork when important visitors come to the house. We may have different opinions about what makes an employee good. Maybe a good employee is one who puts the company first, sacrificing family life and physical health for the profit of the company. Maybe a good friend is someone who is always ready to loan twenty dollars without asking to be paid back. The question we are asking is, what are the qualities of good friends, good employees, or good behavior for young children? But the more fundamental question is why do we consider these qualities to be the qualities of what is good?

It is common in our conservations to use the word *good* to summarize a group of specific qualities that we admire. There is, of course, a sense in which all the qualities of the fruit of the Spirit (love, joy, peace, patience, kindness, goodness, faith, gentleness and self-control) are good because they create a picture of the ideal disciple of Jesus. The fact, however, that Paul includes goodness as one among several other characteristics means that the word is not a general, catch-all word that summarizes all the other respected qualities. Instead, it has a very specific meaning.

The word Paul used in the original Greek text of this verse was *agathosune*, a form of *agathos*, a common Greek word for *good*. It can refer to good in a broad moral sense, describing someone who is good in character, with all the ideal qualities that a morally good person should possess. But it can also refer to a more specific form of good that brings about acceptable and pleasing benefits. Good is what is useful, fulfilling a purpose, and producing beneficial results. We can speak of a thing or person as being "good for something": This year is a good year for growing cotton; This train ticket is good for travel all day long; Dialogue between teacher and student is a good strategy for teaching.

The qualities that form the list of the fruit of the Spirit, as well as other qualities of the Christian life, such as humility and compassion, are good because they produce pleasing and useful results, not only in the lives of people who practice them but also in the lives of those who surround people who practice them. Relationships improve, views of life turn optimistic, and the beauty of life with God becomes evident. At the same time, goodness can itself be a distinct fruit of the Spirit when it refers specifically to living a life that is beneficial to others. When we cultivate goodness, our lives are good for something. Practicing goodness is living a life that benefits others.

We hear people talk about living the "good life." Usually they are speaking about enjoying the physical pleasures of life such as eating delicious food, enjoying free time, having fun with friends, and kicking back and relaxing without cares or worries. A billboard with a picture of a luxurious home on the edge of a beautiful golf course invites us to "Live the good life….Homes starting at $800K!" Not everyone can afford this level of the "good life."

Jesus presents us with an entirely different view of living a good life. A good life is a productive life. Just like a "good tree" and "good ground" bear fruit, Jesus said, "The good man brings good things out of the good stored up in him" (Matthew 12:35). A good person lives a life that is useful and purpose-oriented, generating good results because of the good, beneficial desires and values that already exist in his or her heart. Humility, for example, is the result of learning how to be a servant, learning from lessons about serving that we have stored up in our hearts. A heart of humility, in turn, motivates us to cultivate healthy, productive relationships by focusing on the needs of others. Serving in humility is a way to practice goodness that results in benefits for others. The good life is the beneficial life. Jesus invites us to come and live the good life that everyone can afford to live!

UNDERSTANDING

Beneficial good is a factor that counts for much in the decisions people make. Most people commonly use the amount of possible benefit to calculate the good or bad, right or wrong of the choices that life presents to them. "Will it be good for me to move to another city?" "Will this new job be good for my family?" "Is my son's friend really good for him?" "Am I really going to gain anything by continuing to deceive people into thinking I have quit using drugs?" "If I don't report all my income for taxes, will I have more money to go on vacation with my wife and children?" The way in which people raise such questions involves thinking about doing what is beneficial to themselves or others.

To further understand how often we think about what is beneficial when we make decisions, we should distinguish between different kinds of decisions we make. We can place our decisions into several categories which include preferences, values, and moral decisions. First, we all have preferences concerning an enormous number of options from which we choose in our daily lives. We prefer certain kinds of food, particular places to live, certain jobs or careers, specific kinds of clothing, music, cars, recreational activities, and so on. When we decide what our preferences are, we usually think about the benefits each possibility will bring us. We prefer certain foods because we hope to enjoy the taste, take advantage of the healthy effects of the food, and be able to afford the price. We prefer what brings us the most benefit. Since preferences express something very personal, we do not have to agree from person to person about which ones we choose.

Despite the fact that preferences are personal, we still must consider the effects our preferences have on others. In the first century when the church first began to develop with disciples from Jewish as well as Gentile backgrounds, the issue of eating meat that had been previously offered to idols raised the question of what constituted preferences. Some Christians of Jewish background believed that they could not eat meat that non-believing Gentiles had offered as sacrifices to their idols and then had been sold in the marketplace. They had very strong inhibitions trained for centuries against participating in anything that had to do with idolatry. Actually, for these Christians of Jewish background, eating this meat was a question of faith and not preference; they sincerely believed they could not this meat without supporting idolatry. Many Christians of Gentile heritage, on the other hand, had learned as disciples that the idols were absolutely nothing, only statues and carvings made by human hands with no life or any relationship to reality. They had now come to worship the true, living, infinitely powerful Creator through his Son, Jesus. The Gentile Christians had no compulsions against eating this meat because they knew the idols were nothing. For them this issue was one of preference. The truth was that since the idols were nothing, disciples had the liberty to choose to eat this meat purchased in the market place or not to eat it. Eating was correctly a preference. "The man who eats everything must not look down on him who does not, and the man who does not eat everything must not condemn the man who does, for God has accepted him" (Romans 14:3).

Nonetheless, even though preferences are personal, the practice of our preferences must harm no one. Paul described a scenario that was taking place in the congregation of the Corinthians. A believer who was not sure that eating this meat was morally right sees another believer gladly eating this meat; so, he decides to eat some himself. But because he is not fully convinced, the first believer feels guilty in his conscience for eating the meat. Paul taught that the believer who freely ate the meat should feel responsible for having influenced the other believer to do something that offended his conscience. Amazing! Who would think that we would need to be so careful about influencing someone else to act in a way that would afterwards make him or her feel guilty, even though the guilt was not actually justified? But the inspired apostle Paul wrote, "It is wrong for a man to eat anything that causes someone else to stumble" (Romans 14:20). Imagine if we were to buy a car that causes a friend to be genuinely envious and want to have a similar car, but who really cannot afford such a car. Imagine the friend decides to buy the car and then feels guilty for buying a car he cannot afford. By the preference we exercised in buying a certain car, we influenced someone to stumble and offend his conscience. According to the inspired Scriptures, we ought to avoid causing another brother to stumble. Why? In discussing the issue of eating meat or exercising any other preference, Paul taught, "Nobody should seek his own good, but the good of others" (1 Corinthians 10:24). The good we do ought to benefit others. The choices we make, even about preferences, are no longer so personal. We evaluate every choice not only in view of our own benefits but also in view of the benefits or harm to others.

Besides preferences, we also make decisions based on values. Values hold that one thing is better than another, promising greater benefit in some way. Maybe we value family time more than our careers because the benefits of having a strong family are more important to us than the personal satisfaction of advancing rapidly in our careers. Nonetheless, someone else may value excelling in a profession and decide to not raise a family, thinking that having a family would distract him from his profession. Such a person may have very good reasons for valuing his or her career, especially if such a career will benefit society in general and is so time-consuming that proper, adequate attention to a family would nearly be impossible. Consider another example. We may decide to ride bikes to work because we value exercise and a clean environment. For us the benefits of bike riding outweigh the benefits of driving our cars, so we decide it is a good decision to ride bikes. But someone else may not agree on the value of exercise in comparison to other activities.

Values vary from person to person, depending on how each person judges the benefits of different values. At the same time, the principle concerning the exercise of preferences is also true of values: "Nobody should seek his own good, but the good of others." Since we do not live in isolation but in society, our values affect the lives of others, such as our families, our friends, or our work associates. Obviously, if we value time we spend working more than time we spend with our spouses and children, then our families will suffer. *Good* values are beneficial not just to self but to others. In fact, in a life guided by humility, the benefit to others takes priority over benefit to self.

Moral choices represent a third category of decisions that we describe as "good" versus "bad." For instance, we teach our children to make good moral decisions. In what sense do we label these moral decisions *good?* It is first essential to understand that moral rules are very different from preferences or values. Although we hear people talk about "moral values," this phrase is a contradiction since moral principles cannot be values. We would never say, "I prefer not to lie" or "I prefer not to murder." There is something very weak about these statements that does not express the convictions we have against lying and murder. But neither would we say, "It is better not to lie" or "I value saving life more than murdering someone." Values can vary between individuals without meriting condemnation of one person by another who does not share the same thinking. You do not have to share my value about exercise, and I cannot label you as "wrong" or "bad" for not sharing it. But we ought to agree on moral decisions because agreement about moral principles allows us to live together in society.

How does agreement help us in this case? To live together we have to require each other to be honest, not to steal, and refrain from murder or other similar forms of violence. Members of a healthy society will have to agree that racism is evil and slander is wrong. Such principles describe behavior that is right or wrong for all human beings. Truly moral principles reflect qualities that are essential to human nature and society. Without agreement on such principles, society becomes chaotic and violent. For this reason there are choices we make that we label as moral and that carry a strong obligation and consequent condemnation for not obeying them. There are moral decisions that are good and moral decisions that are evil. Good benefits, evil destroys.

How will we decide or who will decide what is morally beneficial for all humans? Often people make key moral decisions in their lives with lots of emotion and little rational thought. When they do think carefully about moral decisions concerning common, practical issues like whether to cheat on their taxes, whether to lie to their neighbors, whether or not to give their last dollars to people begging on the street corner, or whether to forgive those who have offended them, people generally think about the benefits of the different options. What are the benefits of forgiving someone? What are the benefits of not forgiving?

Using this sort of reasoning, the final decision about some moral question falls somewhere on the scale between benefit to self and benefit to others. Imagine drawing a line between two extremes, with benefits to self at one end and benefits to others at the other end. The natural self-centeredness of humans pushes people to protect themselves and preserve their lives, deciding moral issues by thinking mostly of the benefits for themselves. On the other hand, the willingness to sacrifice self for the good of others will place moral decisions at the other end, focusing on the benefits to others. On this line between two extremes, the decision to abort a baby because it interferes with a career falls at the extreme of benefit to self. At the other end of the spectrum, purely benefiting others, would fall the decision to put our own lives at risk to save others who are strangers to us. Between these two extremes, people make important moral decisions, trying to balance the benefits they want for themselves with the benefits they think others deserve.

In our moral confusion, we move all over this line between benefits to ourselves and benefits to others when we decide what is the moral good that we ought to practice. The confusion is due to the mistaken assumption that moral decisions are similar to preferences or values. Moral obligations are not personal at all, they are universal, meant for all to follow. Consider once again the teaching of Jesus, "Do to others as you would have them do to you." Before making a moral decision, we imagine how we would like others to treat us, whoever the "others" are. They could be our family members, our friends, people from a totally different culture, or even our enemies. We are essentially asking, "How would I like the *world* to treat to me?" To put it another way, "What would the world be like if everyone treated each other the way I am considering treating others?" Such decisions, therefore, are universal, not personal.

In the first chapter we noticed that the principle, "Do to others as you would have them do to you," is parallel to the principle, "Love your neighbor as yourself." This latter principle neutralizes the question of benefit since our neighbors' benefits should be equally as important as the benefits to ourselves. Whatever we believe is morally good for ourselves ought also, at the same time, to be morally good for our neighbors. Genuinely moral rules that we can accept and live by should be beneficial to everyone equally, no matter where we live or who we are. So the question is what behaviors are beneficial to all mankind living in society? Furthermore, we must also consider the consequences of our present moral decisions on the future. What if everyone continued to treat each other in the future in the way I am considering treating others now?

Left on our own, this question can be a difficult one to answer in some specific cases because we are not in positions to know the consequences of our decisions on such a broad, universal level as the "world." From our limited perspectives, we cannot see where all our moral rules or decisions might lead. It is difficult enough to stop in emotionally charged moments and think about the long-term consequences of specific moral choices we have made. In addition, the span of human life is too short to be able to discover on our own what is truly beneficial. We cannot adopt the right perspectives to see all we need to see.

To illustrate our limitations, consider an interesting fact about Yosemite, a beautiful national park on the western slope of the Sierra Nevada Mountains in California. Yosemite consists of a central forested valley surrounded by tall, majestic granite formations. In the spring powerful waterfalls cascade from the summits of these high places. Interestingly, if you drive along the valley floor, you will see various roads that lead from the central road towards amazing sights. But some side roads are posted with "Do not enter" signs. We wonder why because these side roads look beautifully inviting too! But if you were to climb to the top of one of the summits surrounding the valley, you would see that one road leads to a garbage dump and another road leads to a maintenance yard where heavy equipment is stored. From our standpoint down on the valley floor, we cannot see the complete truth about these side roads. In the same way from our limited vantage point in time and human experience, we cannot see where all our possible moral decisions might lead us. Our self-centeredness and our focus on satisfying our physical, material desires in the present moment also blind us from seeing the consequences of our decisions. Despite what the history of human existence has or has not taught us, we are just not in the position to see all we need to see to calculate all the benefits or estimate all the destructiveness of the moral decisions that we contemplate.

If moral decisions must be beneficial to everyone equally, and if, as human experience has proven, we are not capable of understanding what is beneficial in a universal sense, then understanding of universal moral good must not come from within us but from above us.

What is morally right for us flows from the character of our Creator. The Creator, not the creation, has the infinite wisdom to be able to define goodness. God is good, and, therefore, we ought to be good, living and practicing goodness that is in his image. When a young rich man came running to Jesus, asking him, "Good teacher, what must I do to inherit eternal life," he asked the man, "Why do you call me good? No one is good—except God alone" (Mark 10:18). Jesus used the word *agathos* when he asked this question. God's existence is beneficial. He is the absolutely beneficent God. He needs no one to benefit his existence. He is the source of "every good and perfect gift" (James 1:17). Created in His image, he made us to live good, beneficial lives, not to be blinded and isolated by self-centeredness. He has the right to define moral goodness. When Jesus declared, "Be merciful, just as your Father is merciful," he identified mercy as morally good, universally beneficial, because the Creator is merciful.

Jesus, the Son of the Creator, has come from the Father. He came as the Word of God to express in visible human terms the principles and practice of universal moral goodness. Jesus' question for the rich man was intended to make him think about whether he believed Jesus was good in the sense that God is good. If Jesus is the reflection of God's goodness, then we ought to let him teach us how to be morally good. From this unique vantage point, having come from the Father, Jesus can answer our questions about precisely what are the good things we ought to do. When you have some meditative time, read the gospel accounts of the life of Jesus in Matthew, Mark, Luke, and John with the purpose of identifying all the moments that Jesus taught his disciples to live beneficial lives.

An example of one of these moments is the confrontation concerning the Sabbath that Jesus had with the Pharisees, recorded in Mark 3:1-6. Originally God had given the command about abstaining from work on the Sabbath as a principle for the benefit of the Jews. It was to be a day of rest and thanksgiving for what God had done for them from the very beginning of time. The Pharisees, however, had invented many rules concerning what kind of work a Jew could or could not do on the Sabbath. They must have thought they were making the lives of their fellow Jews easier by defining exactly what constituted work, although God had never done this. With so many rules, however, the Sabbath law became a burden instead of a benefit. On this particular occasion, Jesus consciously decided to remind the Pharisees about what was really beneficial. As he was about to heal a man who had a deformed hand, Jesus asked them, "Which is lawful on the Sabbath: to do good or to do evil, to save life or to kill?" What is good (agathos)? What is beneficial? Should we keep the endless traditions of men or heal and save life? Notice that saving life involved more than saving someone from the possibility of death; saving life meant giving a person the chance to live an easier, less burdensome life, alleviating suffering. That day Jesus solved a confusing issue about moral goodness. Jesus, the expression of God's goodness, had the right to solve this question.

Consider other teachings of Jesus that challenge our understanding of what is good. Without the teaching of Jesus, would we discover that forgiveness without limits is truly beneficial? Instead, we might conclude that retaliation, not forgiveness, is most beneficial for everyone involved, because otherwise the offending person would never learn to change his or her behavior. Would we really tend to think, if it were not for Jesus' teaching, that humility is beneficial? Would we not, instead, tend to think that protecting our own interests and putting ourselves forward whenever we have the chance are the ways that everyone ought to act? Would it occur to us that unconditional love, unconditional respect, and unconditional patience could ultimately bear good fruit?

Jesus' parable of the good Samaritan likewise challenged the disciples to think about goodness in a way that would not have naturally occurred to them. Jesus did not call the Samaritan "good," but we do, recognizing the benefit his life was to a suffering stranger from another ethnic group. He bandaged the wounds of the man who had been left for dead by thieves, carefully transported him to an inn, and paid the innkeeper to help the man recover. So many who have read this parable have declared that this Samaritan was the "good" Samaritan, not because he possessed all the qualities that people admired about Samaritans, but, instead, he was good because his life was beneficial to others, even to strangers, and even without regard to compensation for the good that he did. This parable thus served to teach the disciples of Jesus something more about the meaning of moral goodness. The beneficial life is good in its purest sense when there is no thought of compensation. Love, unconditional and self-sacrificing, is the greatest, purest motivation for goodness.

Self-centeredness, the opposite of self-sacrificing love, is a particularly challenging problem in the actual practice of good that benefits others. In reality, we sometimes convince ourselves that specific decisions are for the good of others when, in fact, we make the decisions because we hope to gain benefit for ourselves. Parents spoiling a child may think they are doing what they do in order to give the child what they did not have when they were growing up. Are they simply being generous, or are they actually trying to guarantee a child's love by not withholding any reasonable thing from the child? Are they loving the child in this way to benefit themselves in order to feel loved? What would be genuinely beneficial for the child?

Imagine seeing a person stranded along the highway as we hurry to work. At this present moment while we are reading and thinking about doing good for others, it is easy to imagine that we would stop and at least see if the person along the highway is out of danger—but is that honestly what we would do if we were in a hurry? In practice, if in the moment we were to weigh benefit to ourselves against benefit to others, we might feel more pressured to arrive at work on time and not stop at all.

Remember the judgment scene that Jesus described for his disciples (Matthew 25:41-45)? Jesus taught them not to overlook the small details of living beneficial lives. What blinded the unrighteous from seeing moments to practice goodness was the apathy that self-centeredness produces. If we share this same form of blindness, how could we possibly determine what is morally beneficially, especially in cases that require self-sacrifice? Jesus had to come from the Father to reveal that self-sacrificing love is universally beneficial. Jesus is the "good teacher" because he taught and exemplified in practice what the beneficial good is that the Father created us to do.

REFLECTION

Believer and unbeliever alike know something about living a beneficial life. But Jesus calls his disciples to a higher life and an extraordinary level of goodness. Jesus told his disciples, "And if you do good to those who are good to you, what credit is that to you? Even 'sinners' do that." These words, "even sinners do that," cause us to search our hearts and evaluate the good we do. Are we really any different from other people who stop to do good without being deeply committed to good? Most people, even those who care little about living the right kind of life, at least on occasion give to others or do something that benefits others. Even those whose lives are a burden to everyone around them, because of irresponsibility or laziness, have moments when they spontaneously give to someone else. Jesus challenges us to a higher goodness that characterizes us as his disciples, a goodness that flows from within us and manifests itself in all circumstances. The disciples of Jesus practice goodness that even extends to their enemies. This level of goodness is a fruit of the Spirit because it comes from obeying Jesus' call and committing ourselves to living transformed lives according to the rule of the Spirit.

Remember Jesus' statement, "The good man brings good things out of the good stored up in his heart" (Luke 6:45). Jesus first challenges his disciples to start with their hearts. The heart represents our desires, the deepest emotions motivating compassion, gratitude, mercy, and love for others that blossom into goodness that is sincere and sacrificing. We could think of benefiting others as a responsibility, an obligation that we perform grudgingly. Such a view of goodness would be sufficient to prompt us to do good for others if for no other reason than to be free of the obligation and not feel regret for having failed a responsibility. Much good has been done that has profited many people, even though it was done insincerely or as a mere duty. The Lord wants more from us. He wants good from a good heart.

The teaching of Jesus is transformative, changing us from the inside out, starting with our hearts and then changing our behavior. Obviously, the good we do benefits those who receive it, but the good we do must also transform us. Through experiencing the freedom of shedding our fears, surrendering to generosity, being filled with the joy of giving, and thus feeling connected to our Creator, our hearts are transformed. Now, from the good stored up in our hearts, we bring good to others. What used to be obligation is now enthusiastic willingness. In an earlier chapter we referred to the Christians from the first century Macedonian congregations of Philippi, Berea, and Thessalonica. They serve as an example of this transformation. The apostle Paul had been collecting funds from congregations from Asia Minor to the Greek peninsula in order to help Christians who were suffering from a famine in Judea. When he came to the Macedonian congregations, he discovered that they were suffering from poverty themselves. Nonetheless, they eagerly helped with the needs of the Judean Christians. What might otherwise have been an obligation was now a "privilege." What could have been depressing was now cause for "overflowing joy." Other people in similar circumstances would have put up lots of excuses for not contributing to the need of the Judean Christians, but the Macedonians "urgently pleaded" with Paul to accept their gift. They had a profound desire to give that outweighed concern for their own welfare. Their hearts had been transformed, and now giving would further transform them.

Thinking more about our hearts, Jesus also calls us to practice pure goodness from pure motives. "If you do good to those who are good to you, what credit is that to you?" He taught that we ought to do good, even to our enemies, "without expecting to get anything back." What do we expect when we practice goodness? The Pharisees, religious leaders in the time of Jesus, expected recognition from people. "So when you give to the needy, do not announce it with trumpets, as the hypocrites do in the synagogues and on the streets, to be honored by men. I tell you the truth, they have received their reward in full."

(Matthew 6:2). Jesus taught that even self-recognition is not necessary because our Father, the Creator, understands what we are doing. He said, "But when you give to the needy, do not let your left hand know what your right hand is doing, so that your giving may be in secret. Then your Father, who sees what is done in secret, will reward you" (Matthew 6:3-4). We do not need to convince ourselves of our own goodness by telling ourselves, "You know what? You are a very good and giving person, even better than most people, because you are so generous." We believe the Lord knows what we do, and he is the perfect judge of our actions and the motives of our hearts. Trusting in the Lord, we can go quietly about doing good for others without making a big splash or needing to relish in our own goodness.

What is clear to our Father, though, is not always clear to us. We can easily convince ourselves that our motives are pure when, in reality, we would not be doing the good we do if we were not receiving something in return. At least, we would not be doing good with very much enthusiasm. For example, when doing chores at home or tasks at work that will benefit others who do not share the load, we might feel like telling them, "If you don't help bake the bread, you can't help eat it!" Of course, we want people to learn to be responsible, and if we do their work for them, they will not learn responsibility. At the same time, we want to be generous and beneficial to others. As disciples of Jesus, when we are in doubt about what to do, we ought to do good without reservation or resentment and ask the Lord for wisdom to know how to encourage people to be responsible.

It is also easy to convince ourselves that when we are correcting others, we are benefiting those whom we correct. Of course, people need correction, but we may be benefiting ourselves by creating situations in which we enjoy feeling superior to the people we are correcting. How can we know our motives? Paul wrote that our words ought to be "helpful for building others up according to their needs, that it may benefit those who listen" (Ephesians 4:29). If our gentle, encouraging correction builds people up, instead of building ourselves up and making ourselves feel superior, we know we have served a beneficial purpose with the right motives.

The purest motive for the good we do is to honor our heavenly Father. Jesus taught, "Let your light shine before men, that they may see your good deeds and praise your Father in heaven" (Matthew 5:16). Instead of seeking self-recognition, we want people to see how powerful and good our heavenly Father is. He has forgiven us of evil. He has transformed us. He empowers us to do good. When others see the beauty of a life submitted to the Father and come to live for him too, we have accomplished the purpose for which we have been called.

Jesus also challenges us to do good that overflows, that which benefits people more than they expect or require. In the Sermon on the Mount, Jesus told his disciples, "If someone forces you to go one mile, go with him two miles" (Matthew 5:41). According to Roman law during the time of Christ, a Roman soldier could compel someone to take him a mile in the performance of his military duties. When Jesus said to take him two miles, he was establishing a principle concerning doing good. To take the soldier one mile was an obligation. Everyone, disciple of Jesus or not, like it or not, would have to take the soldier one mile. When we do our duties, even when we do them with enthusiasm, we have not shown any goodness that would surpass the goodness of anyone else who does only his or her duty. But Jesus calls us to a higher goodness, going beyond what is required as duty. By taking people the second mile, we have the chance to reveal the motives of our hearts. The second mile is voluntary, not obligatory. Going farther than required in any act of goodness shows that we do what we do from the sincere desires of our hearts and not because we are obligated. We confirm that goodness comes from our hearts. People need to see our hearts so that they will understand the depth of the beauty of the Christian life.

On another occasion Jesus taught the same principle in a different setting, "Give, and it will be given to you. A good measure, pressed down, shaken together and running over, will be poured into your lap. For with the measure you use, it will be measured to you" (Luke 6:38). When we give, we must not measure out exactly the amount requested, required, or deserved. Instead, give more. If someone asks for a cup of flour, shake the flour down into the cup, eliminating air pockets, and then fill it to overflowing.

What can more can we do? For example, if someone asks for help with a task for a certain length of time, instead of watching the clock, gladly spend more time helping than has been requested. After finishing with responsibilities at work early with time to spare, volunteer to help others finish their work so everyone can go home at the same time. If someone asks for a loan of money in a certain amount, if possible, offer to lend more. With such gestures we reveal the sincerity and joy of genuine generosity.

Of course, the question arises about how to react when people seem to take advantage of our goodness. People whom we are helping are not very fast workers, and the person to whom we loaned money continues to ask for more. First, the choice to go the second mile is the choice to lay aside questions of fairness and what is due; after all, the Lord has been overflowing with grace toward us, beyond what we deserve or what justice requires. At the same time, goodness also consists of helping people to become responsible for their individual burdens. We pray for wisdom. We let goodness rule the decisions of our heart. Then we ask how we can humbly help those who take advantage to grow to become generous with good themselves.

Finally, Jesus also calls us to practice a higher spiritual good. There are people all around us who have physical needs and whose lives we can benefit by being generous and serving. Before we can teach them the good news of Jesus, we may need to feed them or help them overcome physical difficulties so that they will be able to listen. Teachers in school classrooms know that children who come to school hungry do not have the energy to think clearly or to focus well. Physical problems can be very distracting to people and keep them from hearing the gospel. Nevertheless, after compassionately providing the solutions that are within reach, we have not done the greatest good for someone until we have brought them to know the Creator.

One evening, Jesus miraculously fed five thousand people by the shore of the Sea of Galilee. The next morning the people whom he had fed found him on the opposite shore of the lake. As they came to him, he told them, "I tell you the truth, you are looking for me, not because you saw miraculous signs but because you ate the loaves and had your fill. Do not work for food that spoils, but for food that endures to eternal life, which the Son of Man will give you" (John 6:26-27). Jesus had performed a miracle of creation, creating food for this great crowd, proving that he was the Son of the Creator. Instead of looking for him because they were ready to be his disciples (accepting the message the miracle implied, that Jesus was the Son God), they had gone looking for him because they were physically hungry. Jesus had not come just to fill their stomachs; he had come to give them life with the Father. He told them, "I am the living bread that came down from heaven. If anyone eats of this bread, he will live forever" (John 6:51).

He offers us spiritual food that stays with us, food for our spirits. He is the Bread of Life because he provides exactly what our spirits need: to be born again as children of God, receive forgiveness, inner peace and contentment, live in the presence of the Father, possess the power to overcome temptation, and experience spiritually transformed lives. To live a beneficial life means to bring people the chance to benefit eternally from a living relationship with the heavenly Father, the Creator of the universe. Jesus promised, "He who comes to me will never go hungry, and he who believes in me will never be thirsty" (John 6:35).

Jesus invites us not to make ourselves look more righteous than others because of the amount of good we do but, instead, to humbly show the beauty of goodness in the image of our heavenly Father. He calls us to a higher goodness so that we can show what is possible for human beings as we grow into the image of our Father. The greatest benefit is to know what is possible with the Father and to experience the joy and contentment of doing what is possible.

PRACTICE

Among the disciples in the first-century church, there were some who were known for the humble way they lived beneficial lives, doing the good that was possible. Luke, in his account of the early church in the book of Acts, mentions two individuals who were for him models of the good life. One was Dorcas from the city of Joppa who was "always doing good and helping the poor" (Acts 9:6). When she became sick and died, the disciples in Joppa urgently sent for the apostle Peter, who was nearby in Lydda. When he arrived, the poor, weeping with gratitude and feeling the loss of this generous woman, showed Peter all the clothing Dorcas had made for them. She had a talent, and she used it to benefit others. This is the good life.

In a similar way Luke describes the character of Barnabas from Cyprus. In an earlier chapter, Barnabas served us as an example of patience, but Luke also calls him "a good man" (Acts 11:24). His real name was Joseph, but the apostles had changed his name to Barnabas, because the name meant "son of encouragement" (Acts 4:36). He apparently never missed an opportunity to do something beneficial, whether it was great or small. When the Christians in Judea were suffering in need, Barnabas, as well as some of the other disciples, sold property he owned and gave the funds to be distributed among the poorer Christians. Furthermore, when Paul became a follower of Jesus after having violently persecuted Christians, the disciples in Jerusalem did not believe he had really changed; so Barnabas defended him, explaining to the members of the church that Paul was already bravely preaching about Jesus in places where he had previously arrested Christians. Only then did the disciples trust Paul's conversion. Some time later Barnabas accompanied Paul on his first missionary journey. Everywhere he went he encouraged Christians to be strong in the Lord. He was living a beneficial life.

We want to know what can I do. How can I benefit others? But we must answer these questions in personal ways that empower us to practice the higher good, beyond what people commonly do. Our very purpose is to live beneficial lives. By his grace the Lord has "created us in Christ Jesus to do good works" (Ephesians 2:10). By being born again spiritually, we begin our lives in Christ with this new purpose. The Lord creates new life in us, giving us hearts to do good and opening doors for us to practice good works. Now our task is to be imaginative and creative in order to understand what we can do, imaginative to see what people really need and creative to discover ways to benefit those needs.

Imagination is the ability to form images in our minds, especially of things we have never directly experienced. Practicing goodness requires imagining how our lives can benefit the lives of others. Often we begin by imagining how we would like to be useful without first understanding what people actually need. Approaching the problem from this standpoint is backward. We cannot conform the needs people actually have to our ideas of what we want to do to be useful. If we do not begin with understanding the real needs people have, we risk the possibility that all of our efforts will, in the end, not be beneficial.

Many years ago a very kind, older couple had some funds they wanted to invest in the work of spreading the gospel to people who speak Spanish. The woman, who had some acquaintance with the Spanish language, and her husband decided they would compile and publish a bilingual dictionary of all the words in the gospel of Matthew. They believed the dictionary would help people who speak Spanish and English talk together about the gospel. They printed hundreds of copies without first seeing if there was a need for such a tool. Unfortunately, from the standpoint of both Spanish and English speakers, the dictionary was not useful because communicating in a language involves more than just knowing the definition of words. The couple's intent was noble, but the real benefit was minimal because they provided a tool which was not useful according to the needs people actually had.

We cannot imagine until we carefully watch and listen to the people around us. Listening with patience, asking questions, then listening with more patience avoids the problem of jumping to conclusions and offering a quick solution to a need that may be more profound than we realize. "If I were you" are words that come too quickly at times. The objective should not be to imagine ourselves in their shoes but to imagine them in their own shoes, facing their experiences with the history and understanding that they have. We can never stand in their shoes because the experiences of life are too complex and the thoughts of another heart are too private. The best we can do is listen, constantly listen to the expressions of their hearts.

Acceptance without forming our own judgments is also essential to imagining. Remember the occasion when Jesus was the guest for dinner in Simon the Pharisee's house? While they were eating, a woman entered weeping. She began to wash Jesus' feet with her tears and then anointed them with perfume. She apparently was known as a sinful person in the town where Simon lived. Simon could not imagine why the woman had come to his house or why Jesus, if he was a righteous person, would allow the woman to touch him. Simon had no idea that the woman had come to meet Jesus to find forgiveness and new life. As soon as she entered, he began to form images in his mind that were not accurate, judgments that only hindered him from being a benefit. Instead of being a benefit, self-righteous Simon was a distraction to Jesus' purpose of seeking and saving the lost. How different the scene would have been if Simon had simply accepted the woman's presence, accepted the obvious sincerity and humility she had, and listened first in order to be able to imagine the needs she had. His house could have become a refuge for sinners who wanted new life.

Imagine living a beneficial life! Imagine a family who does not have enough food on the table. Imagine an older person who needs his house cleaned or some repairs done. Imagine some children in the neighborhood or from the church who need an older brother or sister to admire as a role model. Imagine a friend or family member who has been feeling down and needs some hope and encouragement. Imagine someone who is trying hard to overcome a destructive habit. Imagine a person who feels isolated and rejected. Imagine a young mother who is struggling with her responsibilities. Imagine what people might need, but first talk with them, spend time with them, understand their lives from their perspectives, and then imagine how to help.

Imagination is one side of practicing the beneficial life; creativity is the other side. Creativity is the ability to develop something new, original, or just different from the ordinary. "I really don't have much to offer." These words could be an escape from the beneficial life. The challenge of practicing a higher goodness is to become creative, especially when we do not think we have much to offer.

There is goodness in sharing what we enjoy. Peter wrote, "Each one should use whatever gift he has received to serve others, faithfully administering God's grace in its various forms" (1 Peter 4:10). The abilities we have are the results of God's gracious love and are not due to some special worthiness we have. The person with a variety of appreciated and respected gifts possesses these gifts by God's grace and not because he or she deserves them. The truth is that no one is any more worthy than anyone else because we all depend on the value he gives us as his servants. He redeemed us from a meaningless existence and gave our lives direction and eternal purpose through living beneficial lives. Instead of complaining about what we do not have or feeling superior because of what we do have, the gratitude we feel toward the Lord inspires us simply to be faithful in using the abilities or opportunities God has given us. Being faithful means doing what we are supposed to do and doing it well. Peter explains that, in regard to our gifts from God, the Lord wants us to use them faithfully to benefit others.

What are the gifts we have? We have the tendency to answer this question by looking at what people around us are doing. We observe what others are doing to serve and decide that if we cannot do the same, then we do not have much to offer. It is a mistake to define (for ourselves) the limits of what counts as a gift by only considering what those who are apparently "gifted" are doing. In this way we limit our vision and blind ourselves to the valuable gifts we actually have. Perhaps a better question to ask is, what do I enjoy doing, and how can I use this enjoyment as a gift for benefiting others? We can imagine the needs of others and then creatively think of how we can use what we enjoy doing for the purpose of serving others.

There was a brother in Christ who had retired after working many years digging graves and doing maintenance work in a cemetery. He had always been very quiet and shy around people. Even when he joked with people, he did so in a gentle voice. Quietly he used to say, "I enjoy my work because I have a lot of people under me." "I feel like I work in an important place because people are just dying to get in." He did not have much in terms of possessions or resources to benefit people except the lovely vegetable garden he cultivated around his humble home. He generously brought the beautiful fruits of his labor to share with his brothers and sisters from the church. Freely and joyfully sharing the labors of our hands is a tremendous gesture of love. But to think creatively about the gifts we have means to think beyond how we would normally use our gifts. In the case of this brother, he could think beyond even sharing his harvest with his friends. He could teach the young children in the congregation how to grow their own gardens. Spending time with the children, teaching them a love for growing vegetables, would leave a lasting impression on them. His gentleness, patience, and smile would form part of their childhood memories. Later in their lives, when they spent time in their own gardens, the lessons they learned about perseverance, responsibility, and tender care would continue to benefit their lives and the lives of those around them. Creative thinking about our gifts means thinking of all the ways we can benefit others with what we enjoy doing. This is the goodness of sharing what we enjoy.

There is goodness in refreshment. Jesus promised that, "If anyone gives even a cup of cold water to one of these little ones because he is my disciple, I tell you the truth, he will certainly not lose his reward" (Matthew 10:42). A cup of cold water is a powerful metaphor for any act of goodness that refreshes others. A cup of water for someone who is thirsty is a small gesture nearly anyone can afford. A cup of cold water is an offering that is certain to quench one's thirst on a hot day and give refreshment and satisfaction in a tired moment. One sister in Christ who had an infectious joy from living the Christian life took this instruction quite literally. On hot summer days in Los Angeles, she used to have a glass of ice water ready for the mailman. That cool drink always gave him a moment of relief in his daily rounds delivering the mail. Imagine, though, the creative practice of this principle represents any moment when we have the chance to give a weary soul some refreshment.

Creatively think of just a few ways to apply this teaching. We help someone carry groceries or lift a heavy load. We smile and say

"Thank you, for your hard work" to a fatigued worker. We enthusiastically greet someone to begin the day well. We share food with someone who is homeless, help to clean up a mess, or let some frustrated, anxious person go ahead of us in line at the store. We listen patiently to someone who wants to complain, giving her relief from her irritation, or we spend time with a shut-in who is tired of being alone. We offer to watch the children of a mother who needs some rest, pay attention to someone who has faced lots of rejection, or simply show extra courtesies by opening doors or yielding to other drivers on the street. We treat someone as an equal who has spent himself serving or take on a responsibility that really belongs to someone else who is overworked. Anything that gives relief to someone who is tired is a form of refreshment.

Everyone, believer or not, understands the beauty of providing relief for someone who is tired, but for a disciple, offering a cup of cold water is a mentality, a way of viewing the world around us. As disciples of the Master who came to serve, our way of life is asking, what can I do to give refreshment? We cultivate the habit of creatively thinking about how to provide relief.

There is goodness in giving hope. Disciples of Christ ought to be optimists who are able to inspire people with hope. We, of all people, have every reason to be hopeful because we trust in God's power and love. We have seen his power in our own lives and in the lives of others who discovered new life in Christ. When people come to Christ looking for help to live new lives, they need to know that it is possible for them to leave destructive habits behind once and for all, rebuild failed relationships, and feel real joy again. Paul's prayer for Christians was that they would "overflow with hope." He wrote, "May the God of hope fill you with all joy and peace as you trust in him, so that you may overflow with hope by the power of the Holy Spirit" (Romans 15:13). Words of hope, expressed with genuine conviction, are necessary. "You can do it with the Lord!" "The Lord will work in you and give you the strength!" "All things are possible with him!" Negativity benefits no one. If we are firmly grounded in the faith and practice of the Christ-life, we will communicate genuine hope that inspires confidence.

There was a man in prison who had spent most of his teenage and young adult years incarcerated for drug use. Each time he was released, he would quickly turn back to drugs. He sincerely believed in God and wanted to live a clean life. But his dad had died in prison, and his two brothers were also in and out of prison until one of them was killed. This young man had repeatedly heard people around him say, "You will never succeed! You will always mess up!" Each time he left prison, he did exactly what people programmed him to do. All he needed was someone to convince him that he could be successful and that the Lord would always stand by him. He needed to know that hope is real.

Sharing another person's joys and sorrows also gives hope. Paul wrote, "Rejoice with those who rejoice; mourn with those who mourn" (Romans 12:15). A sympathetic heart, just like an optimistic heart, has the power to benefit the life of another person, giving support and letting her know she is not alone in her grief or her joy. "I feel very sorry for what you are going through, and if you need someone to listen to the grief you are feeling. I would be glad to just listen." "I am so thankful for your success and proud of what you have accomplished. You have worked so hard and have exhibited so much patience to finish." Every disciple of Jesus can have an optimistic and sympathetic heart because it is the heart Jesus gives us. He sympathizes with us and fills us with hope. Our role as his disciples is to pay attention to people and what they are experiencing. We do great acts of goodness when we lift others up and give them hope.

There is goodness in generosity. One of the first examples of goodness that people generally think of is generosity with our material resources. As we creatively think about ways to live beneficial lives, generosity in helping people materially is just one of many forms of goodness, yet at the same time is a necessary way to practice goodness. People need help to live. Disciples have a special responsibility to other disciples because they belong to the same family, but they also need to look for opportunities to be generous to others whom they encounter in difficult circumstances. The apostle Paul wrote to the Galatian Christians, "Therefore, as we have opportunity, let us do good to all people, especially to those who belong to the family of believers" (Galatians 6:10).

The Lord values our goodness not based on the amount of benefit we can offer people but on the effort and sacrifice our goodness represents. Once, while Jesus observed people putting their money into the temple treasury, the rich were throwing in large amounts of money. Then a widow approached the treasury box and put in two copper coins worth very little but that represented all the monetary resources she had. Jesus told his disciples, "I tell you the truth, this poor widow has put more into the treasury than all the others. They all gave out of their wealth; but she, out of her poverty, put in everything–all she had to live on" (Mark 12:41-44). On the surface the rich appeared to have more abilities than the poor widow to benefit people in need. The widow was in need herself. But goodness consists of more than the actual amount we give; it depends on how much sacrificial love motivates the good we do. When we sacrifice to help someone, we invest ourselves in that person. We lay aside our fears of not having enough for ourselves and suffer the cost to help. When we invest ourselves in people for their benefit, they feel as though we are part of them. We have shared hearts. They receive the hope and strength that comes from a love that is unselfish and sincere.

In truth, we may have more resources than we realize. In her poverty the widow probably understood how little she really needed in life. On the other hand, if we have lots of material conveniences and advantages, we probably believe we need a lot of things to live, everything from multiple cars to multiple cell phones. To be more creative in the goodness we believe we can practice, we will have to view our lives with more simplicity, eliminating what we, in fact, do not need. Then we will be equipped to be more generous. Living simpler lives empowers us to practice goodness. Whatever sacrifices we make in terms of material possessions or the time we spend to chase after more possessions will transform our hearts. If we have benefited from God's blessing, his love compels us to let others benefit from what we have received.

There is goodness in helping people recover. One of the lessons of the parable of the good Samaritan is learning the benefit of helping people recover. When the Samaritan found the man who had been robbed, beaten, and left for dead along the roadside, he could have simply cared for the man's immediate needs, such as bandaging his wounds, giving him some water, and leaving him under the shade of a nearby tree. Instead, he "put the man on his own donkey, took him to an inn and took care of him. The next day he took out two silver coins and gave them to the innkeeper. 'Look after him,' he said, 'and when I return, I will reimburse you for any extra expense you may have.'" Motivated by love, the Samaritan made himself responsible for the full recovery of this stranger. Jesus told the lawyer, whose question had prompted the parable, "Go and do likewise."

We may not find many people laying by the roadside in this same condition, but we have met many people who need to recover in some way. There are those who need to recover from the loss of a loved one, recover from drug or alcohol abuse, recover from the emotional pain of a betrayal, recover from a physical injury or health problem, recover from a costly mistake or failure, or recover from a serious disappointment. Recovery is a process that involves a series of obstacles to overcome and positive steps to take. People need a listening ear, support, encouragement, someone to show them patience and confidence, and help with resources in order to persevere and pass through the process of becoming well. If we are not in a position to help, then we can enlist the help of others, all the while being responsible ourselves to see that people receive the necessary support, just as the Samaritan did when he asked the innkeeper for assistance. Being creative means finding out what we can do and where we can find the necessary help to walk people through their recovery.

There is goodness in encouraging communication. Beneficial communication is another skill that every disciple can and ought to develop in the practice of goodness. "Do not let any unwholesome talk come out of your mouths, but only what is helpful for building others up according to their needs, that it may benefit those who listen" (Ephesians 4:29). There is no need here for material resources or knowledge of recovery methods. Every disciple can learn how to communicate in a way that benefits "those who listen." "Unwholesome talk" is language that is unhealthy for the soul and destroys confidence and self-esteem. It destructively criticizes and disrespects. It humiliates. Beneficial communication "builds others up." Beneficial language praises, expresses gratitude, patiently explains, communicates confidence, speaks the truth in love, and chooses words that make peace and show acceptance. It is the expression of a humble heart.

Just like a disciple develops a mentality of optimism and hope, the followers of Jesus also cultivate a mind that values and respects people, supporting beneficial communication. We cannot love our neighbors as we love ourselves and, at the same time, slander or destructively criticize our neighbors. Each person we speak with throughout the day is a living soul, created and valued by God, and in need of knowing the Savior. As children of God, we communicate the love, mercy, and compassion of God through the way we speak with people. Those who are lost can come to know the Lord and what he is like through the way we communicate. Imagine the need people have to know the Lord and create moments to communicate the acceptance and patience of the Lord!

There is goodness in showing the way. The highest form of good we can do for others is to bring them to Jesus, because the Lord is the source of hope and the way of recovery. He is the only one who can give us new beginnings, new lives, and new purposes. Everything we do to make it easy for others to come to Christ is an act of spiritual goodness. Showing them the beauty of the Christian life through our own transformed lives helps them understand that the Christ-life is possible.

The gospel writer Mark tells about a man who was living an incredibly destructive life, torturing himself because of the demons that were controlling his behavior. Day and night he spent living among the tombs of dead people. When Jesus healed the man and gave him new life, he wanted to leave with Jesus instead of remaining in the town where people had previously feared him. But Jesus told him, "Go home to your family and tell them how much the Lord has done for you, and how he has had mercy on you" (Mark 5:19). Staying close to his Savior would be a comfortable and secure choice, but his life would not be a spiritual benefit to others if he chose not to tell his message to the very people who needed to hear it. "So the man went away and began to tell in the Decapolis how much Jesus had done for him. And all the people were amazed" (Mark 5:20). When Jesus later returned to that place, the people received him with great joy because of the man's powerful testimony. The Lord wants to use us as his instruments. His message can completely transform lives. We have seen people become absolutely new creations in Christ, and we have experienced his power in our own lives. This is the good he asks us to do. We have a story. There are lessons we have learned. Most of all, our love for the Savior fills us with passion to declare his message.

The challenge of goodness is to understand the needs of others from their perspectives and to imagine creative ways to serve those needs. The Christian life is the beneficial life. It begins with a heart that understands and an enthusiastic spirit to imagine and create.

CHAPTER SEVEN

INCREASE OUR FAITH!

"IF YOUR BROTHER SINS AGAINST YOU SEVEN TIMES
AND SEVEN TIMES SAYS, 'I REPENT,' FORGIVE HIM"
(LUKE 17:3-5).

Paul lists faith as a fruit of the Spirit, meaning that it is the result of walking in harmony with God's Spirit; but faith seems to be such a common experience that everyone, whether living a spiritual life or not, requires it simply to survive. We believe, for instance, in the reality of historical events that happened centuries ago without having witnessed those events firsthand. We believe in certain principles and ideals and follow them in our daily lives, even though we do not see the immediate results we might hope to enjoy. We believe and trust in the mechanical worthiness of an airplane and the expertise of the pilot enough to board the plane and travel to some distant place. We believe in a teacher's knowledge of mathematics, and so we dedicate ourselves to learning the material and studying for exams. We believe that our bank records are guarded on a secure computer, so we do not obsess about someone stealing our identities. We believe that if we work forty hours this week, our bosses will pay us for those hours. We believe and trust that family and friends will support us, especially in times of desperation. We believe enough in the possibility of a sunrise tomorrow that we confidently lay our heads down at night with no doubts that we will begin a new day in the morning. Everyone has faith.

We usually distinguish faith from fact by defining faith as believing in things that we cannot see, touch, or sense in any direct way and by defining fact as those truths and realities that we can directly experience ourselves or that have been proven to be reality in an experimental way. For example, we know that hot air rises; nature abhors a vacuum; smoking harms your health; if we do not pay our monthly mortgages, the bank will repossess our houses; colds are caused by viruses; and it is possible for human beings to walk on the moon. We consider these examples to be facts because we can verify them by our own experiences or by the credible experiences of others.

But sometimes faith and fact become difficult to distinguish. Is it fact or faith that convinces us to take the medications that our doctors prescribe for us? Is it fact or faith that persuades us to continue to make deposits in our retirement accounts? Is it fact or faith on which scientists base their theories of the origins of the universe? In truth we have to believe that the doctor has sufficient knowledge of medicine, that the investment counselors for financial institutions understand the ups and downs of the economy, and that scientists have not made huge assumptions without sufficient data to support their conclusions. Even the reality of events that we experience with our five senses depends on how much we trust our own senses. People who are color-blind may not discover for years that they are color-blind and assume that reality is just as they perceive it to be. Emotions also distort perceptions. We know that if we try to listen to others when we are in high states of emotional anxiety, what we hear is probably not what people said to us. To carry on a conversation with people, we need to believe we understand what they are saying. When faith and fact run together, we discover that most phenomena that we consider to be facts in our daily lives actually require some degree of faith. Faith is a fundamental part of our thinking about reality.

If faith is such a common part of our experiences, then why does Paul include faith among the fruit of the Spirit? Since everyone makes decisions and acts from faith, whether or not they are living spiritual lives, in what way is faith a result of living in harmony with God's Spirit? The answer to this question first of all requires a more precise understanding of faith, and, specifically, the faith that a spiritual life in Christ produces.

UNDERSTANDING

Christian faith is similar in certain ways to the common faith every human being needs just to live. In the first place faith is a belief that something is true with some degree of certainty but without a 100 percent guarantee that it is true. Most things that we believe as reality we accept as true even though we are not guaranteed this level of assurance that they are true. Our knowledge of reality and our ability to perceive reality are extremely limited as human beings. Some things we believe as true have an extremely high probability of being true, other beliefs are very probably true, while other things are less probably true. There is a 100 percent guarantee that one plus one equals two, but we can say only that it is highly probable the sun will rise tomorrow and less probably true that we will have the same job at the end of this year that we have now.

Secondly, every instance of faith, whether common or religious, that is worth the risk of believing will be based on sufficient evidence. There must be good reasons why we believe, good reasons why we accept something as highly probable. Blind faith, without reason or evidence, is like jumping out of a plane without a parachute and hoping for a soft landing. It is pure foolishness, not faith. Faith without evidence is not faith. There is no probability for a soft landing unless the plane has not taken off yet.

Next, when there are sufficient reasons for faith, faith may turn into trust. Trust means that we have enough faith to be willing to act confidently, based on what we believe. The risk always exists that what we think is probably true, in reality, is not true. Jumping out of a plane with a parachute does not guarantee 100 percent that the landing will be soft, but with a good parachute and some training, a soft landing is highly probable and the risk is minimal. Nonetheless, there is still a risk that something might go wrong. In order to jump, we have to accept and surrender to the risk. But each time we act despite the risk, faith turns into trust.

Finally, faith leads to faithfulness. When we consistently behave in a trusting manner, we become faithful in our actions. Being faithful means to act in a predictable way, in agreement with what we believe. We faithfully make plans every evening for what we will do on the morrow because of the trust we have that the sun will rise again and we will have sufficient health and energy. The word that Paul used in Galatians 5:22 as one of the fruits of the Spirit that is translated as *faith* can also be translated, and is so translated in some versions, as *faithfulness*. Having faith and being faithful ought to go hand in hand.

A developed faith will always involve these components: a belief in something probable, reasons for that belief, taking a risk, trusting enough to act, and becoming faithful in our behavior with respect to what we believe. Take, for instance, investing money in a retirement account. We may conclude that it is reasonably probable that we will earn money on our investments over a period of time, although it is not guaranteed. We choose a particular financial institution to manage our investments because of evidence showing that the investment fund has earned well in the past. Because of positive evidence from previous performance, we trust enough to take the step of investing our hard-earned money. There is always a risk involved, understanding that the economy could experience depressed times, but we accept the risk because the probability is sufficiently high that over time the investments will be successful. Because of our continued trust, we faithfully invest money in the fund.

Imagine what we mean by saying we have faith in a friend. To have faith in a friend is to believe our friend to be responsible, fair, honest, and dependable. We believe that our friend will always support us and never betray us. We have learned from experience that we have good reasons to believe in the character of our friend because we have observed him consistently manifest those qualities that we respect in a friend. Faith grows with experience and turns into trust when we behave toward our friend in ways that show we truly believe he possesses responsibility, honesty, and fairness. We ask for his counsel. We seek his help. We open ourselves up and reveal our worries and doubts to him. There is always a risk, however, that circumstances could change, and he might reveal to another person what we said in confidence. We accept the risk because of the good reasons we have to trust. After learning through our experiences that we can trust him, we feel safe to become faithful in this relationship by behaving in a predictable, consistent way toward him.

At this level common faith is similar to faith in God. God's existence is a highly probable truth because of the massive amount of evidence supporting the existence of a Creator with intelligence, will, power, and purpose. Our own existence as rational beings with consciousness and free will is evidence of God's intellect and creative power. Paul once wrote, "God's invisible qualities—his eternal power and divine nature—have been clearly understood from what has been made" (Romans 1:20). Some people have even argued that the existence of God is the same kind of truth as the truth that one plus one equals two. We can safely say, however, that God's existence is at least a very highly probable truth. Because of overwhelming evidence of his existence and loving character, we trust enough to commit ourselves to living lives that bring us closer to him, in harmony with his character. There is always the risk that we are mistaken, but the probability for God's existence makes this risk extremely inconsequential. As we trust and consistently practice the life he teaches us to live, we become faithful in our relationships with him.

Faith in God shares these basic elements with a common faith: belief in a probability, evidence for belief, trust, risk, and faithfulness. But faith in God goes beyond these basic elements, distinguishing itself not by the amount of faith required, but by the way faith increases. Spiritual faith grows through the practice of faith in a very distinct way from the common faith we have. Faith in God results in living a spiritual life, but living a spiritual life, in turn, produces a greater and deeper faith.

Faith that trusts in the Lord will, in fact, transform us. James once wrote, "What good is it, my brothers, if a man claims to have faith but has no deeds? Can faith save him? Suppose a brother or sister is without clothes and daily food. If one of you says to him, 'Go, I wish you well; keep warm and well fed,' but does nothing about his physical needs, what good is it? In the same way, faith by itself, if it is not accompanied by action, is dead" (James 2:14-17). If our faith does not make us personally generous toward people in need, then our faith is of no value. If faith does not change how we live, then it is useless and dead. Christian faith is not just about what Christians believe but is also, and most importantly, about how to live.

The qualities that we seek to cultivate in our lives with the Lord's help such as unconditional love, mercy, and forgiveness require faith in God's way. The writer Luke records an important request the apostles made to the Lord: "Increase our faith!" (Luke 17:5). In the context of that passage, Jesus had just taught his disciples about the unlimited nature of forgiveness; they ought to be ready to forgive over and over again when a brother repeatedly sins against them and asks for forgiveness with a penitent heart. Upon hearing of the unlimited nature of forgiveness, the apostles asked the Lord to help them have a more powerful faith. To forgive at this level requires a strong faith that trusts in the Lord to teach us the right way to live, despite the risk. Forgiveness can make us feel vulnerable and involves a risk that people whom we forgive may continue to take advantage of us and pay no attention to how they treat us. We are afraid that forgiveness, especially repeated forgiveness, will just encourage the person to feel free to continue to offend us. To have the power to forgive, we have to believe that the Lord's way is the best way, and that he is wise, just, and merciful enough to deal with those who might try to take advantage. Faith in the Lord and trust in his way frees us to live lives focused on growing spiritually in the imitation of his character, without being anxious or doubtful about possible consequences.

As another example of the role of faith in changing the life of the believer, consider again the most fundamental moral principle that Jesus taught, "Do to others as you would have them do to you." Instead of treating people the way they treat us, which would result in paying back evil for evil, Jesus taught just the opposite. Treat others the way you want them to treat you. This principle means that our behavior and character as Christians are unconditional. Unfortunately, after we treat people the way we want them to treat us, sometimes they do not change their behavior and treat us in the way we want. But whether we are compassionate, generous, or forgiving does not depend on what other people do or do not do in response to our good. Even after treating people with mercy, if they refuse to treat us with mercy, we continue to be merciful because we still want to be treated with mercy. If, ultimately, unmerciful individuals do not change in response to our mercy toward them, we cannot stop being merciful. Mercy is unconditional. Essentially, we behave toward others in the ways we do because of who we are as disciples of Jesus and not based on the behavior of others. Jesus was merciful, and, therefore, we want to learn to be merciful as his followers. To continue to practice mercy under negative circumstances, we will first have to believe that the Lord's way is the right way and then trust enough to practice his way despite the lack of any change in the behavior of other people. Our faith in Jesus empowers us to want to be like him. Faith has the power to transform us.

Furthermore, unlike the common faith we have in every day activities, not only does spiritual faith produce a spiritual life in the imitation of Jesus, but spiritual living, in turn, produces more faith in two ways. First of all, we discover by the practice of Jesus' teaching that the Christian life is the best way to live. The Lord is the Creator and he knows what the best life is for us to live. We are at peace, without resentment or bitterness, when we learn to forgive. Relationships heal when we take the initiative to forgive as the Lord has forgiven us.

Showing mercy and letting God dispense just consequences frees us from being preoccupied with retaliating against people who offend us. Generosity frees us from the ugliness of self-centeredness and greed. Unconditional love gives us hearts like the Lord's own heart. The joy we experience in the Christian life confirms and strengthens our faith in Jesus and his teachings. The good results of faith provide more evidence that the Christian life is worth living, so our faith increases.

Secondly, there will be many moments when people do not respond to our positive behavior, when forgiveness makes us very vulnerable, when somebody does take advantage of our mercy, when people whom we love do continue to betray us. In such moments we must choose to continue to live by faith in Jesus and his teachings. We take a step of faith or, better to say, a leap of faith, without knowing what the consequences might be. When the consequences turn out to be negative, and we determine to trust and continue to live the Christian life, our faith likewise grows. Facing the challenge of living the Christ-life despite negative consequences can make us more determined to trust in Christ. Spiritual living on this deeper level creates more faith. In this way faith is a fruit of living in harmony with God's Spirit. Paul was right, of course.

REFLECTION

Besides having the faith to repeatedly forgive someone, in what ways did the disciples want to have a more powerful faith? In other experiences they had with Jesus, they understood their lack of faith when they could not heal a young boy (Matthew 17:14-20) and when they were astonished that Jesus could curse a fig tree and make it dry up

(Mark 11:20-23). All of these moments share the idea that a powerful faith is a faith that is active, achieving a difficult or improbable result. A powerful faith is not a faith that believes things that are difficult to believe but instead does things that are difficult to do.

What do we want to do? What do we want to do with a greater faith? In the passage from Luke, Jesus told the apostles that if they had even a small amount of faith, as small as a mustard seed, they could "say to this mulberry tree, 'Be uprooted and planted in the sea,' and it will obey you." In another passage he told them they would be able to "say to this mountain, 'Move from here to there' and it would move. Nothing will be impossible for you." But the apostles never seemed to be interested in planting mulberry trees in the sea or moving mountains from one place to another. The New Testament never speaks of them trying to do so. To them, forgiving someone so many times seemed to be a mountain that would be difficult enough to move. To some of the disciples being humble must have seemed as improbable as planting a tree in the middle of the sea. Loving their enemies would be like saying to a mountain, "Go, throw yourself into the sea," and then watching it rise up and crash into the ocean.

Why do we want to have a powerful faith? Do we really want literally, miraculously to move mountains? Some people who would like to impress their friends might excitedly answer yes! But following in the steps of Jesus teaches us that the greatest mountains in our lives are the struggles to imitate the character of Jesus and become like our heavenly Father. When Jesus said, "Be merciful, just as your Father is merciful" (Luke 6:36), he presented us with a very tall but not impossible mountain to climb. We want a faith that is strong enough, persistent enough, and energetic enough to empower us to draw very close to our heavenly Father by letting him transform us into his character. Peter explains that we begin with faith and then "make every effort to add to your faith goodness; and to goodness, knowledge; and to knowledge, self-control; and to self-control, perseverance; and to perseverance, godliness; and to godliness, brotherly kindness; and to brotherly kindness, love" (2 Peter 1:5-7). If we begin with faith, then faith will transform us into the image of the Lord. If we let faith move us to grow in these qualities, then our faith will truly be effective and productive (2 Peter 1:8), even more than if we were to plant trees in the sea!

Notice, however, that when the disciples asked Jesus to increase their faith, he did not directly answer their request by explaining what he would do to give them a more powerful faith. Instead, he told them what they would be able to do if they had just a small amount of faith. What did they expect him to do? What do we expect the Lord to do to increase our faith? Faith is not a gift, but a command. We are the ones who have to do something.

"Moving mountains" gives us an idea of what we ought to do. Mountains, of course, represent challenges or problems we face in the practice of the Christian life. We confront the challenge to forgive when offenses continue, to love when loving is difficult, or to live the right life when people oppose us. Living a spiritual life presents daily challenges that come from choosing to live a God-centered life in a world that generally cares very little about belief in God. Our faith increases when we meet these challenges, determining to trust in the life that Jesus teaches us to live and persistently practice that life. The Lord can graciously allow us to pass through these struggles and even permit us to face increasingly greater struggles. In this way living in harmony with God's Spirit produces more faith, and faith in turn empowers us to live a more God-centered life.

Another question we must ask ourselves is, "How will we know if our faith is increasing?" A common tendency is to answer this question by comparing ourselves to others. Looking at the low level of dedication of some Christians makes us feel like our faith is strong. On the other hand, looking at the impressive accomplishments that other Christians achieve for the Lord convinces us our faith is weak. Comparing ourselves to each other in order to measure the growth of our faith is actually a trap, because we will always find others whom we can judge to be weaker or stronger in faith than we are.

Jesus' parable of the talents (Matthew 25:14-30) teaches us a different, more accurate way to measure our faith. According to the story, a lord who was going on a trip entrusted five talents of money to one servant, two talents to another servant, and one talent to still another. When the lord returned from his trip, the man who had the five talents had increased his to ten, and the man who had two had increased his to four. He commended these two servants for being equally faithful because they had used their master's resources wisely. Trusting in their lord's return and in his sense of justice, they behaved faithfully in their responsibilities toward him. The servant, however, who had one talent buried it, having no profit to offer his lord when he returned. The lord condemned him not for having less than the other servants but for failing to use faithfully what he had. The servant explained his failure by accusing the lord of being, "a hard man, harvesting where you have not sown and gathering where you have not scattered seed." His view of his lord was not correct. In reality the lord was a just man who only required faithfulness. The servant's lack of faith in his lord's justice kept him from acting faithfully.

What does this illustration mean for us as we try to measure the growth of our faith? Instead of comparing ourselves to the level of faith others have, we ought to consider how we began and how we have personally progressed in comparison to how we began. Think of the talents of money in this parable as measurements of how powerful our faith is. The man who had five talents could not become self-satisfied, thinking that since he had five talents, he did not have to progress so quickly; after all, even after the two talent man had doubled his to four, four was still less than five. Did he begin with five talents? Then he needed to progress beyond those five and continue to progress as long as his lord had entrusted him with this money.

The question we should ask ourselves is, "How far have we progressed in faith toward the Lord?" How has our faith made us more forgiving than we used to be? How has our faith motivated us to be more generous, more compassionate, more godly than we were earlier in our lives as disciples of Jesus? We begin the Christian life at different levels of maturity. Some, after having been raised in Christian homes, ironically, may have very little faith because their faith remained unchallenged in such protected environments. Other disciples who benefited from a Christian upbringing may have begun with a relatively strong faith because their parents trained them to carefully face and overcome challenges to their faith. On the other hand, believers who grew up in faithless environments and experienced the destructiveness of sinful lives in all their ugliness may begin the Christian life with a firmly focused faith and progress quickly as disciples because they want to escape destruction and never turn back. Measuring the increase of our faith depends on where we begin and how we progress.

Nonetheless, we still need a way to measure personal progress in order to know specifically how far we have come from where we began. Faith develops and grows according to certain stages and these stages mark our progress. We start with our hearts, we give our faith a foundation in reason, and we come to the point of decision to act on what we believe. Then our faith converts into action through trust, it grows through facing challenges, and finally we can take a leap of faith to do what appears to be improbable in following Jesus. At each stage there are choices to make and behaviors to practice in order to advance to the next stage. As our faith develops, we can gauge our progress according to these stages and come to understand what we need to practice in order to have a faith that is powerful and transforming.

STARTING WITH THE HEART

Faith is not an emotion, but the right emotions can make faith possible; the wrong emotions can make faith difficult and even terrifying. At some time in our lives, we have all refused to believe something because we did not want to believe it. Imagine someone who has trouble exerting herself, difficulties breathing under stress, and pain in her chest. If she has always been proud about being physically fit, she may not want to believe that she has heart problems and refuses to go to the doctor for a physical exam. The possibility that she might be physically weak creates so much fear or humiliation that she does not want to believe it. She may consult several doctors, and, even after all the doctors tell her the same truth, that she is dangerously ill, she may seek to treat herself without the help of a doctor in order to avoid thinking about how sick she really is. In the same way, parents may refuse to believe their children are using drugs despite obvious warning signs. Business owners may refuse to believe that their businesses are failing in spite of the financial evidence. Angry and bitter people may refuse to believe that they can control their reactions, though friends lovingly counsel them about proven ways to conquer these destructive emotions. In the same way, it should not surprise us that people can also refuse to believe in God because their emotions inhibit them from developing faith.

The apostle Paul wrote, "For it is with your heart that you believe and are justified" (Romans 10:10). As we have seen, the word *heart* in the New Testament represents the whole range of emotions that we feel, whether positive or negative, healthy or destructive. Jesus illustrated the role of the heart in belief when he told his famous parable of the sower. He described a man who planted seed in different kinds of soil with varying results (Luke 8:4-15). Seed that fell on the footpath laid on top of the hard soil until birds consumed it. Seed that fell on rocky soil germinated and developed into plants that quickly withered under the heat of the sun because of the lack of deep soil. Seed that fell on ground filled with weeds could not produce any fruit before the weeds choked out the good plants. Only the seed that fell on good ground produced fruit. This story is not a lesson in agriculture but, instead, teaches a truth about belief.

The seed, Jesus states, is the word of God. The different kinds of soil represent the various conditions of a person's heart. How people hear and accept the word of God depends on the states of their emotions. The hard ground of the footpath represents negative, prejudiced emotions that close off a person's ability to rationally hear. The rocky ground represents the hearts of people who listen impulsively with a short-lived joy but without a deeper desire to surrender themselves to living the life despite possible challenges. The ground full of weeds represents the heart that loves physical riches and pleasures of life more than the spiritual contentment of living at peace with God.

The good ground stands for the honest, sincere desires of a person's heart who genuinely wants to know the truth. The central principle of this parable is that a saving, fruitful faith first depends on the heart, what we love and care about, what we desire, what we are willing to hear and carefully consider. Emotions can determine how we listen.

To have an *open heart* means to possess those healthy emotions that allow us to stop and listen to reason. What are some of the emotions that help us listen to reason about God's existence? We can feel gratitude for something that has happened in our lives, something that we know was beyond our control, yet beyond mere coincidence. We deeply desire purposes that will satisfyingly fulfill the emptiness in our lives. We feel abiding sorrow for destroying our own lives with self-centeredness, pride, or greed, and now we want to learn how to live. We experience inescapable confusion about the world because our views of life cannot adequately explain what we understand to be true. We feel terribly insecure and fearful about living alone in an infinite universe. The burden of all the mistakes we have made in our lives has crushed us, and we long to begin again.

Some of these emotions are difficult to bear, but they serve the purpose of convincing us to tear down the walls that we had raised up to protect ourselves from believing. At the same time, emotions should not be so overwhelming that they convince us to believe without reason. Think of people who have such a desire for money that they invest what little money they have in every "get rich quick" scheme that comes along, eventually losing what little they had. Imagine someone in love with another person to the degree that the one in love thinks constantly about winning the beloved's affection, dreams about spending every waking moment in the presence of the one loved, and is certain these feelings are mutual; yet the other person does not even know the dreamer exists. A similar scenario happens in religion if a deep desire for spirituality overwhelms people and they follow their emotions without stopping to reason. They rush to accept the message of the first person who comes along offering them religion, without carefully thinking about the truth of the message. For this reason multitudes have followed false messiahs. The overwhelming desire to believe sometimes convinces people to believe without thinking.

Even when we believe what is actually true, if our beliefs are grounded only in emotions, then faith will always waver and never grow. The parable of the sower predicted that when the seed falls on rocky ground without much topsoil—no depth of reason—people will "receive the word with joy when they hear it, but they have no root; they believe for a while, but in the time of testing they fall away" (Luke 8:13). Trading evidence for emotion means that when the emotions grow weak, faith will be vulnerable and falter. At the same time, those who try to defend their faith based on emotion use emotional arguments, loud voices, searing language, and violent gestures to convince others of their beliefs. Even if what they believe were true, their use of emotional arguments would not be justified because they would only create converts to the truth whose faith is just like theirs, based on the shaky ground of feelings.

Just as emotions ought to help us stop and listen to reason, emotions can also make people deaf to reason. The writer Luke tells us that when Paul taught in the Jewish synagogues in the city of Thessalonica, "he reasoned with them from the Scriptures, explaining and proving that the Christ had to suffer and rise from the dead" (Acts 17:2-3). Paul's reasoning persuaded some Jews to become followers of Christ; others, however, were so jealous of Paul that they hired some violent men to create a riot in the city to oppose Paul and the other Christians. The emotions of these antagonistic Jews blinded them to reason. Through the prophet Isaiah, God characterized such people as, "hearing, but never understanding ... seeing, but never perceiving" (Isaiah 6:9).

What are some of the emotions that can keep us from listening to the evidence for belief? The fear of sacrificing sensual pleasures, the fear of surrender, or the fear of change can shut down and close off our desire to consider quite valid reasons for believing in God. A common emotion that keeps people from listening is anger—anger about frustrations in life and anger against God, blaming him without understanding him. Pride also makes us deaf to the voice of reason. Faith is humbling because we have to admit that we are not perfect and that we depend on God. If we have struggled against constant criticism in our lives to prove ourselves to be worthy and good, then the pride we develop in our defense can prohibit us from admitting to God, if we were to believe in him, that we are worthy and good only in him. If we enjoy feeling that we are the center of the world, that others are here to serve us, and that our needs are most important, we will find belief difficult because genuine belief in Jesus transforms self-centeredness into self-sacrificing love. In such cases, when emotions overrule reason, something—a tragedy, disillusionment, despair—will have to happen to change our emotional states and cause us to understand that we refused to believe because we were not listening. Faith will only grow when healthy emotions open our minds to listen to the evidence for belief. While it is true that faith finds its firmest foundation in reason, our emotions can either convince us to listen or stop us from hearing the evidence. Faith should be the result of careful thinking about the reasons for believing.

FAITH NEEDS THE ROOTS OF REASON

Faith that does not pass beyond emotions will either be fleeting or fanatic. Faith that finds its foundation in evidence and reason will be stable and productive with the power to transform our lives into the image of Christ. The earliest Christians understood the need for clear reasoning in support of their faith. Peter wrote, "Always be prepared to give an answer to everyone who asks you to give the reason for the hope you have" (1 Peter 3:15). The word *answer* in this verse is translated from a Greek word that describes a reasoned defense. The reasoning process that gives faith its foundation is the same logical process we commonly use to verify conclusions. When a detective arrives at a crime scene, he or she will begin to accumulate pieces of evidence like fingerprints, clothing fibers, spent cartridges, and samples of blood. If these individual pieces of evidence are results of a particular crime, they will have a logical relationship to each other. The detective will be able to show what this relationship is and why it supports his explanation of what happened at the crime scene. Scientists work in the laboratory in the same way to accumulate pieces of evidence and determine if the evidence can logically fit together to form a conclusion. This logical process is called inductive reasoning and is common to human perception and experience. The evidence cannot consist of private opinion or personal speculation; on the contrary, evidence must be available to everyone and verifiable. We use this same reasoning method when thinking about the reality of God or the historicity of the life of Christ.

Nature is the source of enormous evidence supporting the existence of God. The world is full of processes and systems that could never have developed by simple chance. Consider, for instance, the process of photosynthesis in which plants use carbon dioxide and water along with light as an energy source to produce oxygen and simple carbohydrates that in turn are used to produce more elaborate molecules necessary for plant growth. Photosynthesis is a complex series of chemical reactions that could not have functioned in a more simplified state, at some earlier evolutionary stage. It is a process that could not have evolved. Nature is full of similar examples. Human life itself depends on complex processes and incredibly efficient systems that could not have functioned in simpler states. Such examples of complex design are clear and indisputable evidence of a Creator who designed and created these processes. As we earlier noted, Paul reasoned that things that are made require a maker. The evidence of design requires a Creator that has intellect, will and creative power. Only a Being can have intellect and will. The design of the universe testifies to the existence of a Creative Being who is also the First Cause. As the First Cause, this Being could not have been caused by any other cause but has eternally existed. As Creator, this First Cause is separate from the creation and has power over the creation. These qualities describe precisely who God is. God is a Being with will and intellect, not a thing. God is divine, that is, separate from the creation and without comparison in the creation.

The evidence supporting faith in Jesus as the Son of God comes from verifiable history, recorded in the New Testament and other contemporary documents, subject to the same scrutiny that we use to examine the authenticity of any other historical event. The New Testament defines faith as being "certain of what we do not see" (Hebrews 11:1). The word *certain* in this passage is translated from a Greek word that describes proof for the reality of something. Faith is a certainty based on proof, though we have not personally seen the thing believed. In the first century, there were thousands of people in Palestine, from Galilee to Judea, who witnessed firsthand the teachings, the character, and the miracles of Jesus. They were certain of what they knew about Jesus because they witnessed him with their own eyes and listened to him with their own ears. They accepted as fact that Jesus came from God. Nicodemus told Jesus, "We know you are a teacher who has come from God. For no one could perform the miraculous signs that you are doing if God were not with him" (John 3:1). Of course, what they accepted as fact depended on how much they trusted their own senses, but there were thousands who witnessed the same evidence firsthand to confirm what each had seen. The consistency of their experiences added tremendous weight to the trust they put in their perceptions of Jesus.

Later, when the next generation of disciples began to follow Jesus without having seen him firsthand, their faith in him meant being certain of what they had not seen. The strength of their faith reflected the degree of their certainty, and their certainty depended on the reliability of the testimony of witnesses. The apostle John wrote about his firsthand experience of Jesus: "That which was from the beginning, which we have heard, which we have seen with our eyes, which we have looked at and our hands have touched–this we proclaim concerning the Word of life. The life appeared; we have seen it and testify to it, and we proclaim to you the eternal life, which was with the Father and has appeared to us" (1 John 1:1-3). Based on his firsthand experience of Jesus, John wrote his historical record of the words and actions of Jesus, explaining that, "Jesus did many other miraculous signs in the presence of his disciples, which are not written in this book. But these are written that you may believe that Jesus is the Christ, the Son of God, and that by believing you may have life in his name" (John 20:30-31). John's purpose in writing his gospel was to provide his readers, who had not been eyewitnesses, sufficient evidence so that their faith would constitute a "certainty" of things they had not seen. The New Testament biographies of the life of Christ represent a bridge from the experience of the eyewitnesses to the faith of the next generation of believers.

The key to the reliability of the writings of eyewitnesses such as John is that thousands of eyewitnesses were still alive who could verify that the writers of the New Testament documents were recording the truth about what Jesus had said and done. This multitude of eyewitnesses could hand over the writings of such men as Matthew, Mark, Luke, and John to the next generation who were not eyewitnesses, with the certainty of historical accuracy. Now that we are separated by time today from that second generation, which first received the historical documents, we must be able to show that the documents we have today in our New Testament are accurate copies of those histories that were originally handed over to them.

First of all, internal evidence indicates a very early date for the writing of these histories, within one generation, a twenty-five to thirty year time period after the death of Jesus. Mark, for instance, interestingly identifies Simon of Cyrene, the one who carried Jesus' cross, as "the father of Alexander and Rufus." Identifying Simon in this way would only make sense if Mark were writing early, to the very next generation of believers who personally knew Alexander and Rufus. In the same way Matthew describes a lengthy conversation Jesus had with his disciples, predicting that Jerusalem would shortly be destroyed, within one generation. The Romans did, in fact, destroy the temple and the city of Jerusalem a generation later in the year 70 CE. Matthew does not record the fulfillment of Jesus' prediction, indicating that he wrote his gospel very early, earlier that 70 CE, early enough for eyewitnesses of Jesus to be living and able to verify Matthew's account of Jesus' life. Furthermore, a careful study of a vast resource of evidence including ancient manuscripts of the New Testament, quotations in the writings of the early church, and very early translations of the documents into other languages give us the certainty we need for our faith that these writings were penned too early, too close to the events they record, to have been mere legend.

On another level of Christian belief, to be certain that we are practicing the genuine teachings of Jesus, we ought to depend only on the New Testament since it is the earliest and most reliable source of knowledge about Jesus. Confidence in what we believe and practice as disciples is the faith, as Paul said, that "comes from hearing the message, and the message is heard through the word of Christ" (Romans 10:17). We can believe that we are disciples of Jesus only as far as we are following his teachings in the New Testament.

To have a certainty of things not seen requires faith, and faith requires adequate evidence to provide this certainty. The evidence is available for us to consider and to cultivate a faith that is stable and firmly rooted. If our faith is struggling at this level, then we need to read more carefully and consider the evidence with open hearts.

FAITH MUST COME TO THE POINT OF DECISION

Carefully considering the evidence for belief is essential for a strong faith, but, at the same time, continued rehearsal of the evidence can become an excuse to avoid the responsibilities of faith. We may convince ourselves that we just need to read a little more, investigate the objections a little more, and become better versed in articulating the faith before we actually surrender ourselves to following Jesus. But a time of decision must finally come. We have to wonder if we are deceiving ourselves into thinking we do not know enough in order to avoid the obligations that come with actually following Jesus as Lord and Savior. Doubt can serve as an escape. Even though we may not know all the possible objections opponents of the faith might raise, we do understand when the evidence outweighs the doubts. The detective investigating the crime scene needs to decide when he has sufficient evidence to arrest someone. The scientist inventing a cure for some disease needs to decide when the results of testing are positive enough to begin administering the cure.

Think about skydiving again. You want to experience a little excitement in life and to overcome some fears, so you go to the local airport with the intention of jumping out of a plane for the thrill of flying. You pay your money and listen attentively to the instructor who will accompany you on the jump, as he patiently explains how to strap yourself together with him and the parachute. You carefully concentrate on learning the release mechanism for the chute and the reliability of the reserve chute in case the main chute does not open. You obediently picture yourself jumping from the plane, folding your legs behind you with your chest arched outwards so that you fall chest first toward the earth. You then climb into the plane and say good-bye to solid ground, hoping no one notices your anxious smile and sweaty palms. "Am I crazy?" you ask yourself several times. When you reach a considerable altitude, the pilot says, "Go!" You waddle to the door of the plane strapped to your instructor, who has the chute strapped to his back. You hope that your instructor is not crazy. Coming to the door, the instructor tells you to cross your arms in front of

INCREASE OUR FAITH! 241

your chest. You think it is part of the technique for jumping, but this final gesture is to prohibit you from grabbing the sides of the door at the last moment. Now is the time to decide. Are you going to jump? Will you scream above the roar of the plane's engines, "Wait, I need to learn some more, practice more, think more"? Enough learning and preparing. You know enough! Now is the moment to decide to trust and jump.

The reasons for faith bring us to this point of decision, a decision we can no longer avoid if we want to fly, living with Jesus. What is involved in this decision? Jesus taught that we must count the cost to understand the obligations and consequences of living lives committed to following him. Jesus gave two examples of calculating this cost.

> Suppose one of you wants to build a tower. Will he not first sit down and estimate the cost to see if he has enough money to complete it? For if he lays the foundation and is not able to finish it, everyone who sees it will ridicule him, saying, 'This fellow began to build but was not able to finish.' Or suppose a king is about to go to war against another king. Will he not first sit down and consider whether he is able with ten thousand men to oppose the one coming against him with twenty thousand? If he is not able, he will send a delegation while the other is still a long way off and will ask for terms of peace (Luke 14:28–32).

Being a devoted follower of Jesus means to think and live differently. What will change? What sacrifices will we have to make? Character qualities such as forgiveness, generosity, compassion, mercy, and holiness represent changes in how we view ourselves and others. We behave in completely new ways with deeper commitments to change from the inside out. Relationships change, some for the better as people benefit from our new hearts, others for the worse because people reject us when we no longer share with them in the sin of our former lives. We do not, however, count the cost in order to decide whether to pay it. We have already come to the conclusion, based on the evidence, that Jesus is the only way. For the one who believes there is no alternative, counting the cost serves the purpose of understanding what is coming and deciding to face the challenges, having calculated that the benefit is far greater than the cost. We already believe that change is possible, necessary, and better; now we have to decide to accept the cost of changing.

John wrote that among the Jewish leaders there were men who believed in Jesus, but who would not admit their faith because they were afraid of being thrown out of the synagogue, losing their place of power. John said, "They loved the praise from men more than praise from God" (John 12:42). Among them must have been Nicodemus who had said to Jesus, "We know you are a teacher who has come from God." They came to the point of decision and decided the cost was too great. They must have mistakenly thought there was some other way to come to God besides Jesus.

John tells us of another occasion when Jesus challenged some people who were following him to live more deeply surrendered lives. Jesus told them, "I tell you the truth, unless you eat the flesh of the Son of Man and drink his blood, you have no life in you" (John 6:53). His language expressed the need for complete commitment to him, as if consuming him, consuming his teachings and the new life. Some of those people decided to follow him no longer because they calculated there was too much risk involved. But when Jesus asked his closest disciples, "You do not want to leave too, do you?" Peter replied,

"Lord, to whom shall we go, you have the words of eternal life. We believe and know that you are the Holy One of God" (John 6:67-68). Peter would later face great challenges to his faith, but he had made the decision to pay the cost, and the rewards far outweighed the risk.

So now we decide to face the risk and trust. At the moment we are going to jump, we may feel a sense of dread, an unfocused anxiety, which can paralyze us into inaction. We review all the right answers we keep offering ourselves to go ahead and jump, but we start to grab the edges of the doorway. In reality this surge of anxiety is normal with most major decisions. In such moments we need to feel a sense of urgency, a gentle push, an inner voice that says, "Be courageous, let go and jump!" "You want to fly, so close your eyes if you need to, but jump!"

In Jesus' parable of the lost son, the young man took this step of faith. He had experienced the tragedy of living a wasted, meaningless life. After losing everything, he "came to himself" and thought about what he would do. "I will set out and go back to my father and say to him: Father, I have sinned against heaven and against you. I am no longer worthy to be called your son; make me like one of your hired men." Then Jesus adds, "So he got up and went to his father." Facing fully the tragedy of his sin motivated him to get up and go back home. In between thinking about what he would do and actually rising up to go and do it was this moment of decision, overcoming whatever dread he might have felt and doing the only thing he could do, return to his father. Overcoming this dread is an act of faith, believing that the good that lies ahead of us is far better than the evil we left behind. Before we move on with faith, we have to come to this point of decision, dismiss the dread—it will always be part of faith—and, letting go of the doorway, fly!

FAITH SAVES
WHEN IT IS CONVERTED INTO ACTION

Of course, you could tell your instructor, "Enough is enough, I have decided not to jump!" He will not force you to jump. You can waddle back to your seat, unhook the harness, sit down, and return to the airport but without faith or trust because they died when you sat down again. Remember that James said, "Faith by itself, if it is not accompanied by action, is dead" (James 2:14-17). Faith has the power to save when it develops into trust and motivates us to act. To trust is to believe in the reliability of someone to the point of surrendering to the care of the one who is trusted. A child trusts his father enough to jump from a high place into the father's arms without hesitation, knowing the father will catch him. In order to motivate us to action, faith has to become trust, no longer just a belief held in one's mind but a confidence to act without dread. James offers the examples of Abraham when he was about to offer his son Isaac as a sacrifice and Rahab when she put herself at great risk to protect the two spies from Israel. Abraham and Rahab both had to trust in God's power to save them in order to act on what they believed about God. They believed that God was powerful and faithful enough to keep his promises. Trust in God's power and faithfulness pushed them to action. In the case of skydiving, trusting the instructor to be sane, calm, expert, and practiced, you jump, completely surrendering yourself to his ability and judgment to release the parachute at the right moment. Trust connects belief with action.

On one occasion when Jesus had been speaking to a large group of people that included opponents to his teaching, curious listeners, and honest seekers of the truth, John tells us that, "Even as he spoke, many put their faith in him" (John 8:30). Their faith was belief at the point of decision. Their decisions to believe were brave because they undoubtedly would face the ridicule and wrath of their religious leaders who were also present in the crowd. Despite the courage of their decisions, Jesus challenged them to take the next step of faith. John continued the narrative, "To the Jews who believed him, Jesus said, 'If you hold to my teaching, you are really my disciples. Then you will know the truth and the truth will set you free'" (John 8:31-32). To "hold" to his teachings meant to live in them by practicing them.

Jesus' statement helps us understand some truths about trust. First, trust takes us from belief to action when we obey what Jesus taught. If we were to say we believe in Jesus and then create our own formulas for a righteous life, we would be trusting in ourselves and not in Jesus. Trusting him means to hold to his teachings. Trusting him implies surrender to his wisdom and power to direct our lives in the path that leads us to the Father. Secondly, when our faith actually does convert into action and motivate us to practice the teaching of Jesus, then we will know the truth and the truth will set us free. We discover the truth about the teachings of Jesus when we practice them. Consider Jesus' teaching that forgiveness is essentially unlimited. At first sight such forgiveness does not seem humanly possible, but trusting in Jesus' wisdom, we begin to forgive as he taught, without limit. Continued practice of forgiveness gives us understanding of forgiveness, its challenges, risks, and blessings that cannot come from just reading about forgiveness. Then the practice of forgiveness brings us an incredible sense of freedom: freedom from resentment, freedom from worry about justice, and freedom from the desire to retaliate. At this point we have learned the truth about forgiveness. Trusting enough to practice sets us free, changes our lives, and saves us. Finally, letting go of doubts and forgiving provides the same exhilaration of letting go of the doorway and flying! We are free!

FAITH GROWS THROUGH FACING CHALLENGES

After jumping a few times with the instructor, we begin to imagine jumping solo at higher altitudes, free falling for longer stretches of time. Trust builds and greater challenges become possible and even desirable. Of course, perhaps, we just wanted to skydive once, feel the freedom of flying, and then return to our normal boring lives. We certainly will never become proficient at skydiving, but perhaps that is not the goal. The Christian life is similar and, yet, different from skydiving. On one hand, the more we trust in Jesus and grow confident in the practice of the Christian life, the more willing we are to accept new challenges to live more powerful lives in Christ. The joy of trusting and growing spiritually creates the thirst for more. On the other hand, we cannot choose simply to start to follow Jesus, make the initial decision, act on our belief, and then decide not to grow in faith. We can decide not to continue to skydive and all will be well; but deciding not to trust in the Lord and continue to grow in faith will kill us spiritually. The Lord is present in our lives. He wants to train us to live a higher life; he wants us to feel the joy of growing; he wants to use us as more powerful instruments. Choosing not to grow is to let faith slowly atrophy and die. Like it is said about learning languages, "Either use it or lose it." The apostles asked Jesus to increase their faith, but he too wanted them to have a more powerful faith. They would have to decide to welcome greater challenges in order to grow.

Challenges cause faith to grow. James wrote that the testing of our faith develops perseverance. Following Jesus involves risk. Dedicated disciples will experience trials, challenges that essentially ask them, "How deeply do you believe?" "How far will you go?" "How much do you trust?" Following the example of Jesus, we humble ourselves, serving others even when no one serves us, even when those whom we serve humiliate us. Treating others the way we want them to treat us sometimes does not change the behavior of people toward us. What will we do? Will we continue to treat them well or decide to treat them the way they treat us? People have needs that call us to give more than we are able to give, sacrificing beyond what we consider to be our capacities to sacrifice. Do we trust that the Lord will supply our need? We pray and do not immediately receive the answers we expect. Will we keep on trusting and praying? We struggle to be compassionate and help someone in need who then takes advantage of our compassion. Will we trust the teaching of Jesus and continue to practice compassion? Faith in action can leave us vulnerable and exposed to the possibility of losing something valuable. Will we continue to believe, trust, and practice?

James said that such trials produce a faith that perseveres, having the ability to stay on course, endure, and continue. How do challenges do this? With each challenge we have to make a decision to trust Jesus, trusting his wisdom and power in our lives, and refusing to give up. Each decision we make to continue practicing his teachings despite the cost strengthens the determination to live the life. The success and growth we experience as we overcome each challenge empowers us and motivates us to meet the next trial. Remember the comparison we made to weight lifting when we were thinking about the patience of perseverance. A weight lifter has to lift increasingly greater weight in order to develop strength. Step by step, one challenge prepares for the next. With each increase in weight, muscles grow, and the power to lift more weight increases. Success and satisfaction from lifting a certain weight is motivation for going on to lift more weight. Lifting the same weight time after time, no matter how many repetitions, will not produce more strength or perseverance. In the Christian life, increasing challenges produce perseverance and perseverance finishes its work by producing a stronger faith with increased trust.

Peter also explained that challenges increase the power of our faith by purifying it. Speaking about serious opposition Christians face, he said, "These have come so that your faith—of greater worth than gold, which perishes even though refined by fire—may be proved genuine and may result in praise, glory, and honor when Jesus Christ is revealed" (1 Peter 1:6-7). At different moments in our lives as Christians, we put faith in various sources of strength, both real and imagined. We may trust in our own abilities apart from the Lord, trust in friends or loved ones to bring us acceptance, trust in the possession of things to bring us contentment, trust in our jobs to give us self-worth, or trust in our own health and physical strength to give us confidence. But circumstances can rob us of any of these people or things in which we trust. We can lose our jobs; a good friend may betray us; we may experience serious health problems. Like the fire that burns off the impurities of a precious rock to reveal gold, trials leave us with faith that is pure and trusts ultimately and absolutely in the Lord. In such moments we learn that we can trust completely only in the Lord for our self-worth, contentment, peace, and purpose. If we feel defeated and tired of living a stagnant Christian life, the answer is not to retreat but to open our faith up to more risk.

A growing faith will always face risk, but it is the risk that keeps faith growing. This stage of faith is where faith ought to be for most of our Christian lives as it continues to grow and mature. We measure its growth by the degree of challenges we are willing to face in order to live ever more closely to the image of Jesus' character.

FAITH LEAPS BEYOND REASON

When our faith is challenged, we naturally have the tendency to calculate the risks involved, turning the decisions over and over in our minds, thinking about the reasons for and against, when we know very well what Jesus is asking us to do. There might be someone with whom we need to talk about the Lord, someone who needs to understand the grace of the Lord and the beauty of new life in him. A door seems to be open to give us an opportunity to speak and we are thinking, "Shall I say something?" "What if she doesn't listen?" "What if I say the wrong thing?" "What if she isn't interested in hearing about Jesus?" "What if she gets angry?" We try to calculate the outcome, but we already know what the Lord wants us to do because we believe we are his instruments. The only choice is to pray and ask for wisdom and then, trusting the Lord, speak with love, respect, and humility.

Imagine another act of trust in the Lord. We decide to make a major change in our life, move to a new city, look for a new job and new friends because we want to help in the Lord's work in the new city. Our friends and family members warn us that the decision does not make sense, and we know it does not seem to make sense economically and socially, but our faith has grown and is ready for the next step, or better to say, the next leap.

Faith is founded on reason. There is a mountain of evidence to support our belief in God and his Son Jesus. But, once our faith has this firm foundation, there will be moments in our Christian lives when we need to take a leap beyond reason, making decisions that do not make sense from our human perspectives. We stop turning it over and over in our minds, trust in the Lord and act. A faith first of all founded on reason now leaps beyond reason.

The earliest disciples learned this lesson. Once Jesus had been teaching near the shore of a lake, sitting in a boat in the water while addressing the crowd that had gathered on the shore. The boat he had been sitting in was Peter's, and, after finishing the teaching, he told Peter to take the boat out to deeper water and let down his nets. Peter at once objected because he and his fellow fisherman had spent the previous night fishing, and they had caught nothing. Peter was a fisherman. Jesus was the son of a carpenter. Peter knew all about fishing, and Jesus' idea did not make sense. Nonetheless, Peter had already come to believe in Jesus. He told the Lord, "Master, we've worked hard all night and haven't caught anything. But because you say so, I will let down the nets" (Luke 5:5). Of course, the catch they brought in nearly capsized the boat!

When the Lord calls us to act, we take the leap, trusting out of pure faith, and faith does not just grow, but it bursts forth from the limits we have placed on it and carries us to new horizons in discipleship that we never imagined we could reach. This is the thrill of faith. This is the excitement of getting out of the boat and walking on water. The Lord uses us to reach people with the gospel that we never imagined reaching. The fear and hesitation we fought against all our lives suddenly disappears. Optimism about life in Christ infuses our plans and desires for the Lord's work. We give in ways we never dreamed of giving. Now we love unconditionally, free to show mercy and patience even in the most difficult moments, when in the past we would have said to ourselves, "Don't do it! Don't you know what will happen?" The truth is we do not know what will happen, but we act because we trust.

There was a young man who had always wanted to be a firefighter though his university studies were taking him in a completely different direction. One summer he trained to fight forest fires and spent the summer doing what he had dreamed of doing, relishing the excitement, suffering the dirty, smoky, exhausting work, and conquering a few fears in the process. While fighting one particularly difficult fire, he and his fellow crewmembers found themselves in a canyon when the fire, blown by winds, jumped from one ridge to another. Suddenly the fire surrounded them and threatened to start burning down into the canyon where they were. At that moment the crew chief, whose job it was to protect his men, told them to wait below while he charged up a hill in the direction of the fire to see where the fire had come from and in what direction it was going. He left the crew members with a radio and disappeared. Soon they heard his voice over the radio instructing them to run in a certain direction. Then, unseen by them, he ran through the smoking trees to another ridge to scout the fire's constantly changing progress. He spoke again, "Turn toward the ridge on your left!" Crossing the canyon to their left, the crewmembers had no idea where they were going, blindly running. But they trusted this man who was leading them. They knew of his experience and his excellent physical condition. They did exactly what he commanded. Their escape from the fire was by pure faith; there was no time to calculate risks, no time to wonder what might happen, just trust and move quickly. When our faith comes to this stage in the Christian life, the Lord will make us powerful instruments for him.

The disciples asked the Lord to increase their faith, but increasing their faith depended much on their decision to trust. Their faith progressed through the same stages as our faith. We can measure the progress of our faith by judging where we are in these stages. Progressing from one stage to the next depends on our decisions, but the Lord will open doors and provide us with resources. He will teach us the meaning of trust. He will protect us and lift us up when we make the wrong decisions. We are the ones, however, who need to trust. Trusting in him, we will fly!

Nathanael, known also as Bartholomew, was one of the twelve apostles. He was amazed when he first met Jesus because Jesus already knew everything about him. He knew that Nathanael was full of integrity. Listening to Nathanael's surprise, Jesus told him, "You believed because I told you I saw you under the fig tree. You shall see greater things than that" (John 1:50). This promise is the promise of a faith that is ready to leap even beyond reason: you will see even greater things than this!

CHAPTER EIGHT

GROWING IN GENTLENESS

"TAKE MY YOKE UPON YOU AND LEARN FROM ME,
FOR I AM GENTLE AND HUMBLE IN HEART"
(MATTHEW 11:28-30).

O f all the fruit of the Spirit, gentleness may be the most radical in comparison to modern values in many contemporary societies. People generally believe in the ideals of love and peace as well as goodness and faithfulness, at least under the best of circumstances. Most people would say that being kind, exercising patience, and having self-control will help us get along better with people and even be successful. And everyone wants to feel joy. But in an age when competition and assertiveness, if not outright aggression, are the rules for advancement in many places in the world, gentleness ranks low on the list of qualities that people might desire to develop. There are, of course, some gentle individuals to be found in most communities, but they are probably unique because of their gentleness. And there are, no doubt, some relatively primitive societies still in existence today in which gentleness might characterize their members as a whole. Perhaps they are gentle because they are isolated from the ambitions of the rest of the world. In any culture gentleness is possible, but in some cultures it will be more costly to possess. During the history of Christianity there have also been plenty of individuals and communities adopting the name of Christ, yet who have been anything but gentle in their treatment of unbelievers or members of other sects. What is the role of gentleness in the Christian life? Is gentleness just for a few Christians who have a natural disposition for being non-combative and accepting?

In truth, Jesus taught the priority of gentleness against the context of cultural confusion, racism, political ambition, and violence that characterized first century Palestine. Although Jesus gained popularity and power that he could have easily used in an attempt to overthrow the Roman domination of Palestine, he refused, without hesitation, to do so. Gentleness was just as radical then as it is now. Jesus had come to manifest the beauty of gentleness that God wants his children to possess. Gentleness ought to describe any disciple dedicated to following Jesus because Jesus himself was the gentle Savior. Imagine the influence disciples could have today if entire Christian communities were known for their gentle spirits!

UNDERSTANDING

Before considering the character of Jesus, a look at the meaning of the word translated *gentleness* in the New Testament will help us understand the nature of this quality. In the list of the fruit of the Spirit in the fifth chapter of Galatians, the Greek word *prautes* is translated *gentleness* in some English translations and *meekness* in others. There is no single English word that absolutely corresponds to prautes. In modern English usage, meekness sometimes suggests weakness. A meek person is quiet and reserved because he is not strong enough to speak out and defend himself. Prautes is not weakness but instead is an attitude that comes from strength. Gentleness in modern usage usually refers to tender treatment, taking care not to harm or damage; but prautes is first an attitude of the heart, a gentleness of heart that is then manifested in gentle behavior toward others.

We can think of gentleness then as beginning with a tender, considerate heart that views people with patience and compassion and then manifests itself in behavior that does not cause harm or damage. Gentleness emanates from a quiet, tranquil spirit that treats others with calmness. It is the opposite of aggression, assertiveness, and self-interest. It is non-violent and does not retaliate. Instead of arguing and becoming angry, a gentle heart listens, considers, and answers with calm. It is the attitude of a master who respectfully and compassionately serves as a servant. Instead of threatening, a gentle spirit quietly reasons and encourages. This level of meekness is not weakness, but, instead, requires consistently strong character.

Think of a wise mother's gentle touch for her small child. She knows just the right amount of support and guidance to give without discouraging. This is the same gentle way that Jesus' heart touches our spirits so that, although he is so strong, he never overwhelms us. The writers of the New Testament, who were witnesses to the beautiful character of Jesus, repeatedly illustrate how the gentleness of Jesus contrasted with the rough and arrogant attitude of those with whom he often found himself. When some parents brought their children to Jesus for his blessing, they must have been worried about the future of their children in a world that was so full of turmoil and confusion. They just wanted this righteous man to pray for their children. Surprisingly, the disciples reprimanded the parents for bringing their children to Jesus. The language and posture of the disciples showed they had neither the time nor the patience to allow the children to approach Jesus. Jesus, however, said, "Let the little children come to me" (Matthew 19:13-15). That day the children felt the gentle touch of the Savior on their heads and the parents felt his gentle touch on their hearts, relieving their worry and putting them at peace.

On another occasion a blind man named Bartimaeus heard the encouraging words of Jesus and felt his gentle touch. Discovering that Jesus had come to his town of Jericho, Bartimaeus went to meet him on the road, shouting, "Jesus, Son of David, have mercy on me!" (Luke 18:35-43). Some of those who were leading the procession (probably the apostles again) rebuked Bartimaeus and told him to be quiet. Their harsh treatment of a blind man revealed their lack of compassion for people who suffer. When Jesus came to Bartimaeus, he asked him, "What do you want me to do for you?" There was no judging, no impatience, no intolerance, just a kind and simple question. The touch of Jesus not only healed his eyes that day but his spirit too.

Then there was the woman guilty of adultery, brought to Jesus by religious teachers who were ready to stone her. These teachers of the law were so blinded by religious zeal and arrogance that they could not see the sorrow and humiliation that the woman felt. They wanted retaliation and not restoration. When Jesus stooped down and wrote on the ground to give the men time to think about their own sins, they suddenly left, one after another, leaving him alone with the woman. She would never forget how different his gentle words felt to her spirit in comparison to the thought of those rocks striking her body, "Go now and leave your life of sin."

There were also some moments when Jesus' behavior did not seem so gentle. Consider the contrast in the behavior of Christ that Matthew presents in chapter twenty-one of his gospel. When Jesus triumphantly entered Jerusalem shortly before his crucifixion, he rode on the back of a donkey's colt. He did not fit the image most people had of a powerful, victorious king, riding a white stallion at the head of legions of marching soldiers. Nonetheless, large crowds of people excitedly and joyfully received him, laying down their cloaks and branches from trees on the path before him. The crowds recognized him as "Jesus, the prophet from Nazareth in Galilee." Matthew explained that his entrance fulfilled the prophecy of Zechariah, who had said, "See, your king comes to you, gentle and riding on a donkey, on a colt, the foal of a donkey" (Matthew 21:5).

Then a short time later he entered the temple, finding a confusing cacophony of people and animals clogging the courts. Temple agents were bartering and haggling with people, exchanging currencies and selling sheep, cattle, and doves for temple sacrifices during the Passover. The greedy temple authorities had turned the sacred place of worship not just into a marketplace but a racket run by thieves. Filled with the highest respect for the holiness of his Father's house and the desire to protect it from defilement, Jesus drove the animals and people from the temple, overturning the tables of the money changers and declaring, "It is written, 'My house will be called a house of prayer,' and you have made it a 'den of robbers'" (Matthew 21:13). Was his behavior on this occasion inconsistent with his gentle treatment of people in other moments? The humble healer from Galilee understood that a subdued voice would not capture the people's attention in the noisy atmosphere of a marketplace. He could not go from person to person quietly asking them to stop what they were doing and inviting them to leave. He could not carefully lead each animal out of the temple, one by one. This moment in the life of Jesus is surprising for the very reason that his behavior, even though appropriate for the occasion, was so different from his normal way of treating people. His reaction astonished people.

Gentleness is not appropriate in moments when we have to suddenly and dramatically get the attention of someone. A gentle voice is not effective when a child is about to run out into the street in front of an approaching car. When a building is catching fire, the question is not about whether to be gentle or not; the question is how to warn people quickly and effectively. A few days later in the life of Jesus, his arrest once again placed his gentle character in stark contrast with the raucous crowd bearing weapons to arrest him. Why did they think they needed swords and clubs to overpower the gentle Savior who did not command even one soldier? If these soldiers and common brutes had known Jesus, they would have understood there was no need for such weapons to apprehend one whose life defined gentleness.

REFLECTION

The apostle Paul urged Christians to "live a life worthy of the calling" they have received (Ephesians 4:1-2). He specifically mentions gentleness in addition to humility, patience, and love as qualities of those who confidently follow their calling as disciples of Jesus. Unfortunately, we might be afraid to be gentle. Will people view us as weak if we are gentle? Will they take advantage of us? If we are not usually gentle, what will people think if we suddenly become gentle?

We can resolve these questions by first understanding the power that supports gentleness in the Christian life. True gentleness is not weakness. Some people seem to be gentle but their apparent gentleness is a mask covering fear. They cannot find the strength in their faith to be bold and firm. They speak softly, avoid any subjects that might offend, and waver when they need to firmly declare their faith. Their gentleness is actually weakness and at the heart of this weakness is fear. Others who lack gentleness seem to have plenty of boldness and do not appear to be afraid of clearly and decisively expressing their faith, no matter whom they offend. In this case their severe and offensive language is also a mask covering fear: fear of losing arguments, fear of being humiliated, or fear of their own doubts. Jesus, on the other hand, empowers us to be bold yet gentle in the confident expression of our unwavering convictions.

The power to be gentle without fear comes from our relationships with Jesus and our heavenly Father. We know that through Jesus we have been forgiven and accepted by our heavenly Father as his children. We know that we have someone who supports us, provides for us, and protects us. We know that he is the one who is just and can judge those who might take advantage of us when we treat them with gentleness. We are only messengers and instruments in the Lord's hand to show the beauty of the life the Lord wants us to live. We defend the life by living the life. We do not have to be aggressive or retaliate because the Lord is our defender. The schemes of those who oppose what is right are against the Lord and not really against us. Trusting in the Lord's providence, we can be tranquil in our spirits, letting go of anxieties and allowing the Lord to work in his way with his wisdom to touch the lives of others. Because of our relationships with the Lord, we can feel safe enough to be gentle with other people. The practice of gentleness is not a sign of weakness but, instead, originates from power, the power of faith in God. Gentleness, therefore, is a fruit of the Spirit because it is the result of walking by faith, in harmony with the purpose and work of God's Spirit

The power to be gentle also comes from humility. Humility and gentleness are companion qualities in passages such as Ephesians 4:2 and Colossians 3:12. Gentleness would be difficult if we were constantly concerned about being first, getting ahead of others, and making sure that we have what we personally want. Gentleness needs humility. Humility motivates us not to think too highly of ourselves but to realize all we have comes from the Lord. It means to consider others better than ourselves, to lift others up instead of lifting ourselves up, and to serve instead of being served. Without humility, we would easily run over people and rush to get what we think we deserve. To feel free to be gentle, we first humble ourselves to be honestly interested in the welfare of others.

Furthermore, the power to be gentle comes from establishing the right priorities in our lives. Paul counseled Timothy to be gentle instead of arguing about useless questions. "Don't have anything to do with foolish and stupid arguments, because you know they produce quarrels" (2 Timothy 2:23). We tend to give importance to subjects that deserve little attention. Many discussions that seem important in the moment are really about trivialities that, with the passage of time, prove to have no value. If our priorities are confused, we can easily become argumentative about subjects that really do not matter. Arguing about trivial matters can also originate from pride or self-centeredness, neither of which is consistent with the humility of gentleness. A secret to having gentleness is to stay far away from matters that incite pride or encourage self-centeredness. The priority should actually be the practice of gentleness.

We can also resolve the fear of being gentle by understanding not only the power that supports gentleness but also by understanding the power of gentleness itself. Of course, thinking that aggressiveness, a loud voice, and strong physical gestures are powerful is natural. Physical strength communicates power, but this power is mainly useful to compel people to respond. A calm spirit and a quietly confident voice can be very powerful in more effective ways to persuade people to respond. Imagine two classrooms of primary school students of the same age and sociocultural mix. One teacher constantly raises her voice, threatens, scolds, and generally maintains a mean presence in the classroom. The students barely remain under control, taking advantage of any moment when the teacher is not paying attention. The teacher assumes the students are naturally unruly and require tough discipline. The other teacher remains calm, speaks at a normal voice level, maintains just limits for the conduct of the students, praises them when they do well, and quietly, respectfully, consistently disciplines them when they misbehave. The students respond with respectful attention and work in an orderly manner. Drawing the conclusion that the students are responsible for the different atmospheres in the classrooms would be wrong. The first teacher has trained the students to react only when she threatens and yells. They react from fear or compulsion but not from respect for the teaching environment. The second teacher has trained the students to react with respect because her gentle but firm treatment of the students demonstrates respect for them. This fascinating contrast in classrooms, played out in real life countless times, illustrates the persuasive power of gentleness.

A firm but gentle demeanor accompanied by a quiet voice is powerful because it is easy to listen to, does not put people on the defensive, and communicates respect. People do not feel compelled or threatened. Gentleness gains credibility for the teacher, the parent, the leader, or anyone in a position to persuade because those listening understand that the one speaking does not wish to overwhelm them with force. Gentleness shows that a person does not have the desire to control or domineer. When gentleness replaces force, people are more willing to listen, to compromise, to agree, and to resolve conflicts peacefully.

What shall we do if a gentle yet firm approach will not produce the results we want? Is there a limit to gentleness? First, before we think about placing limits on gentleness if its results are not satisfactory, we must remember gentleness is a primary quality of the Christian life. It is not an attitude that we practice only when convenient or when we think it might win a favor from someone. Instead, gentleness ought to be one of the first attitudes we think about when we consider how to treat other people.

Secondly, if we were to think that we could dispose with gentleness if it does not appear to bring us the results we wish, then what would we plan to replace it with? Would we think to replace gentleness with verbal abuse or threatening gestures? For the disciple of Jesus, abusive behavior is never the option. If we seem to be losing arguments by being gentle, should we then begin to argue aggressively, raising our voices and using harsher language to overwhelm the arguments of our opponents? Do we really expect to persuade others to accept our views by being severe if gentleness does not work? Do we persuade them or just overwhelm them? Gentleness, in fact, is a decision not to use aggression. As a quality of our spiritual natures, it must color everything we do. If we cannot influence people by being gently firm, then we will not be able to influence them. There ought to be no limits to gentleness when gentleness is appropriate.

At the same time, we can say that gentleness is a relative quality, especially in the ways we express it. Gentleness begins with a heart that views the world with tenderness and care instead of aggression, a heart that seeks to repair and restore instead of harm and destroy. The exact expressions of gentleness are relative, depending on the person or thing that we are treating with gentleness. Think of how to lead a child who is just beginning to walk, carefully holding the child's hand, supporting, encouraging, moving at the pace at which the child can move. Compare the gentle way we would lead children with the way in which we would lead animals such as a burro. A burro, with its tough hide and stubborn spirit, may need the touch of the whip to direct it and encourage it to move. Nonetheless, the burro's master ought to use the whip sparingly with the minimum amount of pressure to control the animal instead of harshly beating the animal each time it takes a misstep.

Jesus spoke differently to the woman who was caught in adultery than he spoke to the Pharisees whom he called hypocrites for the way they had poisoned religion with their false sincerity. Even in the case of the Pharisees, Jesus did not become aggressive with them or abuse them but only used the minimum level of language necessary to call their attention to the errors they were committing. To the woman who was sorry for her sin, he said, "Go now and leave your life of sin" (John 8:11). To the Pharisees who were stubbornly blind to their sins, he said, "Woe to you, teachers of the law and Pharisees, you hypocrites! You are like whitewashed tombs, which look beautiful on the outside but on the inside are full of dead men's bones and everything unclean" (Matthew 23:27). Like the master's touch of the whip to the burro, Jesus' words for the Pharisees represented a relatively gentle way of opening their eyes to their sins. Jesus made his point clear without being brutal. We need to pray that the Lord will give us the wisdom to know what level of gentleness to show in each situation. Often, we are too quick to respond aggressively and then justify ourselves by claiming that gentleness would not work. But if we begin with gentle hearts for all people, the gentle expressions of our hearts will come more naturally and we will be thinking about what gentleness requires in each circumstance.

Remember that the purpose of gentleness is to heal, repair, and restore. It means to direct without damaging and to help without hurting. Imagine a master craftsman building a fine piece of furniture. In the process of working the wood, there will be moments when he uses coarser grades of sandpaper to smooth the finish of the wood and other moments when the material requires only the lightest touch of the finest grade of sandpaper. No matter the stage of the work, the craftsman will always use the minimal amount of pressure necessary, the most gentle of touches, even when using the coarser sandpaper, in order to smooth and finish instead of harming and destroying. The key to understanding the appropriate form of gentleness is to consider the minimum touch required to produce a constructive, positive result.

PRACTICE

Gentleness is difficult to develop when we focus on our physical selves without attention to our spirits. When we live to please our physical desires, we convince ourselves that being assertive, aggressive, and controlling is the way to achieve what we desire. We might use the strength of our bodies to exert power, to be forceful, and to posture and gesture in an intimidating way. The opposite may be true also. We may feel small, insignificant, and intimidated. In this case our spirits surrender to the weak views we have of ourselves, and we resign to living without much ambition. But gentleness is a decision we make about how to treat people and not an act of resignation because we think we are powerless.

Once we are born again and begin to live spiritual lives, we realize that, in order to achieve anything worthwhile and lasting, we have to submit our bodies to our spirits. Our bodies become the instruments of our spirits instead of our spirits being subjugated to the desires of our bodies. When our spirits, empowered by God's Spirit, are in control of our lives, growing in gentleness is possible because gentleness is, first of all, a quality of our spirits. We submit our bodies to the gentleness we cultivate in our spirits. Although we usually think of gentleness in terms of physical gestures such as a tender touch and a moderated voice, gentleness begins with the heart. How can we describe a gentle heart? How do we cultivate a gentle heart?

If we can imagine what a gentle touch is, then we can also think of having a gentle heart. If a gentle touch means to treat people with care, tenderness, and healing, then having a gentle heart means to develop emotions toward people that are caring, tender, and understanding. The heart stands for our emotions and gentle emotions view people with compassion, without aggression, or any desire to do harm. Cultivating gentleness therefore begins with controlling our thoughts and emotions about people.

When a child holds a small animal like a new-born puppy, the parent will likely say to the child, "Be gentle!" Controlling the thoughts of our hearts means giving ourselves the same advice when we feel antagonistic emotions toward someone. "Be gentle!" Just like a parent repeating the same advice to a child, we may have to repeat the same phrase to ourselves over and over again when we are with people who challenge our desire to be gentle. "Be gentle!" "Be gentle!"

Developing a gentle heart means giving up a lot. We discover that treating some people gently is easy. They have never hurt us. Maybe we know they are weaker than we are and depend on us so we cannot imagine harming them. With others, though, we struggle to be gentle. What do we have to change in our hearts to be gentler? We will have to surrender resentment and forgive offenses they have committed or continue to commit against us. We will have to give up prejudices against certain classes of people and stop forming preconceived ideas about people based on their outward appearances. We will have to stop making critical judgments of people without knowing their hearts. We will have to give up the pride that makes us think we are usually right about almost everything. We will have to give up taking the defensive every time people criticize us and, instead, humbly continue to do what is right, letting the Lord defend us in his way. A heart that is doubtful, fearful, critical, judgmental, and defensive will find viewing people with gentleness a difficult task because of all the walls these emotions erect between people. To be gentle we cannot be afraid to let go of these emotions and view people in the best light, giving them the benefit of the doubt, treating their hearts in a tender way, not wanting to offend them or depreciate them.

Leading and following with gentleness. After we start with our hearts, we can then begin to work on practicing gentleness in specific aspects of our lives. Leading and following with gentleness is a good place to begin. If we are not in positions to lead people in some of our relationships, we are probably in positions of following. Parents lead children. Older siblings lead younger siblings. Some friends lead other friends. Supervisors lead other employees. Are we showing someone the way? Are we setting an example? Jesus is our model to practice gentleness as we lead.

Jesus invited the lost to follow him with the words, "Come to me, all you who are weary and burdened, and I will give you rest. Take my yoke upon you and learn from me, for I am gentle and humble in heart, and you will find rest for your souls. For my yoke is easy and my burden is light" (Matthew 11:28-30). The gentleness of Jesus made him a very powerful leader. We can have absolute confidence to follow him because his gentleness convinces us that he has our best interests in mind. Leaders who are proud, assertive, and harsh cannot create a feeling of trust among their followers. No one is at ease in their presence. Jesus, on the other hand, leads us from a gentle heart. We can rest in his presence, feel at peace, and follow him without fear. Jesus calls us as his disciples to develop the same gentle character when we lead. People should be at rest and feel confident when they are following our leads. We put away sarcasm, negative language, ridicule, demeaning remarks, and unnecessary criticism. We praise, we encourage, we appreciate, and we show confidence in others. We lead with humility knowing that we are not always right. We let those who follow our directions know that we care for them as individuals. We want them to feel comfortable and not afraid.

At the same time that we lead some, we must follow others. In fact, following requires gentleness, too. Jesus compared himself to a shepherd, the Good Shepherd who gives his life for his sheep, those who follow him (John 10:1-11). In modern usage the word *sheep* can have negative connotations when describing someone who follows. Sheep could bring to mind images of people who blindly and unquestioningly follow a leader, wherever the leader leads, for good or bad. When Jesus used this image, he had something different in mind. Sheep are submissive animals in contrast to goats which are willful and stubborn. Sheep follow gently. Being a gentle follower means to submit peacefully to someone else's leadership, without demanding to go our own path, without thinking we must continually raise counter-arguments or find every fault with the leader's decisions. Being gentle is more important even than finding fault. When we do need to constructively criticize a leader's decision, then we use humility and choose words that show respect and appreciation.

Giving and receiving counsel with gentleness. Another aspect of our lives that especially requires the practice of gentleness is when we give or receive spiritual instruction. Paul wrote, "Brothers, if someone is caught in a sin, you who are spiritual should restore him gently" (Galatians 6:1). The word *restore* is a good companion to the word *gently* in this passage because, in the Greek language of the New Testament, *restore* expressed the idea of carefully returning something to its original condition, such as setting a broken bone or mending a torn fishing net. The purpose of giving counsel is to help, not to harm. Especially in the case of someone who is weak spiritually, language that communicates care, gives confidence, and points to a positive direction will restore instead of destroy. People who are crushed by the weight of their mistakes do not need to be crushed more. They need gentle counsel that shows them that living pure and productive lives is possible with the Lord's help. Paul also wrote to Timothy about how the Lord's servant ought to conduct himself, "Those who oppose him he must gently instruct, in the hope that God will grant them repentance leading them to a knowledge of the truth, and that they will come to their senses and escape from the trap of the devil who has taken them captive to do his will" (2 Timothy 2:25-26). Those who are trapped in their errors do not need to feel bombarded by the oppressive onslaughts of critical condemnation, no matter how sincere the motives are of those who "instruct." They want to find the way out. They need to learn how to make positive changes in order to live by the truth.

Sometimes parents, in their enthusiasm to correct their children, use language that traps: "You are so lazy!" "You never do your work like you should!" "Why can't you be like your brother!" "You always eat your food like you are going to a race." This kind of language cannot instruct in a productive way. It makes the person feel like they are boxed in by the image that another person has of them. Using the words *never* and *always* closes a person off to the possibilities for change. A person comes to believe about himself that he will always be this way. He will never escape from being this way. We cause similar harm in other relationships when we use this same language which, instead of instructing, demoralizes and destroys the confidence of others.

On the other side of the coin, we accept advice and counsel with gentleness as well. James wrote, "Therefore, get rid of all moral filth and the evil that is so prevalent and humbly accept the word planted in you, which can save you" (James 1:21). The word *humbly* that some versions of the New Testament use in this passage comes from the same Greek word, prautes, translated as *gently*, that we are considering in this study. The one receiving advice needs a gentle heart just as much as the giving the advice. Gentleness when receiving instruction means to respectfully and humbly submit to the instruction just as we said concerning sheep, which gladly follow the shepherd. If we ever think that we already know enough and do not need to learn anything new, we close ourselves off to growth and become stagnant. We guarantee our growth when we have the gentleness to listen, consider, examine ourselves, change what needs changing, and practice the instruction we receive without arrogantly defending ourselves. Just listen! Just think! No need to answer or defend. Just gently receive the implanted word. What can we lose? What are we afraid of?

Addressing differences and agreements with gentleness. Another specific area of life that challenges gentleness includes moments when we involve ourselves in discussions and arguments. These are moments when we are tempted to be aggressive and advance our opinions using forceful language and gestures. Unfortunately, because of the lack of gentleness, we raise walls that separate us even about issues that are ultimately unimportant. In another passage in his letters to Timothy, Paul counseled him about how to handle people who have "an unhealthy interest in controversies and quarrels about words that result in envy, strife, malicious talk, evil suspicions, and constant friction ..." His advice to Timothy was, "But you, man of God, flee from all this, and pursue righteousness, godliness, faith, love, endurance and gentleness" (1 Timothy 6:3-11). He must not only be gentle when instructing but also gentle in the face of controversy. Gentleness gives no room for arguments "for the sake of argument" or "just to prove a point." Divisiveness for the sake of divisiveness originates from pride. Genuine gentleness cannot coexist with pride.

Paul's teaching implies that there are healthy arguments and unhealthy arguments. Of course, we will have disagreements, but how do we know if a discussion about a specific disagreement is healthy or unhealthy? First, ironically, a healthy discussion will not promote our own opinions but, instead, promote the welfare of others. "Nobody should seek his own good, but the good of others." Second, a healthy discussion brings peace, not controversy. There should be movement in the discussion that brings people together instead of separating them even more. "Let us therefore make every effort to do what leads to peace and to mutual edification" (Romans 14:19). Third, Jesus taught, "Settle matters quickly with your adversary" (Matthew 5:25). Sometimes we enter discussions with certain people simply because they are our adversaries, and we believe it is necessary to disagree with them whenever possible. Jesus taught the opposite. We ought to agree whenever we can agree. Fourth, above all, healthy discussions should serve a meaningful purpose. Paul's counsel is that our conversations should reflect what is "helpful for building others up." The problem is that we rarely stop to think if our discussions really have worthwhile purposes that will be important tomorrow, next week, or next year. Does the issue matter? What matters more than winning a discussion is maintaining strong relationships. Relationships have more lasting value than passing disagreements.

If we can first establish the spiritual benefit of some issue, then we can think about how to communicate with gentleness. As in other moments that call for gentleness, we replace arrogance and assertiveness with careful listening, tender consideration of another person's reasoning, and calm expressions of our own perspectives. Without making accusations or putting the other person on the defensive, we gently seek for a solution that is helpful to everyone. Gentleness does not divide but brings people together without fear. Gentleness calms people down and puts them at ease. By evaluating the emotions of the person to whom we are speaking, we can determine the required degree of gentleness.

Providing a defense with gentleness. Peter adds another area of the disciple's life that requires gentleness. Disciples are messengers of the gospel. We live to show others the way to Jesus. We want to show them the beauty of the Christian life by our examples. Naturally, people are going to ask us to give them reasons for our faith. If we hope to convince someone to follow the gentle Savior, we will have to explain the grounds of our faith with gentleness. Peter wrote, "Always be prepared to give an answer to everyone who asks you to give a reason for the hope that you have. But do this with gentleness and respect ..." (1 Peter 3:15).

Perhaps when Peter wrote this passage, he remembered the occasion when he and the other disciples were traveling from Galilee to Jerusalem. On the way they approached a village in Samaria. Remember when Jesus sent messengers into the village to prepare for his arrival, the Samaritan people did not want to receive him into their village because of the prejudice between the Jews and Samaritans. Two of the apostles, James and John, asked Jesus, "Lord, do you want us to call fire down from heaven to destroy them?" These two disciples had forgotten who they were. They were followers of the gentle Savior. Their purpose was not to condemn but to save. Unfortunately, disciples may become so immersed in zealously defending their faith that the power of their words and the force of their voices may seem to the listener like fire coming down from heaven to destroy, instead of filling with hope. Brute force actually betrays a lack of confidence. Remember, gentleness itself comes from power, the power of faith in Jesus. If we really have faith in Jesus, we can speak gently and trust that the power of Jesus' teaching will convince the unbeliever.

Gentleness with our heavenly Father: The most important application of gentleness is not with unbelievers or with fellow believers but in our relationships with our heavenly Father. Despite the fact that his existence comprehends such infinite dimensions, our Creator knows our weaknesses and perfectly understands the limitations of our abilities. Although from our perspectives we might say that his treatment of us is not so gentle at times because of suffering we endure, he knows what we are capable of accomplishing. He carefully allows us to face difficult challenges so we can grow spiritually, developing the faith and courage to be his children. How do we know he has tender feelings toward us? He sent Jesus, his Son, the exact representation of his Being, to show us his gentleness. When Jesus placed his hands on the children, when he protected the sinful woman from the ones who were about to stone her, when he wept at the tomb of Lazarus, and when he tenderly lifted a young boy to his feet after healing him of terrific convulsions, he revealed the gentleness of our heavenly Father. Each time Jesus told someone, "Don't be afraid," he helped them understand that the Father wants to take away all of our fears. The Father wants us to feel at ease and at peace with him because we trust his gentleness.

Knowing the gentleness of our Father toward us, we ought to think about how we can practice gentleness toward him. Of course, he is not weak nor does he require our tender care. Gentleness in our relationships with the Father is the submissive character of a servant willingly obeying his master. Gentleness, for instance, characterizes our prayers. We ask, we ask persistently, we even humbly beg that he will grant us what we need, but we make no demands since he is the Creator and perfectly knows our needs. If we do not receive what we desire, we do not protest or make demands but, instead, accept his will, trusting in his wisdom and love for us. The apostle Paul repeatedly asked the Lord to relieve him of some physical suffering he was experiencing. When the Lord answered him in the negative, saying, "My grace is sufficient for you, for my power is made perfect in weakness" (2 Corinthians 12:9), Paul accepted the answer. Paul gently responded to the Lord's denial of his petition. He gladly thanked the Lord for the power that already worked in him as a disciple.

Furthermore, we practice gentleness in our relationships with our Father when we obey his commands with gentle submission, enjoying the beauty of life with him. Without complaining or objecting, we do what pleases him. John, after years of experience following the teachings of Jesus and submitting himself to the will of the Father, wrote, "This is love for God: to obey his commands. And his commands are not burdensome" (1 John 5:3). A gentle attitude toward the Lord allows him to transform us into his image. Imagine a small child stubbornly crying while his parent tries to dress him for the day. As children of God, gentleness means to allow the Lord to dress us in the "fine linen, bright and clean" (Revelation 19:8) of righteousness. We do not grudgingly resign ourselves to predetermined destinies but, instead, joyfully serve him, praising him for the purpose and meaning he has given our lives.

With some ideas in mind about applying gentleness in specific aspects of our lives, we can constantly look for other similar moments that call for gentleness. Each step we take to grow in gentleness by practicing tender care, compassionate consideration, calm submission, and acceptance takes us closer to Jesus and the image of our heavenly Father. We might become discouraged when the behavior of some people challenges our desire to be gentle, but, in such moments, we will grow more quickly if we trust completely in the Lord's way of gentleness. We have someone who supports us in every moment. We can trust in gentleness because we trust in our gentle Savior.

CHAPTER NINE

SELF-CONTROL: POWER FOR A NEW LIFE

"I PRESS ON TO TAKE HOLD OF THAT FOR WHICH CHRIST TOOK HOLD OF ME" (PHILIPPIANS 3:12).

Paul began the list of the fruit of the Spirit with love, a fitting way to begin because love must motivate and permeate everything disciples do. Without love beautiful deeds are nothing more than a "resounding gong or a clanging cymbal." A clanging cymbal makes lots of noise to attract attention to itself without producing any genuine music for the benefit of others. Without love for others, our efforts to cultivate the fruit of the Spirit would only serve to glorify ourselves as we look for pats on the back and words of praise for being a good person. But with self-sacrificing, unconditional love, the practice of peace, patience, kindness, and gentleness reaches a higher level, supporting the good of others before one's own welfare. When motivated by love, gentleness will not be a tool to manipulate others but, instead, will be a way of making people feel truly safe and accepted. Kindness accompanied by love becomes a joyous way of life instead of a duty seldom practiced. Patience that flows from a heart rooted in love is consistent and enduring.

If love is an excellent beginning, then self-control is a fitting way to end the list of the fruit of the Spirit. This final quality, when properly understood, provides the power to focus our lives on the process of learning and practicing all the other fruit of the Spirit.

UNDERSTANDING

The Greek word translated *self-control* is formed from a root word that means *strength*. It refers to the *inner strength* necessary to control thoughts, desires, and actions to achieve a specific goal. It is the strength to remain focused on the goal despite distractions. At certain times thoughts come rushing into our minds like a roaring flood; at other times just one thought enters our minds, but that one thought becomes a drowning obsession. Some stay briefly, causing momentary diversions, maybe even producing quick, impulsive reactions; others remain with us for some time, coloring our perceptions of the world around us. Such thoughts can either influence behavior for good or for evil, for constructive or destructive results. This brainstorm needs to come under control in order for us to live a productive life practicing the fruit of the Spirit. One could hardly think, for instance, of developing gentleness without self-control. Gentleness needs inner strength to replace an aggressive spirit with calm and respectful acceptance. Without self-control there would be little hope of reigning in aggression. Faith requires inner strength to replace doubts and fears with trust in the Lord. The practice of goodness depends on having sufficient power to choose good over evil, especially when evil appears to be more pleasing and satisfying.

The apostle Paul's well-known comparison between the life of a Christian and the life of a runner paints a brilliant image of the meaning and practice of self-control.

SELF-CONTROL: POWER FOR A NEW LIFE

> Do you not know that in a race all the runners run, but only one gets the prize? Run in such a way as to get the prize. Everyone who competes in the games goes into strict training. They do it to get a crown that will not last; but we do it to get a crown that will last forever. Therefore I do not run like a man running aimlessly; I do not fight like a man beating the air. No, I beat my body and make it my slave so that after I have preached to others, I myself will not be disqualified for the prize (1 Corinthians 9:24-27).

A runner focuses on a goal and determines to achieve it. Paul also said that, in the Christian life, he does not "run aimlessly; I do not fight like a man beating the air." The goal of running might be to finish the day's practice run with a decent time, methodically increase endurance over a period of several months of practice, or ultimately to win a competitive race. The more important the goal is to the runner, the more dedication he or she will invest in training to achieve the goal. Some people run because they enjoy running and have no desire to enter competition, and, in that case, the goal is enjoyment. If for some reason the person ceases to enjoy running, then the determination to train will weaken since the goal of enjoyment is missing.

Self-control is the strength that fuels determination. Determination and, therefore, self-control both require a goal. Self-control just for the sake of self-control does not make sense. Imagine a weight-lifter who lifts weight to become stronger. Once he is fairly strong, with rippling, bulging muscles, we could correctly ask, now what are you going to do with this? The more valuable or the more meaningful the goal is, the more inner strength a person will be willing to cultivate in achieving it. If a person, for instance, has difficulty getting out of bed in the morning and wants to develop more self-control to do so, then the goal will have to be sufficiently valuable, more valuable than the pleasure of staying in bed. If there is not a strong enough reason to get up early, then developing the self-control to triumph over sleep will be difficult. There has to be a good reason behind the effort.

When people struggle to control their anger, the root of the problem may be the lack of desire to achieve the goal. A weak desire for the goal weakens the desire to develop the inner strength necessary to control anger. We assume that everyone should want to control anger, but anger often serves a purpose that is pleasing in a sort of twisted way. Anger gets results. Anger is useful to manipulate and control people. Anger serves as an emotional release. It is a tool to avoid responsibility or guilt. If someone wants to develop the strength to control anger, the rewards of having a calm and peaceful spirit have to be more important than the deceptively appealing rewards of anger. Whether the goal is getting out of bed on time, replacing anger with calm and patience, or developing any of the other fruit of the Spirit, we have to be convinced that the prize is worth the effort. As disciples of Jesus, our prize is very much worth the effort. Our goal in the Christian life is nothing less than enjoying life with the Father through spiritual transformation in his image.

Furthermore, a runner must run to win if he expects to receive the prize. During a long race, a runner's enthusiasm can waver. Doubts can fill her mind, and she might begin to lose heart and think about slowing down. She needs inner strength to overcome those negative thoughts, replacing them with confidence and courage. Working toward achieving a goal is normally a process that involves periods of ups and downs. Maintaining a consistent level of enthusiasm is naturally difficult because it requires constant physical and emotional energy to keep enthusiasm high. The necessary self-control to balance the highs and lows depends on finding adequate sources of energy.

On the other hand, having too much emotional energy can be counterproductive. If a runner, for instance, has too much enthusiasm at the beginning of a race and runs a fast pace, then he may not have sufficient energy at the end to finish the race. He must carefully control his level of excitement at the beginning and pace himself, using wisdom in expending his effort. Self-control in running includes the inner strength to control and channel physical energy and emotions in a productive way toward victory.

In a similar way, the Christian life requires the ability to sustain the emotional and spiritual energy necessary to continue the process of spiritual transformation as we learn to imitate the character of Christ. We are running to follow Jesus. Transformation is a long marathon. We are developing qualities that we hope become consistent habits, manifesting themselves in a myriad of ways in our daily lives. It is not an easy run. As we have previously seen, these qualities we desire to develop grow especially during challenges and crises. The moments of crisis demand unwavering power to pass through them successfully. Love grows most deeply when we learn to love our enemies. Joy becomes an abiding contentment in our spirits after facing disappointment or tragedy. Peace rises out of conflict. If the goal is to develop constancy in the practice of Christ's image, then the inner strength to practice must be constant.

Running well in a competitive race requires physical strength as well as the inner strength of positive, healthy emotions. To build up his physical strength, a runner follows a carefully formulated plan of training that includes various running exercises, weight training, and dietary requirements. To follow this plan of physical development, the runner will also need inner strength on an emotional level. He will need optimism, enthusiasm, determination, courage, and hope. These emotions give him the inner strength to be consistent in his physical training program and focused in the moment of running the race. But this inner emotional strength is, in turn, based on the desire he has to win or at least to run with all his effort. The stronger his desire is for the goal, the stronger his enthusiasm, determination, and courage will be. Inner emotional strength can come from other sources as well, such as the credible encouragement of friends, inspiring stories of successful runners, and even music that directly affects the emotions. He also needs someone he trusts who can confidently tell him, "You can win!"

Running the Christian race—making every effort to live a transformed life—does not require special physical strength but a special kind of emotional strength on a spiritual level. Christians often speak about "spiritual strength," but what does this phrase refer to? What is spiritual strength, exactly? God's Spirit experiences emotions, such as joy (Romans 14:17) and grief (Ephesians 4:30). Furthermore, God created us in his spiritual image and our spirits feel emotions, too, that are distinct from the emotions that are the results of the chemically-based physiological processes of our brains. Physical emotions are not the only kind of emotions we feel. We can also feel emotions in our spirits just like God's Spirit feels emotions. Our spirits are not nebulous, floating things like patches of smoke that occupy containers; rather we *are* our spirits. From our own experience we know that on a physical level we can be enthusiastically involved in a rewarding physical activity while, at the same time, we feel empty and even desperate on some deeper level of our being. In a similar way, feelings of depression may have physiological causes that are treatable with medications that regulate the balance of chemicals in the brain; but we may also feel discouraged in our spirits and the only solution for this kind of spiritual depression is a more immediate sense of God's loving presence near us.

We can think of spiritual strength as the strength of the emotions of our spirits that motivate us to remain very close to the heavenly Father. He created our spirits to enjoy fellowship with him. We feel enthusiasm, joy, and contentment in our spirits when we sense his presence with us. We feel love and peace not just as qualities to cultivate in our behavior toward others but as feelings too. These emotions have the power to motivate us to develop the fruit of the Spirit so that we can live in closer harmony and fellowship with the Father. To be spiritually strong must mean that these emotions are strong and have motivating power.

What are some sources for the inner strength that we develop in our spirits? The emotional aspects of this strength come, for example, from the advantages of living by the direction and rule of God's Spirit. Just like a runner's determination and courage depend on the desire she has to achieve her goal of running, our enthusiasm and determination as disciples of Jesus depend on the desire we have for living a transformed life. Why do we want to learn to practice compassion or mercy? Are we looking for the satisfaction of being recognized and praised by other people as a noble person? If our motivation depends on people then our energy level to live the right life will be up and down, depending on how much people notice and praise our good works.

Instead of attempting to live in harmony with the expectations of people, the focus of living a transformed life is to live in harmony with the Spirit of God, desiring what the Spirit desires. The Spirit of God most deeply desires for us to live a transformed life in the image of our Creator. Through the revealed word, the Spirit teaches us to live in compassion and mercy because these qualities form part of our Creator's character. To live in intimate relationship with our heavenly Father must be the deepest desire of our spirits too. Our spirits thirst for God. We feel empty in our spirits when we live without meaningful, eternal purpose, disconnected from him. Living in love as our Father loves gives us immediate access into his presence. To enjoy this fellowship with God is a powerful motivation that gives us the strength to make difficult decisions and sacrifice even our physical welfare to practice humility, generosity, and forgiveness.

Walking in harmony with the Spirit provides inner emotional strength in other ways besides having a sufficiently powerful desire. There will be others who also share the same profound desire for transformation. Jesus formed the church, his body, with the purpose of providing the strength we need to achieve our goal. We instruct each other (Colossians 3:16), and we stimulate and encourage each other (Hebrews 10:24) to live a transformed life. We watch the lives of those who go before us and learn from their experiences how to practice gentleness and kindness. When we struggle to forgive someone of an offense he has committed against us, we need a trusted companion who can tell us, "You can do this!"

Creating the habit of reading, understanding, and mediating on the Scriptures also gives us the inner strength to keep our emotions focused on our goal. The teachings of Jesus, recorded in the New Testament, have the power to continually open our hearts and minds to the deeper truths about practice. Carefully reading over and over again the narrative of Jesus washing the disciples' feet brings our hearts into harmony with the Spirit. Each time we read, the story reveals something new, on a deeper level. We feel the amazement, the tenderness, and the humility of serving that the Spirit wants us to feel. These emotions give us the confidence to go out and practice serving as our Lord did. Reading over and over again, meditating carefully on the parable of the good Samaritan, opening our hearts to its treasure of truths, the words of God's Son have the power to completely change our views about who our neighbors are and what we can do for them. We feel the enthusiasm for generosity and the determination to freely love that the Spirit of God desires us to feel. With the mind of the Spirit—our minds in harmony with the Spirit's mind—we have the energy to go out and practice loving our neighbors as ourselves. Think attentively, deliberately, and deeply about the story of the sinful woman whom Jesus forgave during the dinner in Simon's house. Understand the sadness and guilt she first felt and then the relief, joy, and gratitude that filled her spirit when Jesus said, "Your sins are forgiven." You will feel what God's Spirit wants your spirit to feel. You will find the inner strength to go out and to forgive as Jesus has forgiven you.

The necessary inner strength to live a transformed life also depends on receiving another kind of power which is communicated Spirit to spirit and that is essential to cultivating the fruit of the Spirit. The greatest problem that we face in the process of developing the qualities of our Father's character is consistency. Our determination waxes and wanes. Some days we thrill at having moments to show compassion. Other days we may feel apathetic or even resentful if we have to take time out of our busy schedules and use funds from our hard-earned resources to help someone who is in need. Our emotions themselves are inconsistent. If someone comes along to try to encourage us to be generous, we might react with frustration at having to listen to the advice of others. Even the desire to read and meditate may be inconsistent. Spiritual consistency requires a source of power that is not affected by our physical well-being or the physical circumstances surrounding us. We can have this level of strength. We can ask for it in prayer.

Paul described a prayer that he was praying on behalf of the Christians at Ephesus.

> For this reason I kneel before the Father, from whom his whole family in heaven and on earth derives its name. I pray that out of his glorious riches he may strengthen you with power through his Spirit in your inner being, so that Christ may dwell in your hearts through faith. And I pray that you, being rooted and established in love, may have power, together with all the saints, to grasp how wide and long and high and deep is the love of Christ, and to know this love that surpasses knowledge—that you may be filled to the measure of all the fullness of God (Ephesians 3:14-19).

Paul prayed that the Lord would "strengthen" the Ephesians in their "inner being." The word *strengthen* in this text is from the same root word in Greek that also forms the word translated as *self-control* in the list of the fruit of the Spirit. Paul was praying that the Lord would provide the Ephesian Christians precisely the inner strength that we desperately need to be consistent in our practice. This strength is Spirit to spirit because it is power that comes from God's Spirit and is communicated directly to our spirits.

The purpose of this strength is to empower us so that Christ can live in our hearts. Remember *heart* stands for our emotions and desires. In other words, this strength allows us to submit our desires and emotions to the will of Christ so that he fills them with his desires and joy. Loving to live the Christ-life is not a passing desire for us but, instead, is the controlling emotion that directs our life.

He lives in our emotions so that we feel what he feels. Then as a result of receiving this strength we become "rooted and established in love." Imagine a strong tree, firmly rooted, that does not move, despite the winds and storms. The Spirit of God can strengthen our spirits with sufficient power so that the teachings of Jesus can consistently rule our hearts. Then we will become rooted in love, unwavering, never tiring, and always growing in our practice. We will have the consistency to practice love even when loving another person is costly to us, when on some level of our consciousness we do not feel like loving, and when we receive nothing in return for love.

The risks and challenges of actually practicing Christ's level of love teach us what we can never learn by simply reading and meditating about love. Through the practice of consistent, unconditional love, we discover that it must be deep enough to never end, wide enough to include even the most distant lost soul, and high enough to reach the heart of God.

Furthermore, the nature of unconditional love is similar to the nature of other spiritual qualities such as mercy, kindness, gentleness, compassion, patience, and forgiveness. The same spiritual strength is necessary to bring practice to the level of habit. There will always be moments that test our consistency and threaten our goal of forming these qualities into spiritual habits. In such moments we can pray the same prayer Paul prayed and believe that the Lord will graciously fill us with this special form of strength in order to complete the power we need to live a transformed life.

Accepting by faith that the Spirit of God lives in us changes the way we view our transformation into God's image. We understand that, not only are we not alone, but that the presence of God envelopes us personally. The fact that the Spirit lives in us means the Spirit knows our hearts, knows what we are feeling, and responds to those feelings. When we occupy our thoughts with bitterness, resentment, anger, or malice, we actually "grieve" the Spirit (Ephesians 4:30-31). In such moments our own spirits become weak and frustrated by the temptation to hate or retaliate. If we surrender to temptation by actually hating and retaliating, the grief we feel in our spirits is also felt by God's Spirit. Our grief, in fact, increases when we realize that our behavior has not only grieved our spirits but has also saddened the Spirit of God.

On the other hand, the joy we experience living in God's kingdom is "joy in the Holy Spirit" (Romans 14:17). The joy of transformation in God's kingdom is also felt by God's Spirit in us. Our joy multiplies, realizing that we have also brought joy to the Spirit of God by practicing the qualities of God's character. Imagine the consolation and strength of having someone by your side who experiences what you experience, shares your grief when you are sad, and celebrates your joy when you are successful. Imagine that the person who participates so intimately with our hearts is the Spirit of God. The incredible joy of this intimate relationship becomes a strong motivation to stay focused and determined in the pursuit of transformation. We are not without help from the Spirit.

We can now understand two important truths about the nature of self-control. First, self-control is a fruit of the Spirit. Having sufficient inner strength to remain firmly in the path of living a transformed life depends on living in harmony with the mind of God's Spirit as well as using the resources we have to increase the strength of our spirits. We should spend much time with the Scriptures and allow our fellow disciples to instruct and encourage us. The inner strength of self-control is also a fruit of the Spirit's work to strengthen us directly in our spirits; but we must develop the discipline of asking for and depending on this strength.

Secondly, we understand that self-control, according to the teaching of the New Testament, is not about self controlling self. It is not about learning to practice grit-your-teeth stubbornness to remain focused on a goal, ignore distractions, and struggle to move forward. It is not about finding the determination to "just say no" when we are confronted by temptation. The English word *self-control* is actually misleading in the context of the New Testament teaching. Ironically, self-control in the New Testament is really about surrendering self. The inner strength we need to imitate the character of our Father comes from surrendering our former mentality with its false goals and misplaced confidence in our own power to change ourselves. Then we surrender to the teachings of Jesus as our Lord, who alone has the right to rule in our lives. We surrender to the mind of God's Spirit who wishes for us to live in the image of the Lord. We also surrender to the special strength that comes from the Spirit who empowers us. Such surrender requires practice but brings us contentment, confidence, and joy in the process of transformation.

If self-control is a fruit of the Spirit then what exactly is our responsibility in developing this inner strength? Our job is to use the resources we have in the Christian life to increase the emotional strength of our spirits; then we use this inner strength to cultivate the other qualities we develop in the image of our Lord. Inner strength must accompany all the other qualities. As we learn to practice love, joy, peace, patience, kindness, goodness, faith, and gentleness, we will need to develop the necessary inner strength to empower practice, especially in challenging moments. Self-control is the power that enables consistent practice.

Turning the fruit of the Spirit into consistent habits is a process that consists of four essential steps—reflection, repentance, replacement, and retraining—which we will now consider. These steps can map the course of transformation on the most specific, particular levels. For instance, if we wish to grow in gentleness, we think of one particular aspect of gentleness that we would like to learn to practice. Perhaps we would like to learn to speak with more gentleness. Then we can think of some specific circumstances or relationships in which we would like to speak with more gentleness. On this most specific level of gentleness, we begin with reflection, proceed with repentance and replacement and then finally work toward retraining to form a new consistent habit. Each of these steps requires strength in our spirits to proceed to the next one without deviating from our goal. As we move from one step to the next, growing in the specific quality, we will discover something surprising: our spiritual strength also increases through the practice of the quality. We grow in conviction, confidence, and joy through successful practice. The process is reciprocal: the inner strength of self-control motivates practice and consistent practice builds more strength.

What follows is a discussion of these four steps of transformation and an explanation about how to develop inner strength for each step.

REFLECTION

Psalm 119:59 says, "I have considered my ways and have turned my steps unto your statutes." The first step toward developing the fruit of the Spirit is reflection: stopping to think about our own thoughts and behavior. God created human beings with the unique ability of self-reflection. Our spirits, created in his image, are that part of our nature that possesses our authentic identities. We change physically from day to day, growing older and, ultimately, lose the physical existence we have tried so hard to preserve. Our spirits, on the other hand, can grow stronger every day. The apostle Paul wrote, "Though outwardly we are wasting away, yet inwardly we are being renewed day by day" (2 Corinthians 4:16). Although we practice the fruit of the Spirit in our physical behavior as we live in this material world, our spirits are that part of our nature that possesses these qualities. The unconditional love that we practice in the image of our Father is first of all a characteristic of our spirits that we then practice in our physical behavior.

Our spirits also give us the ability for genuine self-reflection. Each time we stop to reflect, to think about our thoughts and behavior, our spirits provide the possibility for the deepest level of reflection. The mind, that is the brain, is an organ made up of billions of nerve cells that communicate with each other through electrochemical reactions. The brain receives information from the physical senses and processes the information in view of experiences we have had. Those experiences exist as stored memories. Memories form our images of the world and cause us to interpret and store future information in terms of those images.

For instance, a child who has had an abusive father might have many memories of how cruel someone in authority can be. Those memories can cause the child to grow up with emotions of fear, resentment, rebellion, and even hatred for other people who try to exercise similar authority in his life. Many memories of such negative experiences can form habitual and even impulsive reactions to any authority figures, such as the teacher at school, the boss at work, or even God. In the future as an adult, he may receive new experiences to form new memories with a new understanding that not all authority figures are cruel; however, a mental battle will take place between rebelling against and yielding to authority. Sometimes just seeing someone in authority will cause him to react in physical ways, feeling the desire for aggression or the insecurity of fear as physical symptoms in his body.

The amazing aspect of human capacity is the conscious ability to stop to analyze one's own thoughts. Thinking does not have to be an automatic, uncontrollable reaction to experiences. After critically analyzing our thinking, if we conclude that our thoughts are not rational or justifiable, we can consciously change not only the momentary thought but also the habitual way we think, consciously training our minds to think differently.

If human beings have this power to control the physical processes of the brain in order to stop a certain form of thinking and consciously replace it with a different form of thinking, that power has to come from something distinct from the physical brain itself. Something must be able to control the thoughts of the mind. But what controls the thoughts of the mind to actually change the deeper structure of our thinking cannot be the mind itself. Imagine if a computer program needs to be altered or rewritten, the computer itself, basically consisting of electrical signals controlling on and off switches, cannot create these changes; they have to come from a higher level of power or control. A human mind, separate and apart from the computer, has to create these changes and impose them on the computer.

Similarly the electrochemical processes, representing the activity of our physical brains, need to be restructured to think differently, requiring a higher level of control beyond the physical nature of the brain itself. Electrochemical processes can explain how thinking and memory happens on a physical level; but these processes cannot adequately account for the conscious restructuring of thought—when we consciously decide we are going to think differently. Something is controlling and redirecting the course of our thinking, just like the programmer redirects the actions of the on and off switches of the computer. The power to reflect—to think about thinking—and decide to impose a new structure of thought must be the role of our spirits, and, in fact, represents evidence for the existence of our spirits.

Considering the case of the person who is tempted to rebel against images of authority, his spirit can stop the mind's flood of rebellious thoughts and analyze them to decide if rebellion is really the appropriate response. If he decides he ought to change the usual course of his thinking, he can consciously choose to learn and retain new healthy images that would view authority in a neutral way, evaluating specific examples of authority without prejudice. He would consciously seek to accumulate positive experiences of authority and use them to restructure his mind's response to authority figures.

One of the obstacles to reflection is impulsiveness. Impulsive behavior, acting without thinking, inhibits the thoughtfulness of genuine reflection. Impulsive reactions are necessary in many moments when we have to make split-second decisions without mentally running through all the possible consequences. If we touch something hot, we do not think about the pros and cons of removing our fingers from the hot object, we simply react. If we see someone about to cross the street in front of a car, we impulsively scream at the person, "Watch out!" We do not stop and think whether we will be embarrassed if we scream or whether the person might become angry with us for yelling at her. But there are plenty of other moments in our experiences when impulsive reactions risk destructive consequences.

Impulsive rage is a good example of destructive behavior that detours around reflection and heads straight for the abyss. We feel offended, frustrated, or cheated and react in the moment with abusive anger without thinking. We jump from feeling to action without thinking. Before we express a potentially dangerous emotion like rage, we ought to progress from feeling to thinking and then to action. Unfortunately, sometimes we actually do think, for example, between the moment of being offended and the moment of reacting with abusive language, but the kind of thinking we do is to justify ourselves. Instead of stopping long enough to critically analyze the circumstances and ask whether rage is the appropriate reaction that would produce a constructive result, we only think of why we believe rage is necessary. "If I don't get angry, they won't understand I am serious!"

It is a well-known neurological fact that the emotional centers of the brain can hijack the rational centers of the brain. Instead of rationally thinking through the solution to a conflict, we react with an immediate emotional response. Impulse of this kind is a physical response in which the brain works based on emotional memory. To control impulses that are potentially destructive, we have to shift thinking from emotions to rational thought. How will we make this shift? We will have to think about how we think, consciously analyze what our brains are doing, and then impose a new way of thinking, a new structure of thought.

Genuine reflection is not easy for other reasons besides impulsiveness. Sometimes we are afraid to stop and think. In the mad rush that many people follow toward ambitious goals and even toward goals that are far from ambitious, there is little time for deep, meditative, and honest reflection. Maybe they are afraid to stop and think about their lives because they are not sure of where they are going. Asking serious questions about one's own self can be frightening, especially without a strong faith to provide the foundation for life and its purpose.

Hidden guilt also keeps people from reflecting on their lives because of the fear of discovering who they are. They subconsciously keep running, never standing still to think about themselves, because they cannot afford to think of their mistakes or failures. Pride also inhibits self-reflection. The arrogance of thinking that one is righteous, without the need for changing some behavior, is merely a too obvious cover for insecurity. The sad result of not taking the time or having the humility to stop and reflect is to continue on the same path of self-destruction, repeating the same habits, like a disciplined soldier marching in precise, high-stepping movements toward certain death.

Our natural inclination to defend ourselves also works against self-reflection. On our most basic animal level we defend ourselves against threats just like other animals. When physical threats confront us, we have the choice to escape, surrender, or fight. We also make the same choices when we face emotional threats. People accuse us. They criticize us. They demean us. They abandon us. We even accuse ourselves of not being good enough or failing to be the person we believe we ought to be. In response we feel guilt, shame, and insecurity—feelings that are very painful. We must do something to dull the pain if we have not found the cure for the disease. We have choices to make. Will we escape by retreating from people, creating our own fantasy world, or abusing drugs and alcohol? Will we surrender to the opinions of other people, conforming to their values, and molding ourselves in the image they demand that we bear? Will we defend ourselves with rigorous self-justification, angry retaliation, ambitious attempts to prove ourselves, or arrogant expressions of superiority? Whatever we choose to use to protect ourselves will also serve to blind ourselves from seeing who we really are. If we cannot see ourselves, we will not be able to begin to live a transformed life in Christ.

Reflection is the necessary first step toward transformation that requires the inner strength of self-control. Because of the tendency to make impulsive decisions and the fear of examining ourselves, we need inner strength to reflect on our thoughts and behavior. To practice gentleness we need the power to stop and reflect when we are tempted to react with impatience or aggression. We also need strength to face our habit of being severe, without blinding ourselves with self-justification. Where will we acquire this power?

As children of God we have the incomparable blessing of a Father who is full of grace and patiently forgiving. His acceptance can be powerful enough to enable us to overcome the insecurity and shame that threaten us. When we are born again as children of God, we have a unique relationship with him that is living and powerful. As our Creator his opinion of us is infinitely more valuable than the judgments of our fellow human beings. The truth is that we do make mistakes—sometimes dreadful mistakes with horrible consequences—but our Father is forgiving. Like the father of the lost son in Jesus' parable, God runs to forgive us. The deepest desire of his heart is not to accuse but to forgive and empower us to be transformed into his image. He sent Jesus to suffer in our place so that we would not have to defend ourselves.

His gracious forgiveness is a theme that inspires gratitude and love in our hearts; but in order for his grace to empower us to reflect on our lives without fear, it will have to be more than just a beautiful theme to consider. We will have to internalize his grace. To internalize his grace means to allow it to become part of our essence, controlling what we think about ourselves and how we view other people. Our lives become expressions of God's grace. There is no more self-justification, no more casting blame on others. We, like the tax collector in another parable of Jesus, simply cry out to him, "God, have mercy on me, a sinner" (Luke 18:13). By accepting his grace, we are not surrendering to a tragic view of ourselves, but, instead, we are allowing our spirits to begin to heal. He cures the disease so that we no longer have to escape, surrender, or defend ourselves. He is our defense. About the tax collector, Jesus said, "I tell you that this man.... went home justified before God." We immerse our hearts in his grace and he declares, "Of course my child is not without mistakes but forgiven and on the way to transformation." We will know that we have internalized his grace when we treat others with the same gracious forgiveness. We accept his grace into our spirits and manifest it in our behavior. Internalizing his grace makes self-reflection a joy, not a threat.

When we have become comfortable with honest self-reflection, we need a way of evaluating our thoughts and behavior in order to know when to control them and how to change them. The word of God provides this norm or standard to measure thoughts and behavior. James 3:17-18, for instance, serves as an effective tool for measuring our thoughts by describing the characteristics of true wisdom: "But the wisdom that comes from heaven is first of all pure; then peace-loving, considerate, submissive, full of mercy and good fruit, impartial and sincere." We can use these qualities to judge our own thoughts and determine when we need to control and change our thinking to produce healthy behavior. The teachings of Jesus serve the essential and irreplaceable role of forming the standard by which we can decide, upon reflection, what we must change in our thinking. Now we know what our Creator expects of us and what is possible concerning the practice of forgiveness, compassion, generosity, and humility.

Furthermore, we do not have to be ashamed that we sometimes fail to practice what is possible. We are in the process of transformation. Instead of wasting our energy on self-justification, we can now focus our spiritual energy on learning to practice. Letting the teachings of Jesus guide our practice is what Paul means by "keeping in step with the Spirit" or "walking in harmony with the Spirit" (Galatians 5:25). Knowing the direction we are going, without confusion, gives us inner strength to reflect on our lives.

We also benefit from the gentle, caring counsel of fellow disciples who can help us with self-reflection. A patient brother or sister, who shares our same faith in Jesus and who graciously accepts us the way our Father accepts us, can help us see ourselves. One who has intimate, practical knowledge of Jesus' teaching and who has the gentleness and humility to reveal the ways we can change our behavior is an instrument in God's hands to assist us. We need someone who can tell us, "Run hard! You can do it!" His or her counsel and encouragement is strength for our spirits. Our job is to relax our defenses, calm our spirits, and listen.

The inner strength our spirits need for self-reflection also comes from the Spirit of God. Part of learning to reflect on our lives includes learning how to depend on this help. Remember that we can pray that the Father will bless us with this form of strength. Paul wrote to the Roman Christians about the help of God's Spirit. "Hope does not disappoint us, because God has poured out his love into our hearts by the Holy Spirit, whom he has given us" (Romans 5:5). God's love is not something we just read about on the pages of a book. He can communicate his love to us in a very intimate way from his Spirit to our spirits. Even though we may not be cognitively aware of how it happens, our spirits experience the love that can only come from the Father. Knowing that his love for us is a reality provides us the strength we need to be honest with ourselves and admit the ways we must change in order to live in his image. His love for us is not like a shield that we raise whenever we feel attacked by others. Instead it is our motivation to continue surrendering ourselves to transformation. Because he loves us so deeply, we desire what he wants for us. We want to live in harmony with him, the One who has sacrificed so much to love us.

The patient grace of our heavenly Father, the teachings of Jesus that provide us a standard to evaluate our behavior, the accepting, encouraging counsel of fellow disciples, and the love that God's Spirit pours out upon our spirits are sources of inner strength that empower the step of reflection. Our task is to use these forms of strength to grow strong enough in our spirits to freely reflect on our lives and know where to focus our energy in the process of transformation.

Now imagine a person who is easily irritated, very critical, and quick to respond aggressively. He has been angry for a long time and habitually justifies his behavior as normal. What will make him stop and be open enough to consider his anger and the possibility of changing? What will allow him to accept responsibility for the harm he is causing? Over a period of time, anger had been building a wall that prohibited any meaningful communication, and now his children simply do not listen. He feels ashamed and guilty, but, until now, he has fought to defend himself against the accusations of his conscience. But recently someone has spoken to him about God's gracious acceptance in a very personal way. Considering God's grace, he discovers a feeling of being safe enough to think of his anger as something he needs to resolve instead avoiding responsibility. It is his problem, but it does not make him evil or beyond change. He starts to listen to himself speak with so much criticism and negativity. He thinks about the things that irritate him and realizes how much he must irritate people. With the help of a gentle, caring brother in Christ, he starts to realize that the fear his family members feel when he responds impulsively and aggressively is not healthy and cannot be justified. He does not like what he sees, but at least now he is able to see because of the strength growing in his spirit. He sees his anger in a new light. It belongs to him. It does not depend on anyone else's conduct. He owns it and only he can decide to resolve it.

Self-reflection is the first step toward cultivating each of the fruit of the Spirit. Self-reflection will even help us cultivate more of the inner strength of self-control. Putting aside our fears, we stop to reflect on our weaknesses in the process of transformation and decide how to develop the strength we need. If we determine to put more trust in the strength that comes from our relationship with the Father, we will have to practice trusting him. It is similar to teaching a child to swim. At first the child may be afraid and kick and scream in the water instead of letting the water's buoyancy support his body. Once he learns to relax and trust the water while moving his arms and legs in the appropriate ways, he discovers how easy swimming is. Imagine that the water is God's grace. It supports us, keeping us afloat while we move toward transformation. Through practice we learn to relax and trust his mercy; then we can move on to reflect on our lives without fear. Because of God's mercy and forgiveness, there is nothing to fear from self-reflection, and everything to gain. He is ready to heal us if we are ready to look inside of ourselves and joyfully submit to his rule in our lives.

REPENTANCE

The result of honest reflection can be the discovery of an attitude or behavior that does not harmonize with the image of our Father. Reflection should point us in a very specific direction of spiritual growth, such as the need to communicate with more gentleness in a certain family relationship, the need to show more mercy to a certain individual with whom we work, or the need to put away anger as an impulsive response to offensive behavior in a specific situation. Without fear we humbly uncover and confront an aspect of our character that needs improvement or replacement. Now that we know what to change, how do we change? Repentance is the next step. Just like reflection, repentance also requires the inner strength we know as self-control, and, at the same time, our inner strength increases as we practice repentance.

The word *repentance* in the New Testament is translated from a Greek word that means *to think differently* or *to change one's mind*. Today we commonly use the English word *repentance* only in spiritual contexts and it has come to have a religious sound to it. In the Greek language, this word simply expressed the common idea of changing one's mind. It appears many times in the New Testament. To understand the significance Jesus gives to changing one's mind, read a large sample of the passages in the New Testament that use the word *repentance* and replace it with *change of mind*. For instance, Jesus said, "The kingdom of God is near. Change your mind (repent) and believe the good news!" (Mark 1:15) Read in this way, such passages take on a more practical tone and reveal the Lord's emphasis on changing our minds.

Why is repentance so fundamental to transformation? One difficulty with learning to control any negative or destructive behavior is that, on some level, we still feel pleasure from the behavior or believe that the behavior is not really very harmful. Repentance means to understand the actual harm clearly enough to have a sufficiently powerful desire to change the behavior. People who are very critical of other people may recognize that they need to change this behavior. They have read in the New Testament that our communication should express "what is helpful for building others up according to their needs, that it may benefit those who listen." Reflecting on their own behavior, they have come to see that their conversations with certain friends or family members involve a lot of negative criticism. In moments of clear thinking, they understand they cannot rationally justify so much criticism. Yet, so far they have not been able to curb their habit.

The problem is that, although they understand destructive criticism is unhealthy and morally wrong, they have not completely changed their mind about it. On some level, even subconsciously, they feel a degree of pleasure from being critical. Criticism compensates for their lack of self-esteem, allowing them to feel superior to other people. They feel in control and powerful because, using criticism as a tool, they can manipulate what people think and do. As long as they enjoy this destructive pleasure, even subconsciously, they will continue to criticize. How will they genuinely change their minds?

This question is basic to living a transformed life. So many of us think we have changed our minds about destructive habits, but then we fail to consistently change our practice. We may slow down for a time and appear to change, but, in an unguarded moment, we repeat the same behavior. We know alcoholics and drug addicts have this problem, but we are surprised to find that, in a similar way, we cannot seem to shake our anger or get rid of our bitterness. Whatever the behavior is that we need to change, we face the same threat of relapse that others do. How can we change our minds profoundly enough to avoid relapse?

The apostle Paul explained that there is a specific kind of sorrow that can bring us to genuine, lasting repentance. He wrote, "Godly sorrow brings repentance that leads to salvation and leaves no regret, but worldly sorrow brings death" (2 Corinthians 7:10). We sometimes confuse sorrow for repentance. They are not the same. Paul taught that sorrow itself does not necessarily imply that we have changed our minds, but the right kind of sorrow does produce a true change of mind. There is "worldly sorrow" and "godly sorrow." The former produces death and the latter produces a change of mind.

Worldly sorrow is the kind of sorrow people commonly feel when they accept the fact they have done something wrong. It is a sorrow that flows from the temporary consequences of their mistakes. One person is sorry because he was caught. Someone else is sorry because the lie she told did not achieve what she hoped it would. Another is sorry because he lost the trust of friends, but once he overcomes the loss he forgets the sorrow he once felt.

Imagine a man who is stopped by the police for driving a car while intoxicated. He receives a substantial fine, and he has to perform a number of hours of free community service time. In addition his wife is very angry. With time he pays the fine, serves the time, and his wife calms down. After the consequences pass, he no longer feels the degree of sorrow he once did. With time he starts drinking again. Later

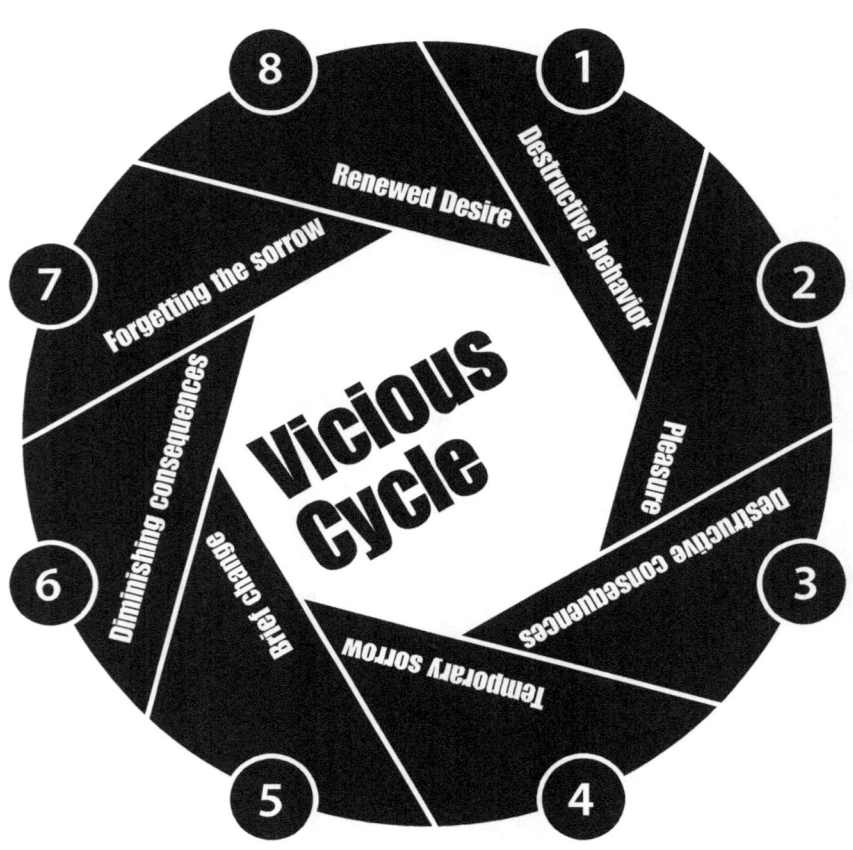

he is stopped a second time for the same offense. As a consequence, the court triples the amount of the first fine and then adds some days in the county jail. With time he pays the fine, does the time, and his wife calms down. A few months later, he repeats the same behavior. He is out-of-control. His sorrow is "worldly sorrow," produced by consequences of a temporary nature that do not leave a lasting impression on his conscience. If we were to ask him if he wants to change, he would confidently answer, yes! But if he still feels pleasure on some level from drinking, then he has not yet completely changed his mind and will struggle to control his desire to drink. Mere worldly sorrow will lead this man to spiritual death.

Whatever we are trying to control, whether actual sin or simply some vexing habit such as eating too much or sleeping too late, the principle is the same. If we have trouble changing the behavior, then our reasons for changing might not be powerful enough. Even if we accept the fact that our habits are unhealthy, the reasons for changing our minds must be more powerful than the pleasure, however twisted it may be, that we experience from the habits.

Without sufficient reasons to change our minds, we find ourselves in a vicious cycle. This cycle begins with the pleasure we experience from the behavior we need to change. The very reason why we continue practicing the behavior is that it provides us some sort of pleasure. The pleasure of being judgmental is the feeling of superiority and power. The pleasure of lying is escaping consequences. The pleasure of overeating is, well, eating! But these pleasures are deceitful because, at the same time they give pleasure, they destroy our well-being.

Next in the cycle, after the pleasure has enticed us, we experience the destructive consequences—the tragedy—of our behavior. The critic has no loyal friends. The liar has no one who trusts him. The overeater experiences, well, the obvious consequences of eating too much. This second step in the cycle, the experience of tragedy, is followed by the third step, sorrow. In the moment we confront the consequences of our mistakes, we start to feel sorry for what we did. As we have already seen, there are many reasons to feel sorry for mistakes we make. Some of these reasons make us feel sorry but not sufficiently sorry to truly change our mind. The reasons for our sorrow will have to be sufficiently powerful enough to outweigh the pleasure we also feel from practicing the behavior. What Paul labels as worldly sorrow is a temporal sorrow that is not lasting, that diminishes with time. If the reasons are not powerful enough and the sorrow does not last, we might change our behavior but the change will be brief. This brief change is the next step in the vicious cycle.

With time the suffering of the consequences diminishes, and we soon forget or ignore the hardship the habit created in our lives. As the impact of the consequences fades, so does the sorrow we feel. Now we slowly begin to recall and enjoy thinking about the pleasure of the old habit. We may begin to fantasize about what we used to do, thinking more about the pleasure than the tragedy, which has now all but vanished from our minds. It may be that thoughts of the pleasure lay just under the surface of our consciousness, ready to surprise us in unexpected moments. Naturally, thinking about the pleasure in this way sets us up to begin the cycle all over again. Jesus taught that we invest our hearts in whatever we treasure. If we once again begin to treasure the pleasure of the old habit, then our desires will lead us directly back to the actual practice of the destructive habit.

This vicious cycle defeats transformation, encouraging the repetition of the negative, unhealthy behavior. We commonly experience the frustration of thinking or behaving in certain ways, feeling bad afterwards, but then repeating the behaviors again and feeling as if we cannot control what we are doing. In such moments we have fallen into the cycle's trap. In summary, the cycle proceeds in the following way: pleasure from the behavior, destructive consequences, temporary sorrow, a brief change of behavior, diminishing consequences, then forgetting the sorrow, desiring the pleasure again, repeating the destructive behavior, followed by pleasure, tragedy, and so on.

In the case of the judgmental person, she experiences the deceitful pleasure of feeling superior, loses friends whom she offends and alienates, feels sorry for having no friends, stops being so judgmental for a while and makes new friendships, forgets the former sorrow, again feels the need to appear superior, repeats the judgmental attitude, enjoys the pleasure of feeling superior, and so on. In the case of the person who overeats, he enjoys the pleasure of eating, experiences the consequences of gaining too much weight, feels sorry for the weight gain and the resulting insecurities, briefly limits his eating or goes on a strict diet, loses some weight, forgets how he felt when he was overweight, thinks about the pleasures of eating again, starts believing that relaxing his diet and eating more would not be harmful, and finally surrenders to overeating, completing the cycle.

The only way to break the cycle and control the behavior is to feel a different kind of sorrow that is powerful enough to consistently overcome the attraction of the deceitful pleasures that lead us to tragedy. When we were trapped in the vicious cycle, the sorrow we felt was due to the tragic consequences of the harmful behavior. Our focus was on avoiding the tragedy. As long as we could avoid the consequences, we habitually repeated the behavior. An essential key to genuine repentance is to consciously change our mental framework.

Instead of thinking about the destructive habit and its consequences, we form an image of the pleasure we hope to receive from a new, healthy habit to replace the old behavior. The more we internalize the value of the new pleasure we hope to enjoy, the more sorrow we will feel for not enjoying it. Now we become sorry not only because of damage we are doing to ourselves but because, if we stay locked onto our path of destruction, we will miss the true, satisfying, healthy pleasure of our new behavior.

With respect to changing habits that are not essentially sinful, such as eating too much or sleeping too long, the positive, healthy results of self-discipline can provide tremendous emotional and physical pleasure. The self-respect from being in good physical shape, the health benefits of keeping weight within reasonable limits, the energy for new, satisfying activities, and the sense of accomplishment we feel when we wake up on time can give us strength to change our minds about our behavior in a way that is permanent.

The more we focus on the benefits and the more we value them over time, the more inner strength we will have to deepen our change of mind. Remember that self-control is really inner strength. To develop more self-control, we have to increase the emotional strength that keeps us focused on the healthy pleasures. In this case, the strength comes from learning to place greater value on the healthy pleasures resulting from the new behaviors. We begin to invest our hearts in the new behavior, treasuring the benefits. We enjoy our new life. We celebrate our accomplishments. We read and learn about more benefits, reinforcing our values. We seek the company of people who can encourage us. Now the thought of continuing the harmful habit fills us with a different kind of sorrow—the sorrow we might experience if we lose these legitimate, productive, and healthy pleasures.

If we are believers and we can align our new behavior with our relationship with God, then our strength to control negative habits increases all the more. Our strength then comes not only from our physiologically based emotions but from our spirits that thirst for intimacy with the Creator. Taking care of our physical health in fact empowers us spiritually with the confidence and energy to be useful instruments in God's hands. Waking up on time also allows us to be more disciplined and faithful in our responsibilities toward God. We will find more time to read his word and pray. We will have more time to lend to those who need our time, such as our children. As a result we feel peace in his presence. We are developing a strong relationship with him that we will not want to surrender by returning to the old behavior. Relapse would mean sacrificing benefits that now have great meaning for us.

Changing our minds about sinful or immoral behavior works in a way that is similar to overcoming less harmful habits but that more profoundly affects our spirits. The godly sorrow that Paul contrasts to worldly sorrow is the kind of sorrow that God wants us to have. He wants us to be sorry for sin because our sins separate us from him, from life in him, from the pleasure of his intimate presence. Our spirits long for his presence, but our destructive behavior builds a wall between him and us. Sin breaks our fellowship with him because he is holy and created us to enjoy holiness with him. By living in sin, we set ourselves against his good purpose in creating us. We cut ourselves off from the only source of eternal meaning and experience the desperation of meaningless existence without God. The more we try to fill the spiritual emptiness with something other than the presence of God, the deeper the desperation grows. Finding ourselves enslaved to the habit of sin, but, at the same time, disillusioned with its deceitful pleasure, we experience profound sorrow that convinces us to change our mind about the way we are living. For the believer this kind of sorrow can produce a lasting change.

The inner strength to continue to change our minds about sin depends on valuing most of all the pleasure of our relationships with the Father. Remember, a change of focus is necessary. Many believers are accustomed to thinking about overcoming sinful behavior in order to avoid punishment. The problem is that if the punishment is not a present reality but an unknown in the far-off future, it will not have much power to deter us in the present. To successfully change our minds, we consciously change our focus to imagine the pleasure of God's presence now, in the present moment. He offers us real forgiveness to remove the guilt from past mistakes, wisdom to make choices that are healthy for us and for those who surround us, a purpose that fills our daily life with meaning, and a relationship with the Father that fills our spirits with confidence, security, and hope.

The New Testament uses special language to describe the intimacy of our relationships with our heavenly Father. We are in Christ. Christ is in us. We live in the Father and the Father lives in us. There is no language that could picture in more simple yet eloquent terms our profound connections to the Father. We feel the closest to another being when we can feel what the other feels, and the other feels what we feel to the degree that there really is no otherness that separates us. Such a mutual empathy means we take joy in what the other enjoys and experience grief when the other grieves. We can come to know the Father through his word and through the practice of the life he teaches us live so that we share his mind and heart. We are then in him as he is in us. Then we will never want to do anything to separate us from the pleasure of living with him. The mere thought of the possibility of godly sorrow from being separated from him will be enough to empower us to make the necessary changes to continue our transformation. Self-control is the inner strength that comes from this level of relationship with him.

Take, for instance, the practice of compassion to help those who suffer and the contrary temptation to ignore the suffering of others and selfishly protect what we believe belongs to us. For many people, the strongest motivation for showing compassion might be to try to guarantee they receive compassion during times when they experience suffering. If, presently, they are not suffering and do not have any real expectations of suffering, the motivation to show compassion will be weak. Denying compassion to a needy person may not make them feel any sorrow or guilt. But if, at some point in time, they do experience some setbacks in their lives, like losing their jobs, they might feel remorseful for not having helped others in the past. Now they may even give a few dollars to people standing on the street corner asking for money. But as they eventually overcome the misfortunes and find new jobs, they forget about how they felt when they were without work. In fact, from their perspectives, they helped themselves by aggressively looking for work. "Why don't other people help themselves in the same way?" Whatever sorrow they might have felt for not showing compassion has now vanished. They relapse to practice self-centeredness instead of compassion.

For the believer compassion has a different motivation. Our motivation to relieve suffering is to be like our heavenly Father and live with confidence in his presence. Having strong, living relationships with our Father gives meaning and purpose to our lives. We witness the spiritual transformation he is producing in us. Whether or not people show compassion to us, we will still be compassionate because, most deeply in our hearts, we want to feel God's presence in our lives. As we live in love, he lives in us and gives our lives eternal meaning.

Imagine, though, that we start working long hours, making more money, enjoying the benefits of more resources, and slowly forgetting to notice the needs of others. Our lives continue in this direction for a time. We are busy. We still think about God, but we think mostly about our jobs. We think even less about the needs of others. Then the economy suddenly goes south. We lose our jobs and even lose our houses that we heavily financed, thinking that the good times would always continue. Our loss can make us look at life differently.

Now that we are in need, we may look at other people who struggle to pay their rent with more compassion. We feel sorry for not helping, but we also feel sorrow on a deeper level. The loss of our job and the sudden halt to the materialistic direction of our lives cause us to evaluate our relationships with God. Because of our faith, we see how far we have drifted from his presence through our self-centeredness. What makes us deeply sorrowful in our spirits is the separation we feel from his presence. What we feel is not sorrow from contemplating some kind of punishment for being selfish but, instead, sorrow from the potential loss of the pleasure of living in God's presence. Now, whether or not someone helps us in our moments of need and whether or not we find jobs that return us to our former economic status, we determine to put aside selfishness and start practicing compassion so we can once again feel close to our Father. This level of sorrow in our spirits is godly sorrow, the sorrow that God wants us to feel when we sense in our spirits that we are drifting away from him, missing the pleasure of his presence.

To genuinely change our minds requires the inner strength of a strong, living relationship with the Father. An unbeliever will not feel godly sorrow. Even believers may not feel much sorrow when their relationships with the Father become weak if their relationships with him were not very strong to begin with. The key then to having sufficient self-control or inner strength to repent is to develop a powerful relationship with the Father.

As we grow as children of God, there is so much we must change our minds about. If our relationships with the Father are living and growing more powerful, if his presence in our lives is the energy that sustains us spiritually, and if being his children is the most precious relationship we have, then we will never want to leave him. When self-reflection presents us with some aspect of our behavior we must change to live in his image, we will gladly change our minds about that behavior. The very thought of the possibility of being separated from the Father and the pleasure of his presence should move us to quickly change our minds in moments when we are tempted to be arrogant, selfish, unmerciful, impatient, or angry.

Since having sufficient inner strength to repent depends on having a strong, intimate relationship with our Father, how can we strengthen this relationship? When we think in a purely rational way, we easily understand it is not reasonable to value anything in this world more than we value our relationships with our heavenly Father. But we usually do not make decisions based on purely rational thinking. Emotions always enter the equation. Emotions motivate us and enliven us. To increase our inner strength, we can encourage the emotions of our spirits that draw us more closely to the heart of the Father. Each of us has different emotional connections to our Father and different ways of strengthening those connections. Some of us have been saved from a wretched life of addiction and realize that we exist only by the loving grace of the Father. Others, because of personal experiences, have faced the desperate reality of an absolutely meaningless and hopeless existence without God and, for this reason, never want to be without him. Some have committed tragic sin that has affected the lives of others and feel so grateful for the Father's mercy and forgiveness to be able to begin again. Others blindly thought for a long time that they were quite righteous and deserved the blessings of God and then suddenly saw themselves as they truly were, sinners needing redemption from sin. They were surprised, humbled, terrified, and overcome with grief; now they never want to be without the Father's forgiveness. Such emotions have the power to keep us close to him. In order for our change of mind to be persistent, we must remember what we feel, keeping the gratitude, humility, and love we feel toward the Father ever present in our minds.

What we specifically do to encourage the positive emotions that we feel in our spirits will depend on our experiences and what works for each of us; but each of us will have to practice the Father's presence in some manner to increase our inner strength and have the necessary power to change. Spending a quiet time in the morning, reading his word, meditating on it, and talking with the Father in prayer can make the knowledge of his presence a part of the beginning of each day. During the day we view moments to show mercy, patience, kindness, or gentleness as ways to serve as instruments in his hands to show the beauty of life with him. In this way we interpret the events of each day as moments in his presence, feeling the joy of serving him in whatever we are doing. We also consciously practice the qualities of his character, the fruit of the Spirit, as expressions of his life in us. When the practice of forgiveness or patience challenges us, we take the risk of trusting his way and make the choice to obey his teaching, despite the consequences or cost. The trust required in such moments strengthens our relationships with him. The times when we understand the Father has forgiven us, accepted us, changed us, and used us to show others the way to him are reasons to celebrate. Celebrating by giving thanks or by telling others what has happened reinforces the joy we feel from our relationships with him.

In fact, Paul explained that contemplating God's kindness also leads us to repentance (Romans 2:4). Reminding ourselves about the abundant life that God offers us helps break sin's vicious cycle. We never want to offend someone who has loved us so much, giving us such abundance. The more joy, contentment, and peace we feel from being free from guilt and living the right life in communion with God, the more strength we will have to control ourselves and escape the destructive cycle of sin. The pleasure of life with God offers us incomparably more meaning and value than the pleasure of sin.

Destructive habits that have developed to the degree of addictions especially require godly sorrow to break the vicious cycle. Many addictions have a powerful physiological component to the pleasure received from the substance or the behavior. The long repetition of the addiction has trained the brain to react by producing chemical substances that increase the intense feelings of physical pleasure. Overcoming the addiction to this degree of physical pleasure requires a profound change of mind on a spiritual level. The kind of pleasure our spirits are capable of feeling in God's presence is powerful enough to replace the physical desire for the addictive behavior. Contemplating the possible loss of the pleasure of God's presence produces sorrow sufficiently powerful to defeat the attraction of the addiction and change our minds. The solution is to consciously shift from thinking about losing the pleasure of sin to missing the pleasure of God's presence.

Now think again about the man who is struggling with his anger. Having enough faith in God's grace to confront his anger, he can now clearly see the consequences of his negativity, irritation, and aggression. He understands that he is responsible for alienating his children and building a wall between him and his wife. He accepts the fact that his anger is his problem, no matter how his family is behaving. But stopping his aggression for more than brief moments is difficult. After each of his angry episodes, everyone stays out of his way until he cools down. Once there is calm again, the family atmosphere eventually returns to a somewhat normal state. Then people tentatively start talking together about subjects that will not cause arguments. In reality his family is making it easy for him to repeat his destructive behavior by smoothing over the consequences. But he does not want to keep going through this cycle. His own father was a very angry person until he died. He does not want his children and wife to go through what he went through. At the same time, because of his faith, he sees he has drifted far from God. His family is a blessing of God's grace. He realizes on a deeper level what he was trying to ignore before: his behavior was leading him away from God. He feels alone, helpless, and genuinely lost. He prays, opening up his heart to God in a way that he has never done before, refusing to justify himself, and simply asks for forgiveness. He wants to feel the joy of being close to God again and he wants his family to feel safe in God's presence too.

REPLACEMENT

After reflecting on our thoughts and behaviors and changing our minds about what we are doing, the next step toward transformation is replacement: practicing good in place of the evil that we were habitually practicing. Replacement means to advance beyond repentance and, in the words of John Baptist, "produce fruit in keeping with repentance" (Luke 3:8-14). Fruits of repentance are the practical changes in behavior that will follow true repentance. A genuine change of mind will result in a changed life. Of the thousands who came to listen to John's preaching outside of Jerusalem by the shore of the Jordan River, some were of the Pharisees, a self-righteous sect of the Jews, who prided themselves on how carefully they kept God's law, at least in their own opinion. When they came to John, pretending to be interested in the message of the gospel, John warned them to produce evidence that they truly had changed their minds.

Others in the audience who humbly wanted to change their lives asked John, "What shall we do then?" This question was the correct one. The question showed true repentance that leads to action. John gave them some very practical answers. "The man with two tunics should share with him who has none, and the one who has food should do the same." He told the tax collectors who wanted to repent of greed, "Don't collect any more than you are required to." Even some soldiers asked John, "And what should we do?" John answered, "Don't extort money and don't accuse people falsely—be content with your pay" (Luke 3:8-14). John gave them very practical, specific advice about what they should do to replace evil with good. Now they understood not only what not to do but also what they ought to do.

Controlling what we eat is not just a matter of not eating unhealthy food but also eating food that is nutritionally beneficial. In the struggle to live transformed lives, we usually think a lot about what we should not do, but replacement implies a change of focus to think about what we ought to do. Focusing principally on the bad causes discouragement, pessimism, and stagnation, filling our minds with reasons why we are "not good enough," without giving us the confidence to do what is right. The object of transformation is to cultivate the heart of our heavenly Father. This goal is positive and therefore powerful.

What happens if we fail to replace, in a conscious, deliberate manner, the destructive and unhealthy habits with something positive? Jesus presents the answer to this question in a parable about a man who was possessed by evil. "When an evil spirit comes out of a man, it goes through arid places seeking rest and does not find it. Then it says, 'I will return to the house I left.' When it arrives it finds the house swept clean and put in order. Then it goes and takes seven other spirits more wicked than itself and they go in and live there, and the final condition of that man is worse than the first" (Luke 11:24-26).

Compare the man possessed by an evil spirit to a person possessed by a destructive habit. The habit is out of control and dominates his life. Then imagine that he finally sees the deepest tragedy of his behavior, repents, and stops participating in it. Now his life is clean, free of the disorder and confusion caused by the dominating habit—clean and free but empty. The danger is that, although his life is empty of evil, it is also empty of good. What does Jesus' parable predict will happen if he does nothing to fill up his life with good to replace the evil? The habit will return to enslave him to an even worse degree.

Continued transformation depends on replacing the evil with good, the unhealthy with something healthy, the destructive with something constructive, and the negative with something positive. If a person with a drinking habit stops drinking, he will have to replace the time normally spent drinking with something healthy. If he spends the time doing nothing, he will go back to drinking. A person who had the habit of lying will have to consciously and deliberately tell the truth to everyone in every circumstance in order not to return to lying. Why is replacement so necessary? We return to what has been customary and natural to us. If we choose not to fight habits, we will return to what is easiest and least demanding, giving in once again to the habits. Without experiencing new and different pleasures from something positive and constructive in our lives, we return to the old pleasures, even though we have experienced their deceptions.

The burden of the disciple of Jesus who teaches other disciples to follow the teachings of Jesus is to explain exactly what to do in order to follow Jesus. Telling people what not to do is easy. We simply observe how they behave and describe their unhealthy, destructive behaviors to them. Explaining what people ought to do is more difficult. For example, telling someone not to gossip is simple. We listen to how he is talking behind someone's back, and we describe his destructive behavior. The question that is just as important is what he ought to do to replace gossip. Simply quoting a verse such as, "Let your conversation be always full of grace" (Colossians 4:6) is the easy answer, but how to teach someone to speak with grace is also the burden of the teacher. What is the meaning of grace? Which aspects of grace ought to characterize our speech? What would gracious speech sound like in his particular relationships with members of his family, members of his congregation, his neighbors, his critics, or even his enemies? What are the conditions under which he could talk to one person about another person without gossiping? Answering these questions requires more meditation and wisdom.

Replacement does not happen automatically when we stop negative behaviors. We have to consciously make the effort to replace the bad with good. Paul taught this principle in Colossians 3:5-14. First, he explained what Christians ought to stop doing, the behaviors from which they need repent. He gave examples of behaviors and habits they needed to abstain from completely in the Christian life such as immorality, greed, anger, slander, and lying. He used the language "put to death" and "rid yourselves" to describe their responsibilities to reflect on their lives and change their behaviors.

Then Paul explained exactly what they ought to practice in order to replace the evil. Here he used the language, "clothe yourselves," to describe the practice of new qualities in their character that ought to replace the old. He gave them specific examples of qualities such as compassion, kindness, humility, and gentleness, concluding with the words, "And over all these virtues put on love." The original Christians who read his letter knew exactly what was expected of them as they followed Jesus. Imagine if Paul had told them what not to do without telling them what to do, the picture of the Christian life would have been only half finished. Paul would have left the Christians without a clear idea of the righteous life.

In another sense, the list of positive attributes in the Colossian passage is general in that each quality refers to a wide range of behaviors. Imagine that we need to replace prejudice and condemnation with compassion. Compassion refers to understanding the suffering of another person and helping to relieve the suffering. It includes, among many possible applications, taking the time and spending resources to help a sick person recover, listening to a person who is depressed and giving encouragement and hope, helping a person economically who has lost a job, providing shelter and food for a needy person, being a friend to someone who is lonely, giving new direction to someone who has made a serious mistake, or consoling a person who has lost a loved one. These examples represent specific applications of compassion.

In Philippians 4:6-8 Paul gave wise and practical counsel about replacing destructive thoughts. Instead of allowing anxious thoughts to control our thinking, we ought to pray. Replace the worry with prayer, and God will replace the worry with peace. In verse eight Paul explained the kind of thinking that should replace negative, critical, and impure thinking. "Finally, brothers, whatever is true, whatever is noble, whatever is right, whatever is pure, whatever is lovely, whatever is admirable—if anything is excellent or praiseworthy, think about such things." These characteristics of healthy thinking require careful meditation and practice to discover how to use them to replace unhealthy thinking. For example, thinking true thoughts means to refuse to entertain thoughts of suspicion, gossip, and rumor. Instead, we ought to think thoughts that we know to be true about people. Thinking right thoughts means replacing thoughts of revenge, manipulation, and cheating with thoughts that are forgiving, transparent, and just. Thinking about things that are admirable implies replacing negative criticism with reasons to respect and praise someone.

These behaviors are not automatic. Plenty of people have grown up in social and cultural atmospheres where compassion on this level is not common. They will have to learn the specifics of exactly how to think in compassionate ways, how to show compassion, and what language to use to communicate compassion. Our role as disciples is to think creatively about how to practice replacement. If the New Testament taught in such detail about every quality a disciple of Jesus should practice, the book would be too huge to handle. Furthermore, the meditation and search for creative applications requires faith.

Our faith in the teachings of Jesus develops and grows as we constantly seek to discover new moments to practice the qualities of his character. The job of the teacher is to work together with the student as fellow disciples to imagine and create applications of compassion in their particular social and cultural contexts. Simply saying, "You need to be more compassionate," is not enough.

Imagine a runner, who wishes to run competitively, asks for the help of a coach to train for a significantly difficult race. Imagine the coach tells the aspiring runner, "You need to run faster if you want to win!" Such counsel would compare to a Christian teacher telling a disciple, "If you want to go to heaven you need to be more humble!" This "counsel" may be true, but it is not helpful in any genuine way to promote progress. The coach needs to assist the runner in developing a very specific plan for daily training to build muscle strength, develop flexibility, increase lung capacity, adopt an efficient running style, and understand strategies for competing well. In this way the runner would have a very precise plan to follow in order to be able to run faster.

Having a plan provides us the inner strength necessary for this step in our transformation. Without a plan for change we would be adrift, paralyzed into inaction by the question of how. The more specific and practical our plans are to replace one conduct with another, the more successful transformation will be. If someone is trying to control overeating, and we simply tell him, "Eat nutritious food," we may leave him without understanding what to do. The fact that he has a problem with eating should indicate to us that he does not know the details about which foods are nutritious and which are not. The teacher's role is to explain exactly which foods, what amounts of food, and what kind of food preparation contributes to healthy meals.

Then the student will know exactly what to do to replace the former habit of eating unhealthy food.

In the same way, a disciple who wishes to teach a fellow disciple to become more humble must help her to understand the various facets of humility, including seeking the welfare of others above her own, serving even when it is not her position to serve, adopting the perspective of a child to recognize her dependence on others, freely admitting mistakes without self-justification, and being content to let others occupy the best places of honor. Furthermore, the disciple needs a very specific plan that helps her creatively imagine and discover moments in her varied range of relationships, including with her heavenly Father, to practice all of these aspects of humility. What can she do in her family to serve even when serving is someone else's obligation? What can she do to free herself of the language and gestures of self-justification and to accept responsibility for her own mistakes? What can she do to advance in her job through the practice of humility? How can she show that she is ready to learn from others and accept their help, even when she thinks she has everything under her control?

Here is another place in which we require inner strength to continue our transformation into the image of our Father. Remember that, in the process of transformation, self-control refers to the inner strength to remain focused on our goal, moving constantly toward it. If we have come this far, after reflecting on our lives and repenting of some specific unhealthy or destructive behavior, we have already developed an admirable degree of inner strength. Now, remaining focused on the practice of replacement also requires inner strength.

The strength to practice replacing destructive behavior with new healthy habits comes from faith in Jesus. Our lives are very busy, full of responsibilities at home, at work, and in the community. When we are not busy fulfilling these responsibilities, we just want to relax and rest, without thinking about anything serious. When is there enough time to think about how to practice compassion or to discover new ways to serve with humility? We do not have time to think about our character! But if we believe in Jesus as Lord and have faith in his teachings to transform us, consistently surrendering to the process of transformation is how we live. It is not as if we have to allot a special time to learning compassion just like we allot a special time each day to doing exercise. Instead, living a transformed life is the way we fulfill all of our responsibilities. Learning to practice the character of Christ covers, surrounds, envelops, and supports everything else we do. Practicing his character is how we do everything we are called to do. It is how we live. To immerse our life so completely in learning to practice his character requires great faith, enough faith to understand that life only makes sense and is enjoyable only when we are totally engaged in his life. Paul wrote, "to live is Christ" (Philippians 1:21). This faith is the inner strength necessary for replacing the old with the new.

Practice increases our faith and faith increases our practice. As we replace old patterns of thinking and behavior with the patience, humility, peace and gentleness of Jesus, we see how beautifully his way works. We feel the contentment and joy that comes from realizing we really are changing. In this way we come to believe even more deeply that living the Christ-life is really living. This faith in turn gives us enthusiasm to constantly look for new ways to practice. Then the more we practice, the more our faith deepens.

We return to the man who has the anger problem and who has been successful at reflection and repentance. With these successes his self-control is growing. Now he must learn to practice healthy behaviors that can replace the anger. At first he does not quite know what to do because he has been impatient, demanding and aggressive for so long. Anger is all he knows. He decides to ask for help from a trusted brother in Christ who truly practices patience. He also reads more deeply, meditating on passages that describe how Jesus treated people with gentleness and mercy. He focuses on learning to listen carefully without speaking, take his time to think about how to respond with gentleness, lower his voice, and relax his body language. He spends more time in prayer to approach potential conflicts with calm and wisdom. When he does make a mistake, falling back into his aggressive behavior for a moment, he immediately asks forgiveness from his family members when he offends them. His faith in Jesus and in the beauty of the Christian life keeps him strong in his spirit. His success motivates him to continue to creatively think about new ways to carefully avoid reacting impulsively and, instead, to communicate gentleness.

RETRAINING

Transformation into the image of our Father begins with reflection to stop and think about our thoughts and behaviors. Next, we repent or change our minds about the destructive aspects of our lives, understanding the tragedy of being alienated from the purpose and presence of the Father. Then we begin to replace the destructive behaviors with thoughts and actions that are spiritually healthy, keeping us in close communion with the Father. With each step of transformation, our inner strength increases, empowering us to focus on this incredible goal and enthusiastically expend every effort to grow in the image of our Father. The fourth step that follows replacement is retraining. At this stage, we continue the practice of replacing the bad with the good until the good becomes the new habit. A destructive habit does not come into existence overnight but develops by repeatedly practicing the same behavior, while gradually silencing the accusations of our conscience with self-justification. The consistent practice of new habits of righteousness does not develop overnight either. We have to retrain ourselves over time in the face of challenges in order to form new habits that can become part of our new nature in Christ.

Retraining is the discipline of self-control. The word *discipline* can refer to punishment, but discipline can also refer to training one's self to perform an activity that is difficult to do. Discipline is the consistent, constant practice that produces lasting change. Paul counseled Timothy to avoid useless myths and instead to "train yourself to be godly" (1 Timothy 4:7). The need for training implies that the understanding and abilities to live godly lives do not come to us automatically after being born again.

If we were to ask disciples who have grown up in very dysfunctional surroundings, without role models and with little instruction about developing healthy character, these disciples would confirm the truth that living godly lives is the result of patient learning and practice. No doubt some Christians believe that godliness is automatic, but they probably grew up in a safe environment that taught them, more or less, how to live right. Such disciples should pay attention to Paul's instructions to Timothy. Timothy was already a young evangelist, who had been raised by a godly mother and grandmother, when Paul advised him to train himself to be godly. If we are honest with ourselves, we will have to admit that we all need more training, no matter where we have come from. Overconfidence is disastrous for spiritual growth.

Training is a different project from learning. We can learn about godliness by reading the Scriptures and considering the life of Jesus. We train ourselves, however, through the experience of practicing what we learn in a consistent manner. The goal of training is to produce new habits of living that come to form part of us on such deep levels that we cannot imagine living or behaving any other way.

Being a disciple and being disciplined should go hand in hand, since the two words share a common root meaning. The original Greek word that is translated *disciple* means *student*. Jesus gave this word a deeper meaning than just describing someone who might sit and listen to a teacher. He said, "If you hold to my teaching, you are really my disciples" (John 8:31). Being a disciple of Jesus means to keep his teaching, to hold to it, to live in it. His teaching is our spiritual home, our way of life. In the same way, the word *discipline* suggests practice in a consciously consistent manner. The disciples of Jesus live disciplined lives. Through the discipline of training, they become like their Master.

Training involves repeated practice. A runner who is training for a race must run many miles, do countless repetitions of exercises, and mentally rehearse many times exactly how he will run the race. His life is a disciplined life because he must not allow anything to distract him from consistent practice. The object of his discipline is to train his body to respond just as he would like it to respond during the race. Such a predictable response comes only through repeated practice.

The disciplined life of a disciple of Jesus is no different. In the step of replacement, she determines what she will practice in the place of the former unhealthy habit. Now, as she retrains herself, she consciously looks for moments when she can practice the replacement behavior over and over again. The critic who decides to control her destructive criticism determines to replace criticism with words of encouragement and praise. Now, she must consciously look for moments to encourage and praise. At first, such language feels strange and awkward coming from her lips, just as awkward as a runner feels when first training with a new style of running. With time and practice, the runner's body feels more comfortable running with the new form, and the critic feels at ease showing appreciation and affirmation for other people.

The key for the critic is to look for a variety of situations in which she can show special attention to encouraging others. She must encourage others with the same effort and discipline that a runner trains for a race. The person who is overcome with anxiety must practice over and over again ways of thinking and behaving that replace worry, such as giving the worry over to the Lord in prayer, talking himself through the worry to decide if it reflects reality, and sharing the worry with a close friend who can give counsel about how to make a plan to resolve it. The person who is seeking to control greed must practice over and over again moments of sharing generously what she has with others, expressing thanksgiving to the Lord for specific blessings, and serving the needs of others in a self-sacrificing way.

Our training must also involve doing what we can to control our surroundings to make the practice of new habits as easy as possible, at least at the beginning, when we first make the changes in our lives. Paul wrote, "Don't give the devil a foothold" (Ephesians 4:27). We give evil a foothold or an advantage when we put ourselves in situations that may weaken our determination and leave us vulnerable to temptation. We know that certain people, specific circumstances, physical conditions like being tired, or emotional conditions like being frustrated or anxious can affect our mental states and rob us of strength to practice the habits we are trying to change.

Just watching a particular movie or listening to a certain kind of music can easily alter our frame of mind. Instead of surrendering our thoughts and behavior to our surroundings, we can decide to control whatever is within our power to eliminate distractions. We decide with whom we want to spend our time, under what circumstances we want to spend time with those people, what entertainment we choose to enjoy, whether we get enough sleep, and whether we let anxiety overcome us or not. Transformation of heart and life is worth the sacrifices we have to make.

Of course, there will be situations that we cannot control and that will, in fact, challenge our perseverance. We do not necessarily have to avoid these challenges. As we have previously shown, the fruit of the Spirit grow tremendously in moments when we face challenges to their practice. The runner strengthens his endurance by running increasingly difficult distances and paces. Practice is more effective when it is difficult, not so difficult as to defeat us but difficult enough to help us extend our abilities. The alcoholic who has stopped drinking cannot afford at the beginning of his struggle to be around people who are drinking. When he is first developing the inner strength not to drink, he must avoid circumstances that might encourage him to drink. With time and practice, however, he will be able to face conflicts, anxious or frustrating experiences, or discouraging problems, which in a former time would have tempted him to drink. The person working to eliminate greed can practice increasing levels of generosity. The person trying to change her critical spirit can learn to appreciate and encourage even the people who are very critical of her.

To face these challenges, though, we need to have a special plan prepared ahead of time to deal with them. Peter's advice is excellent: "Prepare your minds for action" (1 Peter 1:13). If we know ourselves and understand our weak moments, we can honestly predict when practicing the new habits might be especially difficult. Carefully reflecting on potentially difficult circumstances, we devise plans to avoid, solve, or overcome such situations in peaceful and productive ways. Run away! Gently confront! Come to an agreement! Call someone who can encourage us to do what is right! Pray! If we cannot think of a plan, then perhaps we can ask trusted and wise friends about what we ought to do when faced with provoking situations.

Then we have to rehearse these plans in our minds over and over again until we can easily remember what we must do when challenging circumstances present themselves. School children practice a strategy called, "Stop, drop and roll," to prepare for fires. If their clothing catches on fire, they must immediately stop, throw themselves to the ground, and roll over and over on the ground to extinguish the flames. School children practice this drill until it is etched in their memories. If and when they find themselves in a fire, they will remember exactly what to do because they practiced a set plan. We, too, will know exactly how to react to our fires of temptation if we rehearse our plans over and over in our minds ahead of time. Now, with these plans recorded in our minds, we are set to react in the moment of temptation by doing the right thing. When we consistently practice the new habits, even when practice is difficult, then our levels of consistency will grow and the habits will become a deeper part of us.

Challenges to our new habits are not the only moments we have to prepare for. Ironically, when we begin to experience success in practicing new habits, we might have the tendency to relax and think that we no longer have to expend so much effort to fight against the old habits. Successes lull us into inattention. But training ourselves to adopt new habits requires constant focus. Losing focus because we become satisfied with our successes leaves us open to break our discipline. When we experience successes, we want to celebrate, but celebrating by relaxing is not an option. There are other more effective and safe ways to celebrate: we can give thanks to the Lord for his grace, tell friends why we are so happy, and share our excitement with others who are struggling with the same habits in order to give them confidence.

James has something very interesting to say about disciplining ourselves to control what we say. He wrote, "No man can tame the tongue" (James 3:8). He does not mean to say no one can control the tongue, but that no one can tame the tongue. There is an important difference between control and tame. James gave examples of taming animals as an illustration of his point. We can control a dog by tying the dog up to a tree, but this does not mean the dog is tamed. A tamed dog is an animal that no longer needs our constant attention. We can leave the animal at home in the house, knowing that it will not dirty or destroy the inside of our home. We can leave the animal untied, certain that it will not jump on anyone or escape.

James taught in this passage that we can control the tongue, but we cannot tame it. We can never come to the point in our lives, no matter how strong we think we might be, that we can simply stop paying attention to how we talk, assuming that we will always say the right thing in the right moment. The truth is that we always have to think about what we are going to say and how we will say it. Some careful reflection teaches us that there are very few situations in which we find ourselves confronting a totally new challenge. In fact we can easily predict our moods, the kinds of people we will deal with, and possible problems that might arise. If we are serious about controlling our speech, we should begin our day by rehearsing a plan for responding with patience, gentleness, and compassion during difficult conversations we might have. Even if we happen to avoid the conversations we thought we would have, our mind will easily resort to our rehearsed plan when other, unexpected conversations confront us. A good plan can prepare us for challenges that might otherwise surprise us. Having a plan gives us inner strength.

In the process of retraining our thoughts and actions, relapse to our old behaviors is always possible. It happens, even to those who are really trying hard to be disciplined, but it does not have to happen. Slipping for a moment does not have to lead to a complete fall back into a former habit. If the behaviors we are trying to change were habitual then our reactions to temptation used to be nearly automatic. What has been automatic for so long may require time to abandon. Trying, for example, to replace vulgar vocabulary is a challenge because, although we really want to change the way we speak, words seem to escape from our mouths in the most embarrassing moments. "Oops! Sorry about that! Working on it!" is about all we can say when it happens. What can we do?

First, we do not need to beat ourselves up about it. It happens. We are really trying. The Lord is gracious and patient with us, and we therefore need to be patient with ourselves. Feeling overly guilty about slipping in a given moment can actually tempt us to surrender to the guilt, give up trying, and fall into complete relapse. There are usually family members, so-called friends, or even voices inside us who are ready to say, "Just give up. Changing is too hard. You will always be this way." The Lord, however, is the One who will always forgive us and lift us up to try again. Just as he said to the woman caught in adultery, "neither do I condemn you. Go now and leave your life of sin." Inner strength to persevere comes from seeing ourselves the way the Lord sees us.

Second, we ought to stop to think about why the relapse happened and what we can do to prepare ahead to avoid similar situations in the future. Sometimes relapse happens because success, as we said, can lead to inattention. We want to rest and enjoy the confidence from our successes, and, as a result, we stop taking temptation so seriously. A person who is overcoming the temptation to drink alcohol may come to think that he or she is strong enough to be around friends who are drinking or strong enough to face emotionally difficult moments without extra support from family or brothers and sisters in Christ. Temptations can surprise us in our most confident moments. Sometimes relapse happens because we become tired of fighting every impulse and desire. We convince ourselves that we lack the inner strength to keep going. It also happens because we are not really as determined to control the habits as we thought we were. The moment of relapse is revealing. We discover that we still feel some pleasures from certain behaviors, though we have told ourselves and others that we hate the way we used to live when we were enslaved to sin. Understanding why we fell back into the former behavior should help us modify our plan to overcome the weaknesses we identified. How will we pay more attention, remain alert to temptation, find the inner strength to keep fighting, and never allow false pleasure to deceive us again?

It is clear that the discipline of retraining calls for constant inner strength in our spirits, emotional as well as spiritual. It requires the strength that fuels that form of patience that we call perseverance. Retraining is a long project. It is the marathon of the Christian life. The threat of relapse, the challenging moments when practice is difficult, the possibility of overconfidence, the negative voices along the way, and gradual spiritual exhaustion constantly force us to make a decision between surrender to our past or perseverance toward a new life.

What shall we do to fortify our power to persevere? Should we slow down our lives so that we have the time to focus on the changes we must make? Should we spend more time in prayer, reading, meditation, and fasting? Should we put more effort into discovering creative ways to practice the new habits? Should we honestly identify the moments when we feel most tempted and prepare a plan to face those moments? Should we flee or fight? Should we be more honest with ourselves about the deceptions of sin and how they have fooled us? Should we continue to remind ourselves of the tragedies and enslavements of our former life until we truly decide never return to them? Should we internalize the Father's grace more deeply in our spirits to appreciate our relationship with him? Should we find a brother or sister in Christ to whom we can be accountable and from whom we can receive practical, useful encouragement? Each of us is different as disciples of Jesus. Our struggles are different. The solutions that provide us the inner strength to persevere will be also different. Each runner in a race prepares for the race with a plan of training that specifically suits her individual needs. The key is to keep in mind the pleasure of running and the joy of winning so that she determines each day to follow her plan.

Despite our different circumstances and needs, we can all rely on the special strength that comes from God's Spirit, Spirit to spirit. The Father has not left us alone in our struggle. We need to ask for his help, believing he can strengthen us with power in our inner being. He has also promised to give us wisdom to make decisions along the road to transformation. James encouraged us to ask without wavering in our faith (James 1:5-7). Wisdom is his gift that bolsters our confidence to face hard decisions. Most of all, to have the spiritual strength to persevere, we focus on Jesus. Following him to cultivate the image of our Father is the priority of our lives. The writer of Hebrews said,

> Therefore, since we are surrounded by such a great cloud of witnesses, let us throw off everything that hinders and the sin that so easily entangles, and let us run with perseverance the race marked out for us. Let us fix our eyes on Jesus, the author and perfecter of our faith, who for the joy set before him endured the cross, scorning its shame, and sat down at the right hand of the throne of God. Consider him who endured such opposition from sinful men, so that you will not grow weary and lose heart (Hebrews 12:1-3).

If, from the beginning, we commit ourselves to Jesus as Lord, our humble commitment to him will carry us through the trials as well as the successes. Our focus will be on him and not on the moment's distress or the glory of success. As we progress in our abilities to practice and realize the joy that comes from genuine spiritual growth, our commitment to Jesus as Lord increases, providing us even more strength. Total, loving, unconditional surrender to him fills us with the power to never give up.

Consider, finally, the progress of the man who is learning to control his anger. He has learned to be aware of when he is becoming irritated or anxious by the physical symptoms of tenseness in his body. He has also been practicing several options for calming himself including taking a break to breathe more deeply and consciously relax his muscles, talking to himself about the situation to critically examine his emotions, and praying to ask for strength. Furthermore, he has begun actively to practice listening, take time to respond, and speak with gentleness.

But he still lacks the consistency of habit. Although he knows what he ought to do, he does not always do it. Once in a while he still reacts impulsively. There is one thing, though, that he is certain about: he wants to change. The Lord has been so gracious to bring him this far. He feels forgiven for all the vicious anger that flowed from him in the past. Now he just wants to remain focused on Jesus and keep practicing no matter what happens. When he first began to replace anger with his new behavior, he felt like he was being challenged and put to the test every day. To prepare for the challenges he made plans to deal with moments of irritation and anxiety in specific circumstances at work and with his family. In moments of calm, he rehearsed these plans in his head to prepare for moments of frustration. This rehearsal has worked because now he responds quickly but with patience and gentleness to situations that would have triggered impulsive anger in the past. He really believes the Lord is changing him and is humbly grateful for the Lord's patient mercy. Gentleness and peace are now becoming part of his nature. They will soon be habits.

When the new habits become consistent and even impulsive in a healthy way, we reach points in our experiences when we cannot imagine thinking or doing anything different than practicing the new behavior. Our minds and our hearts have changed and our consistent practice reflects that change. The new habits have become part of our nature. The Lord has transformed us into his likeness. It has happened, just as Paul beautifully wrote, "And we, who with unveiled faces all reflect the Lord's glory, are being transformed into his likeness with ever-increasing glory, which comes from the Lord, who is the Spirit."

CONCLUSION

CONCLUDING THOUGHTS

Understanding, reflection, and practice are all equally necessary to spiritual growth in the image of Jesus, but transformation can only come after practice. We can carefully listen, read, and research. The Lord can fill us with strength in our inner beings, bless us with wisdom and present us with challenges to help us grow. But we still have to practice. At the end of the Sermon on the Mount, Jesus compared the person who listens to his teachings and practices them to a man who built his house on a rock. A life of practice changes thought into solid reality. When the winds blew and the rains descended upon that house, it stood firm. The one who listens but does not put Jesus' teachings into real-life practice is like a man who builds his house on sand. A house built on sand will not withstand the storms. A person's life that consists only of listening and contemplation will likewise be a disappointing failure. Continued, consistent, and challenging practice turns a transformed mind into a transformed life.

In another story, Jesus told of a young man who demanded his inheritance from his father so that he could leave home and fulfill every worldly desire he had ever had. Later, in a distant country far from his father, he lost everything and became horribly lost himself. After experiencing tragedy upon tragedy as a result of his deceived decisions, "he came to his senses," Jesus said. At that point he understood the depth to which he had fallen and thought about what he would do, "I will set out and go back to my father and say to him: Father, I have sinned against heaven and against you. I am no longer worthy to be called your son, make me like one of your hired men." He changed his mind and reflected on what was necessary for him to do. He had a plan. His words, though, at that point, only expressed the desire of his heart but did not represent complete transformation. The pivotal point of the young man's experience came next in Jesus' narrative, "So he got up and went to his father." Without taking this action to practice the desire of his heart, he would never have enjoyed new life with his father. The one who was lost became found; the one who was dead became alive. Practice is transforming.

Practice transforms our understanding by revealing the meaning of character qualities that cannot be known by reading only. Practice transforms our spirits by giving us peace in the Father's presence, knowing that we are living as he is. Practice transforms our hearts so that we feel the celebration that our heavenly Father feels when his creation is restored to new life. Practice transforms our bodies from instruments of evil to instruments of righteousness in his hands. The imagination and creativity to discover new, more challenging moments of practice transform the very purpose for which we are living. Practice is the excitement, the passion, the joy, and the reward of transformation.

www.ingramcontent.com/pod-product-compliance
Lightning Source LLC
Chambersburg PA
CBHW031613160426
43196CB00006B/123